Religious and Sexual Nationalisms in Central and Eastern Europe

# Religion and the Social Order

AN OFFICIAL PUBLICATION OF THE
ASSOCIATION FOR THE SOCIOLOGY OF RELIGION

*General Editor*

William H. Swatos, Jr.

VOLUME 26

The titles published in this series are listed at *brill.com/reso*

# Religious and Sexual Nationalisms in Central and Eastern Europe

*Gods, Gays and Governments*

*Edited by*

Srdjan Sremac
R. Ruard Ganzevoort

BRILL

LEIDEN | BOSTON

Library of Congress Cataloging-in-Publication Data

Religious and sexual nationalisms in Central and Eastern Europe : gods, gays and governments / edited by Srdjan Sremac, R. Ruard Ganzevoort.
     pages cm. – (Religion and the social order, ISSN 1061-5210 ; volume 26)
     ISBN 978-90-04-29747-0 (hardback : acid-free paper) – ISBN 978-90-04-29779-1 (e-book) 1. Homosexuality–Political aspects–Europe, Eastern. 2. Homosexuality–Religious aspects–Christianity. 3. Church and state–Europe, Eastern. 4. Religion and politics–Europe, Eastern. 5. Nationalism–Religious aspects–Christianity. 6. Gays–Europe, Eastern–Social conditions. 7. Europe, Eastern–Politics and government–1989- 8. Europe, Eastern–Religion. 9. Europe, Eastern–Social conditions. 10. Europe, Eastern–Moral conditions. I. Sremac, Srdjan, 1976- II. Ganzevoort, Reinder Ruard, 1965-

HQ76.3.E852R35 2015
  306.76'60947–dc23

                                                                                    2015012323

This publication has been typeset in the multilingual "Brill" typeface. With over 5,100 characters covering Latin, IPA, Greek, and Cyrillic, this typeface is especially suitable for use in the humanities. For more information, please see www.brill.com/brill-typeface.

ISSN 1061-5210
ISBN 978-90-04-29747-0 (hardback)
ISBN 978-90-04-29779-1 (e-book)

This book is printed on acid-free paper.

Printed by Printforce, the Netherlands

# Contents

# How European is Eastern Europe?

The break-up of the former Soviet block has led to a variety of forms of differentiation among the various nations that have resulted across the last several decades. As sociologists of religion, we often look toward the extent to which religious "options" are increased as indices of democratization and inclusion. In the United States, in particular, the "melting pot" image is one that may not be specifically "sacred," but is certainly put forward as one that characterizes our society over time. Other western nations may have a different metaphor that encapsulates a similar vision within their particular national context and social space.

Volume 26 in the Religion and Social Order series looks at one specific index of differentiation between western and Eastern Europe: the extent to which "space" is made available in the society for LGBT persons. This refers to both social space and actual space, the latter of which is to be sought through Gay Pride parades—not merely for the act of the parade but for the symbolism attached to it, namely that LGBT have a right of inclusion within the national society as a whole. Gay Pride parades continue to be held in a variety of Western cities, though perhaps not as frequently today as was so a decade or two ago. In short, in the democratic West, LGBT persons are generally accepted as a part of the socio-political community. There have been, for example, a number of gay mayors, gay persons in state and federal legislatures, but also as television "stars," news commentators, sports figures, and even clergy. A number of states allow gay persons, if otherwise qualified, to be adoptive parents. Quite simply, in general, the LGBT person is accepted as part of the civil whole as long as she or he otherwise remains within our laws. The situation is basically the same in England, the Netherlands, France and so on.

This has not been the case for the most part in Eastern Europe, where a different sexual ethic continues to be informally (and occasionally formally) enforced. In general, gay persons are marginalized and—to get to the point of this volume—specifically so in religious settings. In general, the Eastern European religious establishments have taken a relatively hard line against the incorporation of LGBT persons in both civil society and the churches and mosques themselves. The "Prides" were organized as a protest against this condition and continue as a means of protest against what is seen by the LGBT as a denial of civil rights. The current volume looks at a variety of case studies of the Prides and the social processes surrounding them in the context of post-Soviet Eastern Europe, in so doing giving us a very different picture of how "freedom" can be constructed and deconstructed. I am grateful for the offering of this volume and hope it will enable you as a reader to assess and reassess the value of a comparative-differential sociology of relgion.

*William H. Swatos, Jr.*

# The Interplay of Religious and Sexual Nationalisms in Central and Eastern Europe

*Srdjan Sremac and R. Ruard Ganzevoort*

*Religious and Sexual Nationalisms in Central and Eastern Europe: Gods, Gays and Governments* is about the interplay between religion and nationalism in the context of conflicts around sexual diversity in Central and Eastern Europe. Religion, nationalism, and sexual diversity have long been contested terms, both in academia and outside. The debates on these issues, however, have changed over time. Previously nationalism was considered to be intrinsic to the public sphere, while sexuality was a matter for private consideration and religion connected the public and the private or alternated between the two, dependent on political circumstances. Since the political transformations of the last decades in Central and Eastern Europe, the public perception of both religion and sexual diversity has changed fundamentally and gained unpredicted public importance in a highly antagonistic way.

One of the prominent and fiercely contested issues in cross-cultural encounters regards precisely the position of religion, nationhood, and sexual diversity—more specifically homosexuality. Whereas several Western societies consider acceptance of sexual diversity the litmus test of tolerance and essential to human rights, hence a criterion of good citizenship, other societies see homosexuality as a threat to national, cultural, and religious identity. In these struggles, religion serves to bolster particular national and cultural identities as can be seen, for example, in the fiercely contested Gay Pride parades. Religion is at the same time embraced as a means to unite the country, a process in which sexual minorities are often seen as the "imagined or excluded others/intruders" (Ahmed 2006). Conflicts about religion and homosexuality thus not only show shifts and tensions in changing public perceptions of homosexuality, but also of religion and its function to create, facilitate, or foster nationhood (Van den Berg et al. 2014). In this way religion and nationalism are mutually reinforcing. Nationhood in this context does not necessarily refer to an institutionalized nation-state, but rather to what Anderson (1991) calls "imagined communities" or Gellner's (1983) notion of "invented communities".

This volume explores whether and how the oppositional pairing of religion and homosexuality is related to the specific religio-political configurations in different multi-layered cultural and national contexts. We therefore will examine the cultural discourses at work and explore the differences in several contexts and the cultural and political role of religion and nationhood in conflicts about sexual diversity in CEE. The "cultural discourse negotiations" represent an interpretation of homosexuality as a massive Western conspiracy and a threat to the traditional values of national and religious identity. Homosexuality is portrayed as an assault against patriarchal norms of sexual expressions and a danger to the integrity of family, tradition and the nation-state. Religion is called upon to protect morality and social norms. This discursive strategy has evoked the response in Western countries of framing Central and Eastern Europe as the "European homophobic Other" in the ongoing debate of "homoinclusive Europe" (Kulpa 2013). This tendency to orientalize Central and Eastern Europe as a "homophobic" and "undeveloped Other," dangerously premodern and religiously and sexually conservative, is problematic because it produces a discursive power of Western moral and cultural superiority over an assumedly intolerant and traditional Central and Eastern Europe.[1] These polarized perceptions obviously don't contribute to dialogue and mutual understanding but instead foster the creation of orientalizing stereotypes and the establishment of hegemonic political and cultural discourses on both sides that become instrumental in new forms of cultural colonialism.

Any attempt to understand the nature of the relationship between religious and sexual nationalisms in Central and Eastern Europe requires terminological clarification. In the academic literature the conceptual frame of sexual nationalism is often understood in terms of inclusion with an integration of homosexuality (or what has been called "sexual citizenship") into the Western nation-state building thus promoting sexual progressive rhetoric and politics as well as "pro-gay" discourse as part of the configuration of national and cultural identity (Dickinson 1999, Dudink 2011, El-Tayeb 2011, Geyer and Lehmann

---

1  Orientalism in Edward Said's (1978) terms describes how the West produces knowledge and dominates "the Orient" through academic, artistic, ideological, political, cultural and discursive processes. Orientalist rhetoric, therefore, builds its strength on the ontological and epistemological distinction made between the East and the West (between "the civilized" and "the uncivilized" societies). In this way, orientalist discourse stigmatizes other societies that do not fit into the Western-type democracy (Bakić-Hayden 1995). Maria Todorova (2009) in her book *Imagining the Balkans* applies Said's notion with "Balkanism," a discourse that creates a stereotype of the Balkans. See also Bauman and Ginrich's (2004) interpretation of Oriental Otherness, as one of the "grammars" of identity and alterity. Their interpretation allows us to see orientalism as an identity strategy that can occur in every context and not only from a Western perspective.

2004, Hayes 2000, Kuntsman and Esperanza 2008, Mosse 1985, Kulpa 2013, Puar 2007, Sabsay 2012, Stychin 1997, Walker 1996). We consider this one-sided connection of sexuality and nationalism to be flawed, because it inadvertently prioritizes Western views rather than offering an analytic tool to understand cultural discourses. We therefore use the term sexual nationalism in a broader sense to include every perspective that links nationalism with a certain view of sexuality. Both in "pro-gay" rhetoric of Western sexual citizenship and in "anti-gay" discursive practices in the Central and Eastern Europe, the role of the state is invoked to regulate sexuality through restrictive politics (pro- or anti-gay discursive regimes) in the process of justifying national self-determination. Similarly, religious nationalism refers to nationalist discourses and practices that use and regulate specific views on and practices of religion. This volume explores the crucial features of divergent configurations of religious and sexual nationalisms in Central and Eastern Europe. It shows how the interactions of sexuality, religion and nationalism are multidirectional and multidimensional and cannot be accounted for in oversimplified models.

### Religious and Sexual Nationalisms: Theoretical and Methodological Perspectives

As a highly relevant and sometimes contentious notion, religious nationalism continues to spark debates as to how it is and should be approached, particularly in relation to sexuality and sexual nationalism. What is specifically religious about religious nationalisms and what is sexual about sexual nationalisms? What is the place of religion and sexuality in the modern nation-building processes in Central and Eastern Europe? And how do religious and sexual nationalisms intersect?

The starting point for unpacking the notion of religious nationalism is the recognition that religion and nationalism share what Rieff (2008) calls a common social and/or sacred order. As Friedland (2011: 1) refers to it, they are "two ontologies [...] of divinity and of the nation-state." Both state and religion are mode(l)s of the performativity of authority and power, the regulation of social cohesion, and the governing principle of collective orders. Many theorists of religious nationalism (Aburaiya 2009, Arjomand 1994, Barker 2009, Brubaker 2012, Fukase-Indergaard and Indergaard 2008, Grigoriadis 2013, Geyer and Lehmann 2004, Leustean 2008, Juergensmeyer 2006, 2008, Requejo and Nagel 2014, Smith 2003, Friedland 2002, 2011, Van der Veer 1994) have noted that nationalism adopts some of the key religious functions and can become a "new religion of the people" (Smith 2003: 4–5).

In post-communist Central and Eastern Europe, religion and nationalism are intertwined to the degree that religion provides central elements of the symbolics of the nation, and nationalism functions as one of the key materializations of religious inspiration and morals. Religion increasingly serves as a constitutive element of nationalism and a powerful political mobilizing force. In the Western Balkans, for example, religious communities were the main catalyst of nationalism and the key discriminating marker that defined parties in the conflict. In a similar vein, Rogobete (2009: 566) notes that ethnic conflicts can rehabilitate religion and cause a revival of traditional religiosity which can often provide the impetus for more violence in conflict zones. Consequently, religious institutions have acquired unpredicted political importance, and post-communist societies are still searching for an adequate understanding of religion. Although these countries are secular by constitution, intermingling between the religious and the national (political) is clearly evident in the public discourse. Religious nationalisms, therefore, emerge as collective identity markers in political debates and popular culture. It should be noted, however, that religious nationalisms must be understood in a concrete social and national context, and the patterns of religious nationalisms vary from country to country. This is the reason why we use the terms religious (and sexual) nationalisms in plural.

Mark Juergensmeyer (2008: 152), a dominant voice in interpreting religious nationalisms, rightly recognizes that the fall of communism and the rapid changes and transitions in political and economic systems in Central and Eastern Europe ended one form of secular transnationalism and provoked the tension between secular and religious nationalism in the years to come. As secular ties have begun to unravel in the post-Soviet and post-communist Eastern Europe and the ideological vacuum of post-socialism becomes unbearable, local leaders have searched for new political capital to incorporate religious elements into their ethnonational ideological matrix. In the post-communist transformations, religious nationalisms emerged as a reaction to a secular nationalism that had proved to be ineffective, weak and unable to provide sufficient differentiation between ethnic or political entities (Abazović 2010).[2] However, not only the communist system had failed them. Juergensmeyer (2008:167) argues that religious nationalists also lost their faith in Western-type secular nationalism, since they "reject its antireligious bias and its claims of

---

2   Mitchell (2006: 1140) argues that religion is support for ethnicity and nationalism because
    religion "is not just a marker of identity, but rather its symbols, rituals and organisations are
    used to boost ethnic identity." In other words, religion is "the fabric of ethnicity."

universality." This departure from "secular replacement" to "neo-traditionalist" models (Grigoriadis 2013) and its incorporation of religious elements into national ideology can to some extent explain the evidence of desecularization in several Central and Eastern European societies and the sociopolitics embedded in extreme ethnoreligious ideologies. Religious nationalisms in these contexts are not a premodern backlash but emerge from modernity and appear mostly as a substitute for post-civil or post-ethnic nationalism (cf. Topić and Sremac 2014).

Roger Friedland (2011) classifies three main characteristics of religious nationalism. According to him:

- Religious nationalists understand the nation-state as a collective religious subject.
- They seek to extend and derive the authority of the state from an absolute divine act rather than from a subjective accumulation of the demos; and
- For them the nation-state in which they live and operate is construed as an instrument of the divine.

It seems that the goal of religious nationalists is to establish the institutional and national infrastructure that would allow people (or at least their followers) to live their lives in obedience to God's will. Therefore, the political theological program of religious nationalists and its project of "sacralization of the nation-state" propagates a return of religion to the public domain. The objectives of religious nationalisms thus are both political and religious, and we would misunderstand the phenomenon if we would entertain a functional-reductionist interpretation in one direction or the other.

Juergensmeyer, Friedland, Smith and other theorists pay much attention to the institutionalized forms of religious nationalisms (e.g., focus on political and religious elites) and less on religious nationalisms of "ordinary people" or what Billig (1995) calls "banal nationalism." Similarly, Hobsbawm (1983: 10) argues that nationalism "cannot be understood unless analyzed from below, that is in terms of the assumptions, hopes, needs, longings, and interests of ordinary people." Future research on religious nationalisms, therefore, needs to focus more on what we call "lived (religious) nationalism," which engages with religious nationalistic practices and performativity of "real people."

Based on the literature review and the material in this volume we identify the key elements of religious nationalisms: sacralization of politics, exclusivity and the promotion of group homogeneity and aggressive separation from racial or sexual "others", the employment of religious rhetoric and symbolic resources, disciplining the body and sexuality, totalitarianism and extremism. Religious nationalisms also give people an ideological justification and a set of discursive practices for the radical transformation of society, culture, politics, and institutions based on its ultimate religious values and purpose. These elements have proved to be crucial for the creation of national identities and a sense of nationhood and eventually led to "the establishment of a preferential relationship between the dominant religion and the state" (Grigoriadis 2013: 10). This makes religious nationalism prone to becoming militant and violent, tapping into a distinctive ontology of power and control. It comes as no surprise that, in many cases, this accumulation of nationalism creates deep-rooted religious and/or ethnic conflicts that are almost impossible to resolve (e.g., the conflict in the Western Balkans or more recently in Eastern Ukraine).

While in some cases it is relatively easy to identify this ambivalent relationship or what Grigoriadis (2013) calls the "sacred synthesis" between religion and nationalism or nationhood, it is more difficult to conceptualize the ways in which religious discourse frames and shapes this interaction. Rather than asking what the relation between religion and nationalism is, Brubaker suggests that the more fruitful conceptual and methodological approach might be to specify how the relation can be investigated productively. He offers four approaches to scrutinizing the relationship between religion and nationalism. The first is to consider religion and nationalism (along with ethnicity and race) as *analogous* phenomena. The second way seeks to specify how religion helps explain nationalism—its origin and power. The third way explains religion as part of nationalism rather than an external explanation of it. The fourth and final way of exploring and explaining the connection between religion and nationalism is to posit religious nationalism as a distinctive kind of nationalism. Brubaker (2012: 16) suggests that the interplay between nationalist political and religious discourse can "accommodate the claims of religion, and nationalist rhetoric often deploys religious language, imagery and symbols. Similarly, religion can accommodate the claims of the nation-state, and religious movements can deploy nationalist discourse."

The next step in constructing our theoretical framework is to make the connection to discourses about sexuality and therefore to sexual nationalism. Friedland (2011) helpfully claims that religious nationalisms have an erotic component. Along the same lines of argument, Parker and colleagues (1992: 1) note that "[w]henever the power of nation is invoked—whether it be in the media, in scholarly texts, or in everyday conversation—we are more likely than not to find it couched *as a love of country*: an eroticized nationalism." In this view, there is a link between religion and sexuality and nationhood that needs further exploration, not because the religious and erotic are contested terms, but because religious nationalisms are organized around erotic discourse, heteronormativity, patriarchal (often militarized) masculinity and the gendered order of society, leading to specific moral regimes. For analytical simplicity, we make reference to interactive dimensions and main analytical tools for understanding religious and sexual nationalisms: *the nation-state, family,* and *body.*

If we take the lens of gender as a starting point, we can observe that CEE nationalisms idealize masculinity as the basis of the nation-state and emphasize the family as the cornerstone of the nation and society. The ideal of masculinity is threatened as a symbol of national regeneration and self-defense (Mosse 1985, 1998). In this regard, religion serves not only as a conservative force protecting the traditional, national and moral value systems but also as the obligation of regulating and controlling sexuality through public discourses. As Peterson (1999) rightly argues, the conjuncture of (religious) nationalist ideologies and practices and their connection to (homo)sexuality is inseparable from the political power of nation-state building. Accordingly, these religious nationalisms can be understood as sexual nationalisms rejecting non-normative sexualities. Religious and sexual nationalisms as understood in Central and Eastern Europe give primacy to family issues, group reproduction and the defense of the patriarchal order of society. In some cases it is framed around the discourse of blasphemization of the western culture or the heretical devastation of the sacredness of the nation, tradition, family, and body.[3] On this ground, Peterson (2010) claims that heterosexism is "naturalized" through multiple discursive strategies and religious doctrines as the only "normal" mode of sexual identity and practice. In this discursive normativization of heterosexuality, nationalists seek to "masculinize the public sphere" (Friedland 2011: 401), and protect the sanctity of marriage and the family (Mosse 1985). The regulative principles of sexual order are thus based on a "rigid sexual moralism" and "hetero-normative politics of desire" (Cooper 2008: 27, 32). For religious and sexual nationalists, homosexuality is construed as a threat to society and a force that emasculates, destabilizes or weakens the national body. It is depicted as excessive, transgressive and dangerous. Consequently, the national regeneration program often promoted by religious and sexual nationalist movements seeks to discipline, in various ways, the sexuality and sexual behavior of its members for the

---

3  In Serbia, for example, the emergence of homosexuality as a topic of debate has been interpreted in Church circles as an imposition of the "decadent West" and as foreign and dangerous to Serbian identity, morality, tradition and culture (see Van der Berg et al. 2014 and Sremac et al. in this volume). Similar discursive framing of homosexuality as a Western conspiracy may be observed in Russia and other Central and Eastern European countries.

well-being of the nation (Pryke 1998). Therefore, those who deviate from heteronormative sexuality are treated as either "sick" or "abnormal." In this way,
homosexuals become "biologically dangerous" (Lemke 2011: 43) and have to be
eliminated from the national body. The politicization of sexuality, therefore,
serves to divide society radically into the "healthy" and the "sick"—those loyal
to tradition and nation and those who have betrayed it.

It then comes as no surprise that these religious nationalists consider themselves to be the protectors of the social order and advocates of strict moral
programs that target and prohibit the public expression of homosexuality. It
is usually justified on the basis of divine rather than secular sexual politics,
allowing religious nationalists to establish the rules of "sacred" social order as
the only moral order prescribed by God (Cooper 2008). The sacred social order
is fundamentally antagonistic toward the constructed enemies of that sacred
social order. The authority of their ethno-national and religious powers thrives
on the principle of exclusion. In this way, the sacred-social order becomes crucial to the process of nation-building, providing ontological force to notions
of identity and exclusion, authority and subordination. In many cases, as we
shall see in this volume, religious nationalist and clerical movements create
a social atmosphere of public hatred to further their agenda. The interplay
between religious frontiers and "national threats," therefore, has important
ramifications for national preservation, the biological survival of a population
and "moral" defense.


### The Structure of the Volume

For better understanding of religious and sexual nationalisms in Central and
Eastern Europe and the academic reflection on their dimensions and ramifications, this volume offers a variety of perspectives. The authors not only show
the ambivalent relationship between nationalisms, religion and (homo)sexual-
ity, they also highlight the fact that to understand these configurations we need
to look beyond the usual perception of (homo)sexuality in Central and Eastern
Europe and take into account both global processes and very contextual trajectories. The authors will thus not only describe the oppositional pairing of
religion and homosexuality in contemporary discourse in Central and Eastern
Europe but will also provide in-depth insights into some of the religious formations informing the sexual politics of the nation states.

In the opening chapter, anthropologist Marek Mikuš describes the role of
religious nationalism and ultranationalist groups in sustaining resistance to the
Pride Parade and LGBT rights in Serbia. He argues that the social and political

ideology of radical nationalist groups made appeals about the nature of Serbian (Orthodox) identity, morality, the "true" Serbian nation, and calls for a clear anti-EU stance and desecularization of the public sphere. In his analysis, Mikuš shows that the Pride Parade has become one of the main lines of confrontation between liberal civil society and the "Europeanizing" state, on the one hand, and nationalist organizations and movements, on the other. These struggles expressed two antagonistic visions of a legitimate social order. While the LGBT activists and the government voiced a liberal discourse of individual freedom and equality framed by the policy of "Europeanization," the nationalists called for a complete political sovereignty and cultural autonomy of the Serbian "nation." The author concludes that the nationalists have failed to build a strong social and political coalition to challenge the advance of Serbia's EU integration and liberalization.

In his contribution to the volume, Mihai Tarta demonstrates how the secularization/modernization thesis appears as a powerful form of cultural imperialism in emerging countries like Poland and Romania, where religion's vitality is strongly connected with nationalism. He argues that in Poland and Romania there is a close link between the Church and state, which he calls civil religion, a hybrid of nationalist discourse and traditional religion. The emerging dispute centers on national identity, (homo)sexuality and the role of religion in public, and the specific actors are the traditional Churches with sufficient power and bureaucratic influence, and secular forces backing the European Union's laws regarding minorities. Minority rights, human rights, abortion and the importance of religion in politics form the theme of a new social pact that would bring Christianity to Europe's center. In reply, Tarta argues, minority rights promoters mostly challenge the churches' political role using the orientalist and secularist rhetoric of the culture wars.

Srdjan Sremac, Zlatiborka Popov Momčinović, Martina Topić, and Miloš Jovanović offer comparative perspectives on religion, nationalism and (homo)-sexuality in the media context of the former Yugoslavia. They show how the fall of communism triggered the revival of ethnicity and religion within the national spaces. In this context, the status and application of LGBT rights remains one of the most polarising political issues in the countries of the former Yugoslavia. In their discourse analysis, the authors show how both in Serbia and in Bosnia and Herzegovina the media, with their lack of critical distance, contributed to the circulation of hate speech, lending support to well-established power structures and hierarchies. Croatia presents a different case where the media do not openly agitate toward discrimination of LGBT groups and where Gay Pride manifestations are regularly held more-or-less without incident. However, the overall continuing influence of the Catholic Church should not be underestimated. The authors conclude that the conjuncture of (religious) nationalist ideology and practice and its connection to (homo)sexuality is inseparable from the political power of nation-state building in the post-Yugoslav space.

Drawing on the poststructuralist discourse theory developed by Ernesto Laclau and Chantal Mouffe and the examination of press cuts gathered in the Polish Central Archives of Modern Records, Dorota Hall presents public debates about religion, nationalism and homosexuality conducted in Poland since the end of 1980s. Her chapter shows that the opposition between religion and homosexuality is neither an obvious nor a static phenomenon. Engaging various discursive components within the social field, in close correspondence to articulation practices enabling the formation of various subject positions within the social struggle for hegemony.

Mariecke van den Berg and Zlatiborka Popov Momčinović investigate the construction and representation of minority discourses in responses to Papal statements on homosexuality in Bosnia and Herzegovina and Sweden. The authors argue that while the socio-political configurations of both countries are very different, similar processes and strategies are at work in the construction of a coherent national Self through both the silencing and the strategic representation of minority discourses. They clarify the paradox that dominant discourses of religion and homosexuality are both in opposition to, as well as dependent upon, counter-discourses from the margins against which the desired national identity is framed. Van den Berg and Popov Momčinović understand religious and sexual nationalisms as the simultaneous formation of national, religious and sexual identities in a particular geographical context of the nation-state. Furthermore, the authors show a number of case studies of public debate, using a multi-method approach: critical discourse analysis of minority voices from the "hidden spaces" of the Internet such as blogs, forums and religious websites, as well as the "echo" of these voices in public discourse.

Alar Kilp shows highly problematized public controversies over the legal rights of same-sex couples in the Baltic states. The success and failure of the attempts to introduce same-sex union laws is explained by the balance of power between the discourses advanced by the change (mostly supranational courts and institutions and transnational activist networks) and blocking coalitions (alliances of mostly national religious, social and political actors) of the legislative change. The author argues that churches strive not only to impose a particular sexual order, but also to re-define the existing state-religion relationship in a way that would give churches more power over what have so far been regarded as secular domains.

Tamara Pavasović Trošt and Koen Slootmaeckers analyze the relationship between religious institutions, nationalism and homosexuality by examining how the major religious institutions in the Western Balkans (specifically the Catholic Church in Croatia, the Orthodox Church in Serbia and Montenegro, and the Islamic Community in Bosnia) are playing a role in *defining the nation* through their statements about homosexuality. While these institutions are vocal in their opinions on, for example, same-sex marriage and gay parades, the authors focus only on those statements in which parallels were drawn between the nation and positions about homosexuality. The authors take a "top-bottom" content analysis approach, systematically exploring the discourse utilized by these religious institutions examining how these prominent institutions play a role in defining discourse about the nation.

In our final chapter, Magda Dolinska Rydzek and Mariecke van den Berg analyze present-day discursive strategies associating the homosexual minority with the notion of the "Antichrist," which are applied in texts published in the Russian Internet by nationalist and religious movements. Implementing critical discourse analysis as a methodological frame, the authors aim at explaining how the Antichrist-based discourse may be understood and valued. The authors show how the dominant ideology that labels homosexuality as a "threat" to the heteronormative character of contemporary Russian state may be reproduced and constructed by religious nationalists.

### Conclusion

While we engage with the transnational dimensions and discussions of the contested notions and effects of present-day constructions of (homo)sexuality, nationalism and religion, the volume retains a major focus on its context-specific debates in relation to the respective and very different national settings, histories, cultures and religious traditions. Undoubtedly the contributors in this volume provide alternative mappings of this intertwining territory of religious and sexual nationalisms in Central and Eeastern Europe, yet this only demonstrates more keenly the need for further work in this manner from a global perspective.

As the contributors show, the debates about religion and homosexuality are produced by much more multifaceted and multidirectional discursive framings on culture, nation and gender. The interplay between religion and homosexuality is not only defined by specific moral, philosophical, or spiritual presuppositions. These positions emerge from discursive negotiations in a wider public arena, in which cultural and national identities play a crucial role. Thus the discursive negotiations of (homo)sexuality in Central and Eastern Europe not only rely on religious and/or theological arguments, but on a combination of religious, sexual, political and nationalistic discourses. In this way, religious nationalist movements present themselves not only as religious and moral, but also as political agents. Paradoxically, their political-theological programs aim to establish the institutional and national infrastructure according to secular principles. The discourses about (homo)sexuality are usually presented as a danger to the societies of Central and Eastern Europe, either in political, moral or religious terms. It is often framed as a reinforcement of new cultural norms and propagation of (homo)sexual propaganda by the "decadent West" (certainly in Serbia and Russia). Homosexuality is therefore framed as a threat to traditional values of the nation, family and the gendered order of society.

Taken together, these chapters show that is it not correct to treat religious performances and debates as purely political nationalist instances with a religious guise or the other way around. The dynamic interplay between religious and political actors, negotiating powers and meanings against the background of cultural narratives and international politics, results in this wide variety of configurations. The views on sexuality, notably homosexuality, play a role in both these cultural narratives and international politics and are therefore important social-discursive elements in how political and religious actors position themselves vis-à-vis each other.

## References

Abazović, Dino. 2010. "Religijski nacionalizam na Zapadnom Balkanu." Pp. 13–23 in M. Sitarski, M. Vujačić, and I. Bartulović-Karastojković (eds.) *Iščekujući Evropsku Uniju*. Beograd: BOS.

Aburaiya, Issam. 2009. "Islamism, Nationalism, and Western Modernity: The Case of Iran and Palestine." *International Journal of Politics, Culture and Society* 22: 57–68.

Ahmed, Sara. 2006. *Queer Phenomenology: Orientations, Objects, Others*. Durham, NC: Duke University Press.

Anderson, Benedict. 1999. *Imagined Communities* (2nd edn.) London: Verso.

Arjomand, Said A. 1994. "Fundamentalism, Religious Nationalism, or Populism?" *Contemporary Sociology* 23: 671–675.

Bauman, Gerd, and Andre Ginrich. 2004. *Grammars of Identity/Alterity: A Structural Approach*. New York: Berghahn Books.

Baker, Philip W. 2009. *Religious Nationalism in Modern Europe: If God be for Us*. London: Routledge.

Bakić-Hayden, Milica. 1992. "Nesting Orientalism: The Case of Former Yugoslavia." *Slavic Review* 54: 917–931.

Billig, Michael. 1995. *Banal Nationalism*. Thousand Oaks, CA: Sage.

Brubaker, Rogers. 2012. "Religion and Nationalism: Four Approaches." *Nation and Nationalism* 18: 2–20.

Cooper, Melinda. 2008. "Orientalism in the Mirror: The Sexual Politics of Anti-Westernism." *Theory, Culture & Society* 26: 25–49.

Dickinson, Peter. 1999. *Here is Queer: Nationalism, Sexualities, and the Literatures of Canada*. Toronto: University of Toronto Press.

Dudink, Stefan P. 2011. "Homosexuality, Race, and the Rhetoric of Nationalism." *History of the Present* 1: 259–264.

El-Tayeb, Fatima. 2001. *European Others: Queering Ethnicity in Postnational Europe*. Minneapolis: University of Minnesota Press.

Friedland, Roger. 2001. "Religious Nationalism and the Problem of Collective Representation." *Annual Review of Sociology* 27: 125–152.

———. 2002. "Money, Sex, and God: The Erotic Logic of Religious Nationalism." *Sociological Theory* 20: 381–425.

Fukase-Indergaard, Famiko and Michael Indergaard. 2008. "Religious Nationalism and the Making of the Modern Japanese State." *Theory and Society* 37: 343–374.

Gellner, Ernest. 1983. *Nations and Nationalism*. Ithaca, NY: Cornel University Press.

Geyer, Michael and Hartmut Lehmann (eds.). 2004. *Religion und Nation, Nation und Religion*. Göttingen: Wallstein Verlag.

Grigoriadis, Ioannis N. 2013. *Instilling Religion in Greek and Turkish Nationalism: A "Sacred Synthesis."* New York: Palgrave Macmillan.

Hayes, Jarrod. 2000. *Queer Nations: Marginal Sexualities in the Maghreb*. Chicago: University of Chicago Press.

Hobsbawm, Eric. 1983. "The Invention of Tradition." Pp. 1–14 in E. Hobsbawm, and T. Ranger (eds.), *The Invention of Tradition*. Cambridge: Cambridge University Press.

Juergensmeyer, Mark. 2006. "Nationalism and Religion." Pp. 357–367 in A.R. Segal (ed.) *The Blackwell Companion to the Study of Religion*. Malden: Blackwell.

———. 2008. *Global Rebellion: Religious Challenges to the Secular State, from Christian Militias to al Qaeda*. Berkeley: University of California Press.

Kuntsman, Adi and Miyake Esperanza. (eds.). 2008. *Out of Place: Interrogating Silences in Queerness/Raciality*. York: Raw Nerve Books.

Lemke, Thomas. 2011. *Biopolitics: An Advanced Introduction*. New York: NYU Press.

Leustean, Lucian N. 2008. "Orthodoxy and Political Myths in Balkan National Identities." *National Identities* 10: 421–432.

Mitchell, Claire. 2006. "Religious Content of Ethnic Identities." *Sociology* 40: 1135–1152.

Mosse, George L. 1985. *Nationalism and Sexuality: Respectability and Abnormal Sexuality in Modern Europe*. New York: Howard Fertig.

——. 1998. *The Image of Man: The Creation of Modern Masculinity*. New York: Oxford University Press.

Parker, Andrew, Mary Russo, Doris Sommer, and Patricia Yaeger (eds.). 1992. *Nationalisms and Sexualities*. London: Routledge.

Pryke, Sam. 1998. "Nationalism and Sexuality, What are the Issues?" *Nations and Nationalism* 4: 529–546.

Puar, Jasbir. 2007. *Terrorist Assemblages: Homonationalism in Queer Times*. Durham, NC: Duke University Press.

——. 2013. "Rethinking Nomonationalism." *International Journal of Middle East Studies* 45: 336–339.

Requejo, Ferran and Klaus-Jürgen Nagel (eds.). 2014. *Politics of Religion and Nationalism: Federalism, Consociationalism and Seccession*. London: Routledge.

Rieff, Philip. 2008. *Sacred Order/Social Order: The Jew of Culture—Freud, Mosses, and Modernity (Vol. 3)*. Charlottesville: University of Virginia Press.

Rogobete, Silviu E. 2009. "The Interplay of Ethnic and Religious Identities in Europe: A Possible Mapping of a Complex Territory." *Europolis*, 6: 563–584.

Sabsay, Leticia. 2012. "The Emergence of the Other Sexual Citizen: Orientalism and the Modernisation of Sexuality." *Citizenship Studies* 16: 605–623.

Said, Edward W. 1978. *Orientalism*. New York: Vintage.

Smith, Anthony D. 2003. *Chosen Peoples: Sacred Sources of National Identity*. Oxford: Oxford University Press.

Stychin, Carl F. 1997. "Queer Nations: Nationalism, Sexuality and the Discourse of Rights in Quebec." *Feminist Legal Studies* 5: 3–34.

Todorova, Maria. 2009. *Imagining the Balkans*. Oxford: Oxford University Press.

Topić, Martina and Srdjan Sremac (eds.). 2014. *Europe as a Multiple Modernity: Multiplicity of Religious Identities and Belonging*. Newcastle: Cambridge Scholars Publishing.

Van den Berg, Mariecke, David Boss, Marco Derks, R. Ruard Ganzevoort, Miloš Jovanović, and Srdjan Sremac. 2014. "Religion, Homosexuality, and Contested Social Orders in the Netherlands, the Western Balkans, and Sweden." Pp. 116–134 in G. Ganiel, H. Winkel and C. Monnot (eds.) *Religion in Times of Crisis*. Leiden: Brill.

Van der Veer, Peter. 1994. *Religious Nationalism: Hindus and Muslims in India*. Berkeley: University of California Press.

Walker, Brian. 1996. "Social Movements as Nationalism or, On the Very Idea of a Queer Nation." *Canadian Journal of Philosophy* 22: 505–550.

# CHAPTER 1

# "Faggots Won't Walk through the City": Religious Nationalism and LGBT Pride Parades in Serbia

*Marek Mikuš*

Over the past 15 years, the rights of LGBT persons have been a contentious public issue in Serbia. Stigmatizing and discriminatory attitudes toward LGBT people are frequently expressed in public discourse and through social practices (Greenberg 2006, Kahlina 2014, Mikuš 2011, Nielsen 2013, Stakić 2011). Struggles over the attempts to hold an annual LGBT Pride Parade in Belgrade have become a symbolic focus of the LGBT controversy. In 2010, the first Pride with a full security backing from the state was held, but threats, riots and other forms of violence overshadowed the apparent success. The Ministry of the Interior subsequently banned the Prides scheduled to be held in 2011–2013. The next Pride took place in 2014.

Numerous public actors argued that Pride was unacceptable for the Serbian nation because it contravened Serbian Orthodoxy. The concept of religious nationalism has been used to analyze such articulations of the idioms of religion and nation around the world (e.g. Barr 2010, Brubaker 2012, Grigoriadis 2013, Van der Veer 1994, Juergensmeyer 1993, 2006, 2008), including Serbia and other post-Yugoslav states (Drezgić 2010, Perica 2002). In this chapter, I build on my ethnographic fieldwork to examine how nationalist NGOs and movements, or the "patriotic bloc" as they sometimes call themselves, used religious nationalist discourse in their struggle against Pride. In the first part of the chapter, I offer a brief account of their history, organizational practices and external relationships. I show how these organizations and their supporters, including the Serbian Orthodox Church, fought against an alliance of the state, LGBT NGOs and a broader liberal civil society over which issues and norms had a legitimate presence in the public sphere. I illustrate this further with the example of the anti-Pride "Family Walks" in the second section. In the third part, I focus on the historical roots, social ideology and current uses of religious nationalist discourse. Finally, I highlight the nationalists' populist presentation of their anti-Pride campaign as a defense of the collective rights of the Serbian nation, and consider the audience and achievements of this strategy.

© KONINKLIJKE BRILL NV, LEIDEN, 2015 | DOI: 10.1163/9789004297791_003

### Patriotic Bloc

Nationalist NGOs and movements started to emerge in the late 1990s. At the time, they criticized the regime of Slobodan Milošević for being insufficiently nationalist and traditionalist while, ironically, the liberal and "pro-European" opposition found it to be intolerably so. However, their number and level of activity have been growing much faster since 2000. In this period, Serbia's political, economic and cultural globalization advanced while nationalism in institutional politics was progressively marginalized. This has led the nationalists to adopt an increasingly oppositional and even insurgent posture. In recent years, they became highly visible in the media and urban landscapes, and domestic public figures have expressed concerns over their radical ideology, propensity to violence and constituency among youth, including football hooligans (Kostovicova 2006, Nielsen 2013).

Nationalist organizations could be described as a specific type of NGO, although some have gradually become political movements with parliamentary ambitions. Many registered with state authorities as "associations of citizens," just like most other NGOs. They usually possessed, at least nominally, decision-making structures typical for NGOs, such as management boards. Although many of these groups call themselves "movements," their members often referred to them as "associations" or "organizations" (but never as "NGOs") during public speeches and interviews they gave me.[1] The core group of activists of these organizations tends to be relatively small, as was obvious from the modest turnout at the meetings that I attended. In interviews and meetings, the leaders complained that often only a fraction of Facebook "attendees" actually came to a rally. Large crowds were more likely to attend protests that addressed burning issues of the day, and the participants at these often do not consider themselves members or supporters of any particular nationalist organization.

Nationalist organizations focus on doing politics—by means of protesting, organizing talks and discussions (*tribine*), and spreading what they call *propaganda* through posters, stickers, graffiti, banners, fanzines, magazines and the Internet. All major organizations regularly update their websites, and many run email newsletters and busy Facebook accounts. They use these channels

---

1   I interviewed high-ranking members of the 1389 Serbian National Movement, the Dveri ("Doors of the Iconostasis") Serbian Assembly, the Naši ("Ours") Serbian National Movement, the Nomokanon ("Nomocanon") Association of the Students of the Faculty of Law, and the Obraz ("Honor") Fatherland Movement. I refer to these organizations, in keeping with the convention in Serbia, by the non-generic part of their names, e.g. Dveri.

to advertise their activities, present their political agendas and comment on current issues. A lot of effort is spent on "campaigns," consisting of putting up posters and stickers with political messages and the organizations' logos and names.

Because nationalist organizations do not "implement projects" like other NGOs (and obviously because of their politics), they do not receive funding from foreign donors. The nationalists I interviewed told me that their work was voluntary and that the organizations' main source of funding was donations from activists and sympathizers. The groups invited their supporters through newsletters and website banners to send donations to their accounts or buy "patriotic" merchandise. The diaspora was also targeted. Dveri worked with the Serbian Orthodox Church eparchies[2] in Western countries to organize visits to Serbian communities, with fundraising being one of the goals. In a small number of cases, Dveri received funding from ministries, municipalities or state-controlled enterprises.

### Public Pride?

The thirteen-year-long history of the Belgrade Pride Parade (*Parada ponosa*) is to a great extent one of sustained resistance to it. The participants in the first Pride of June 2001 were beaten, in some cases severely, by a thousand-strong crowd of young men. The police reported that the attackers included football hooligans[3] and members of the nationalist organization Obraz, whose leader is captured on the footage of the incident. The next two attempts to organize a Parade, in 2004 and 2009, were met with nationalist threats and called off for security reasons. After the 2009 cancellation, the Public Prosecution Office asked the Constitutional Court to ban Obraz, the 1389 Movement and Nacionalni stroj ("National Formation"). One of the reasons was their supposed involvement in anti-Pride activities. In 2011, the Prosecution submitted a new request for a ban on the 1389 Movement, the 1389 Serbian National Movement[4] and the Naši Serbian National Movement. The Constitutional Court banned Obraz and Nacionalni stroj but refused to ban the other organizations. The

---

2  In the Eastern churches, an eparchy (in Serbian *eparhija*) is a territorial diocese governed by a bishop.
3  The involvement of football hooligans in anti-Pride mobilizations is long-standing and significant (Nielsen 2013).
4  The 1389 Serbian National Movement (hereafter "1389") splintered from the original 1389 Movement in 2008. It is larger and more active than the rump 1389 Movement.

leaders of Obraz and 1389 were judged guilty of inciting hatred against LGBT persons before the 2009 Pride (one of these rulings was later overturned).

In October 2010, the first Pride since 2001 was held. On that sunny Indian summer morning, I joined a group of friends, all employees of a large liberal NGO.[5] We entered the designated downtown area through the calmest of the three "entry points." Normally busy boulevards were hermetically closed and eerily vacant, patrolled by a helicopter and thousands of policemen, gendarmes and military policemen who formed three concentric "rings" around the zone. We saw few opponents of the Pride, but our seemingly relaxed conversation barely masked the tension. In the safe zone, I heard distressed participants sharing the news—inaccurate as it turned out—that "they broke through the blockade." As 1,000 of us listened to mostly formal and dull speeches, walked the route of some 800 meters to the Student Cultural Centre, where the closing party, I suspect, never really took off, and finally boarded armored police vans which transported people to their respective neighborhoods. Simultaneously, the biggest riots in recent years were unfolding throughout central Belgrade. An estimated 6,000 young men, who split into smaller groups but coordinated via cell phones and messengers on motorbikes, were fighting the police. They set ablaze vehicles and bins, looted shops, attacked the seats of the three political parties in power, and pushed two abandoned trolleybuses downhill. More than 140 people were injured, mostly policemen. About 250 rioters were detained, but the vast majority were released without charges. A small number were given penalties at the legally prescribed minimum, but even these rulings were mostly overturned.

Before the Pride, the nationalists repeated for the media, with a prophetic matter-of-factness, that "there won't be a gay parade" but avoided explicit calls for violence. Posters reading "We're expecting you!" and depicting a rowdy crowd waving Obraz flags appeared in downtown Belgrade. Other organizations had their own "campaigns" limited to posting stickers. Numerous anonymous graffiti read "Blood will pour on the streets / There won't be a gay parade," "Death to faggots," or "Stop the parade." After the Pride, the nationalists blamed the "regime" and the organizers and attendees for "provoking" the righteous anger of patriotic youths. In 2011, four leaders of Obraz were found guilty of planning and coordinating the riots, and ten more people, including Obraz members, of taking part. (This ruling too was overturned.) Given that little information about the evidence raised became public, and the rioters neither wore symbols of nationalist groups nor were so identified in the media (with

---

5   Author's fieldnotes, 10 October 2010.

the exception of Obraz), the exact relationship between the organizations and the riots is largely unknown. However, the publicly available information and my own data discussed below suggest that at least some nationalists took part.

The 2010 Pride was organized by a group of LGBT NGOs and attended, apart from some Serbian and foreign officials, by many people from what could be termed a liberal civil society: members of liberal and human rights NGOs, political parties, artists and journalists. The practices of these people and their opponents may be understood as a struggle for public space—in the literal sense of the symbolically valuable space of central Belgrade, but by extension the entire public sphere.[6] The official slogan of the 2010 Pride was "Let's walk together." This brought up the symbolism of "walks" (šetnje)—protest marches through central urban spaces originally associated with the anti-Milošević opposition (Jansen 2001: 39–40). In the context of Pride, walking represented a claim to an open and legitimate presence of LGBT people and issues in public space. That the nationalists understood this was obvious from their focus on preventing Pride but not indoor LGBT events, such as exhibitions or talks, which comprised the run-up to each Pride from 2010 onward. Some of the anti-Pride graffiti vowed quite specifically that "the faggot won't walk through the city."

During the interviews they gave me, as well as in their verbal and written statements, the nationalists invariably denied that their members committed any offence to stop the Pride. They claimed that the arrests, lawsuits and rulings against them were "illegal," "unjust" and motivated by "political persecution." However, their discourse was rather different in an evening meeting I attended in November 2011. Naši called the meeting in a Belgrade café to discuss "whether the patriotic bloc could at all unite."[7] The crowd consisted of smaller groups of men and some women mostly in their teens and 20s. While some youths wore hoodies and sweatpants, associated with football hooligans, a boy at the next table was clutching his Orthodox prayer rope. In their speeches, the leaders of several organizations called for more unity in the fragmented "patriotic bloc," though with few specific proposals for action. Ivan Ivanović, leader of

---

6  I understand "public sphere" as an arena in modern societies where political deliberation occurs through discourse and where social identities are constructed and enacted (Fraser 1990). Access to the public sphere is often restricted for people of a certain gender, class, ethnicity or, as the present case illustrates, sexuality. Some practices, including religious (Asad 2003: 181–186), may be also excluded from the public sphere and restricted to the private sphere. This chapter shows how such exclusions and private/public distinctions become themselves the object of struggle.

7  Author's fieldnotes, 17 November 2011.

Naši and teacher of religious education in his 30s, complained that the organizations arranged their own events, which attracted fleeting media attention, but did not "contribute anything concrete." Mladen Obradović, leader of Obraz, intervened: "Don't say that, brother, what about the parade?" He referred to the cancellation of the 2011 Pride a month earlier, which the nationalists experienced as their grand victory. Ivanović conceded: "That's an example of when we all united for a joint action." Shortly afterwards, all the speakers were asked to answer the same set of questions, including which organizations they considered "patriotic." Ivanović responded:

> [P]eople who came to the [2010] gay parade and clashed with the cordons of police and were ready to die in the defense of Serbhood (*srpstvo*) and Orthodoxy, those are real patriots. Every organization that showed up on that day and brought its people on that day specifically, and which wasn't embarrassed and afraid to come out on the street, those are patriotic organizations.

In an insider setting, Ivanović effectively admitted that his organization and other "patriotic" organizations participated in the riots. However, the nationalists did not only attempt to stop the Pride with symbolic or physical violence, but they held their own performances of an occupation of public space as well.

### Family Walks

Days before the 2009 Parade was to be held, Dveri organized the first of a series of events called "Family Walk" (*Porodična šetnja*). In hindsight, this marked the beginning of their expansion from an association of citizens to a fledgling party. Dveri was established in 1999 by a group of students of the Faculty of Philology at the University of Belgrade. These people now constitute the leadership of Dveri as both association of citizens and, since 2011, a political movement. As trademark activities, they used to publish a fanzine and later a magazine *Dveri srpske* ("Serbian Doors of the Iconostasis") and organize debates. They enjoyed exceptionally close ties to the Serbian Orthodox Church whose high dignitaries attended and spoke at their events. Until late 2010 or early 2011, prominent Dveri members worked in the editorial team of *Pravoslavlje* ("Orthodoxy"), the official magazine of the Patriarchate. They also worked with Church-affiliated youth organizations to prepare several "assemblies of Orthodox youth." Dveri announced they would "enter politics" in 2011 and have participated in various elections since then. The 2009 and 2010 Family Walks may be thus interpreted as a part of Dveri's gradual shift from rather "intellectual" activities to mass political mobilization, and the launch of a discourse on family as the *leitmotif* of their party rhetoric.

The 2010 Walk replicated many of the pragmatic, discursive and iconographic elements pioneered by the 2009 Walk. At one o'clock on that Saturday, a day before the Pride, the plaza near the Faculty of Philosophy in downtown Belgrade was teeming with men, women and children of all ages and social backgrounds. Apart from Serbian flags, banners provided by Dveri could be seen in the crowd, reading "We defend the family," "The movement for the family" and "Life is on our side." A large banner above the improvised podium assured onlookers that "We are not a party, we are a family." Srđan Nogo, a member of the Dveri management board, welcomed everyone at "a family protest in the defense of the family and for the cancellation of the gay parade." He yelled that nobody asked "us" whether we agree to pay the costs of "this shameful event," which is against the constitution, public morals, and the opinion of the "Serbian majority" and the Church. Miroslav Parović then blamed the Parade on the anti-family "system," in addition to unemployment, a bad economy, privatization, and food shortages. The audience booed, shouted and whistled in support of his points, and some broke into football-style chants of "Kill, kill the faggot" and "The faggot won't walk through the city." Vladan Glišić, Dveri's 2012 candidate for president, concluded in his priestly, theatrically tranquil diction: "Brothers and sisters, we are the majority of Serbia. We don't need violence, we are strong and there is the quiet decisiveness of this nation behind us that represents a strong river, a river that will change Serbia. We are not a party, we are a family!"

The crowd then marched by the National Assembly and the state TV, covering a much larger section of the downtown than the hermetically segregated Parade would on the next day. People chanted invitations for President Tadić to "kill [himself] and save Serbia" and the refrain of a rap song about the police: "You are the regime's servants / You defend the rich / Beat the people for peanuts / Protect thieves," with some singing "faggots" instead of "thieves."

### National Sovereignty and Orthodox "Symphony"

Through Family Walks and other anti-Pride activities, the nationalists expressed their vision of the public sphere and social order. In this section, I focus on the religious nationalist foundations of this vision: its emphasis on the political sovereignty and cultural autonomy of the nation defined in religious terms.

Apart from using the multicultural discourse of the recognition of diversity and the liberal discourse of individual freedom and equality, the organizers and the government linked the 2010 Pride to Serbia's integration into the European Union (Mikuš 2011). The organizers I interviewed hinted that this enabled them to ally with the state keen to demonstrate its commitment to EU integration.[8] That the Pride promoted Serbia's acceptance of "European values" was reiterated in the media, by speeches at the event (mostly by representatives of European institutions), and by the subsequent European Commission report and European Parliament resolution which expressed satisfaction over the state's support for the event. The iconography and language used at the Pride itself were Western or global in character, which only added fuel to the critiques that it was something alien and imported. The EU flag could be seen in the crowd, along with rainbow flags and a purple Union Jack, but no Serbian flag. The music in background was Western pop. If the speakers (mostly foreigners) mentioned Serbia, they usually denoted it negatively, as a place that lacked the European norms of human rights. Little attempt was made to evoke local traditions of diversity and tolerance.

The nationalists responded to this linkage between the Pride and European integration. They repeatedly argued that their persecution, including for their anti-Pride activities, was meant to break their resistance to Euro-Atlantic integration. They portrayed the EU-driven Pride as an assault on Serbia's sovereignty that they looked to defend. This resonated with their branding of the present "regime" as "betrayers," a "puppet government" or "occupation government." From their perspective, the incumbent government extradited "Serbian heroes" (i.e., suspected war criminals) to the International Criminal Tribunal for the Former Yugoslavia, "betrayed" Kosovo, and allowed foreigners to enter all state institutions and decide about everything. By resisting this state of geopolitical subalternity, which they variously described as "occupation," "colonization" or "national humiliation," the nationalists were fighting for "freedom" equated with collective ethnonational sovereignty.

Against the Pride's liberal and globalizing narrative, the nationalists stressed the central role of Orthodox Christianity and the Serbian Orthodox Church in

---

8  Some LGBT activists *not* involved in the organization of the Pride were critical precisely of this political alliance of the organizers with the government. They repeatedly described the Pride as the "State Pride" (*državni prajd*) and pointed to the personal linkages between the Gay Straight Alliance, the main organizing NGO, and one of the ruling political parties (the Socialist Party of Serbia). They also argued that the organizers "monopolized" the Pride and that the Pride was not useful, or was even harmful, for solving the practical, everyday problems of LGBT people in Serbia.

the governance of society. They used quasi-clerical discourse to describe the Pride as a "sinful," "shameful" and "satanic" attack on the Orthodox values of the "vast majority" of Serbs, and a negation of the will of the Church. The Church itself encouraged such invocations. On the eve of the 2010 Pride, Metropolitan Amfilohije Radović, one of the highest Church dignitaries, described the event as "Sodom and Gomorrah" and "violent propaganda." The Holy Synod, the executive body of the Church, released another statement hours later in which it called for non-violence but also condemned those who "threaten public morality" and publicly express their sexual orientation. During the Pride, several priests wearing black cassocks and carrying crosses led groups of the rioters and used their special status to get through police cordons. Some of the rioters also carried crosses and Orthodox icons and sang religious songs. Churches served as rallying points from which the rioters launched their attacks on the police and where they hid to avoid arrest.

The nationalists' view on where non-heteronormative practices properly belonged was compatible with the position of the Church. In interviews, the nationalists claimed that they "had nothing against" such practices *in private* (except that they were sinful) and "did not care" and "did not ask" what anybody's sexual preference was. Vladan Glišić even vowed that Dveri would support a ban on discrimination against LGBT persons in employment, and pretended that Russia gave them such rights while banning their "propaganda." What Dveri (and other nationalists) supposedly opposed was "homosexualism"—their own idea of what Pride was about—public shows of homosexuality and a conspiracy to destroy the traditional family by imposing a gay "ideology."

This goes to the very foundations of the Pride controversy. The Pride sought to establish that LGBT individuals and issues had a legitimate presence in the public sphere, unlike religious norms militating against that. The nationalists claimed precisely the opposite. This was in line with the opinion of both the Church and a majority of the population. In a 2010 national survey, 58 percent said they had "nothing against homosexuals, as long as they keep their activities private," 64 percent supported the Church in "condemning homosexuality," and 53 percent believed the state should "suppress" it (Gay Straight Alliance 2010: 8). This shows that religious injunctions against LGBT rights are seen as a legitimate source of public policy, in contrast to some other European countries such as Sweden or the Netherlands (Van den Berg et al. 2014).

Those invoking a public authority of the Serbian Orthodox Church can point to a long history of its closeness to the state. In the Middle Ages, members of Serbian royal dynasties served as Church dignitaries and were canonized as national saints. This reflected the Orthodox Christian principle of "symphony," which some of the nationalists who were interviewed evoked under that name, according to which the church and the temporal power "should work together for the common good" (Ghodsee 2009: 228). After the Ottoman conquest, the Church started to undertake some functions of the former Serbian state. For much of the history of the modern independent Serbia, it was legally defined as the state church. Its repression in socialist Yugoslavia started to unravel in the 1980s, simultaneously with the Serbian national "awakening" and rejection of Yugoslavism. Socialist secularization was replaced by two decades of a dramatic resurgence of religiosity (Blagojević 2006) and the rapprochement of the Church and the state, particularly since 2000 (Drezgić 2010, Perica 2006, Vukomanović 2005). However, according to its Constitution and laws, Serbia is a secular state where all churches and religious communities are independent from the state and equal before law. The nationalists detest such arrangements, which they see as a debasement of the Church, and call for the latter's return to its former prominence. More broadly, the bond between religion and ethnonational belonging is an important element of the myth of the nation on whose behalf they claim to act.

### Saint-Savaism and Populist Politics

On the eve of the 2010 Pride, Dveri told the media that "[i]nstead of the problem of white plague (i.e., demographic decline) and whether there is bread and milk,[9] our state is concerned with [trivial] problems of one aggressive minority group" (Nedeljković 2010). This illustrates how the nationalists constructed Pride as an elite political agenda oriented to the illegitimate, particularistic interests of the "aggressive" LGBT minority and the demands of the EU (Greenberg 2006, Mikuš 2011). To this they counterposed the legitimate, universal rights of the "nation" (*narod*),[10] such as employment, social justice, biological survival, and reproduction. This was a characteristically populist strategy that exploited pre-existing resentments and anxieties and constructed a simplistic dichotomy of "us" against "them" (Comaroff 2011, Mudde 2000). More than 400,000 people lost their jobs in the period of 2008 to 2010, and the already high unemployment rate soared. The 2011 census confirmed what was already assumed—Serbia (without Kosovo) had lost almost 5% of its population since

---

9       This refers to food shortages which, however, were episodic, localized and limited to a very few foodstuffs at the time of my fieldwork.
10      *Narod* may denote, depending on the context, (ethnic) "nation" as well as "the people."

2001. Swaths of rural areas and most provincial towns were being depopulated as people flocked to Belgrade, Novi Sad and Niš in search of subsistence. This was generally considered alarming, but the nationalists especially were spreading the fear that the "white plague" would eventually lead to the extinction of the nation. They discussed these issues in apocalyptic terms as the "brink of catastrophe" or the "complete collapse of the state and society," and blamed them on the "regime" that was looting and destroying the economy with a vicious disregard for the nation. Thus framed, Pride went far beyond the issue of LGBT rights. Through resisting it, and being subsequently supposedly victimized, the nationalists aligned themselves with the ethnonational masses against the corrupt elites and their colonial overlords.

In general, the nationalists claimed to act on behalf of the nation—indeed as its organic part. They would tell me that they "were educated that the interest of the community is above the interest of individuals," which is why they joined their respective organizations, some of which styled themselves as "National Movement," "Fatherland Movement," or "Movement for Serbia." The nationalists saw the nation they defended as first and foremost Serb in that its properties were natural for Serbs, as their ancient origins proved. Sharing such an essence, the nation was "united" and "harmonious." Although some "divisions" (*podele*) were acknowledged, these were constructed so as to fit the nationalist and populist framework. The elites were considered as self-excluded from the nation by their actions and marked as "anti-Serbs" and "Serb-haters." Other than that, divisions were relatively recent aberrations imported from "the West" or "Europe." At the meeting on the unification of the patriotic bloc, Mladen Obradović, the leader of Obraz known for his clerical rhetoric, warned against looking for "human, earthly" solutions, especially "ideologies," for the problems of Serbia.

> [T]hat way, we will keep going around in the same vicious circle in which the Serbian nation, unfortunately, finds itself since almost a century and a half ago [when] two evils had been imported to this space—one evil, that's sects, and the other, that's [political] parties.

In that period of emancipation from the Ottoman Rule, Obradović continued, Serbs made a key historical mistake—instead of turning to Russia, they turned to the West and thus "divisions" reached Serbia.

> Why did the Serbian nation in all its glorious and holy history, until most recent times, not know social unrest, peasant rebellions, worker uprisings and so on? We never had that, especially not in the time of the

holy Nemanjić.[11] Why? Because the whole state and society was imbued
with that which is the holiest, the most important—the Orthodox belief
...

The solution was for all Serbs, and especially all nationalists, to "gather around
a single idea," namely Saint-Savaism (svetosavlje),[12] suggested Obradović. He
concluded with a number of quotes from the work of Bishop (and, since 2003,
Saint) Nikolaj Velimirović, one of the godfathers of Saint-Savaism. Speaking
next, Ivan Ivanović of Naši reiterated: "There aren't any ideologies for the
Serb, as Mladen said, the only ideology at this point is Orthodoxy and Saint-
Savaism."

The nationalists proclaimed Saint-Savaism or "Saint-Savaist nationalism"
their most important or even only ideology. It was mostly church-affiliated
nationalist intellectuals like Velimirović who articulated this blend of messian-
ism and anti-Western, Slavophile nationalism in the interwar period. Saint-
Savaism stresses the importance of Serbian Orthodoxy and the Church for
the Serbian national being (Falina 2007). This resonates with the vernacular
ideas of Orthodoxy. Most Serbs who declare themselves "Orthodox" understand
Orthodoxy primarily as a "political religion" that sacralizes the Serbian nation,
rather than something necessitating an intense personal relationship with God
or frequent public displays of piety (Ilić 2009). This is why "sects" and "ideologies" threaten the unity and welfare of the nation.

As Obradović's comments imply, this amalgam of religion and nationalism
was invoked as the ultimate solution for all kinds of social problems. Since the
nation was constructed as inherently internally solidary, all of this would wane
once it reclaims its complete sovereignty. EU integration and globalization in
general was "colonization" destructive not only for the identity of the Serbian
nation, but also its welfare. Vladan Glišić of Dveri thus explained their "Saint-
Savaist approach" to me:

> [T]o be Christian in the Serbian nation [today] means to take care of a
> nation which is disempowered, (...) socially humiliated, (...) nationally

---

11    The House of Nemanjić ruled medieval Serbia in its period of expansion (1166–1371). It is
      known as a "saint-bearing lineage" (*svetorodna loza*) because many of its members were
      canonized.

12    Saint Sava, son of the founder of the House of Nemanjić, was consecrated in 1219 as the
      first Archbishop of the Serbian Orthodox Church, which by this deed achieved auto-
      cephaly.

ruined and defeated and subjugated and enslaved, and when you put it all like this, then to be Christian today and to be socially active means to fight for national freedom and social justice in Serbia.

The nationalists argued that poverty and "social differences" in Serbia had never been so great and shameful as today, and emphasized that "social justice" was one of their main priorities. Igor Marinković even told me that Naši could be as well considered "leftist." However, one would struggle to find anything leftist in the nationalists' programs. Class almost never features in their discourse, unless they talk about the "political" or "ruling class." Social inequalities and struggles are reduced to the populist dichotomy and collective subjugation of the Serb nation by the anti-Serb elites and colonizers. Once the nation is liberated, the interests of capitalists and workers, men and women, parents and children, and LGBT people and homophobes will all be effortlessly reconciled. Inequalities will not disappear—they will be normalized by an organicist social order in which everybody knows his or her rightful place. The nationalists styled this as the "spiritual vertical of God in heaven, king in the state, and [male] master (domaćin) in the house." They called for a rebirth of the spirit of medieval and early modern Serbia, and often quite literally demanded the restoration of the monarchy and a feudal "estates society." Their Saint-Savaist fusion of Orthodoxy and ethnonational statehood legitimated and called for clerical, feudal and patriarchal forms of domination intrinsic to one's position within the holistic order of the nation. But the latter was threatened by individualized inequalities and particularistic rights (minority, women's, LGBT, and so on) emerging in the liberalizing Serbia.

The nationalists constructed "family values" as the natural cornerstone of solidarity and social justice within the nation. They evoked family, with recurrent epithets like "numerous" and "patriarchal," as the prerequisite of the nation's biological survival. Once in power, they promised to make family the primary welfare beneficiary, in contrast with its woeful neglect by the current "regime." Although the nationalists claimed not to oppose the involvement of women in public life, they had no doubts that their natural purpose and wish in life was to be a "woman of the family." Dveri consistently styled themselves as a "family" and a "movement of family people" rather than a party. Their relatively elaborate election program did not include a section on social policy, but it talked at length about "family policy."

The nationalists also implied the primordial idea of the nation as a family (Verdery 1996: 63). They would address their audience in meetings and protests, and the readers of their texts, as "brothers and sisters," often preceded by the rather archaic greeting "God help you" (pomaže Bog), to which the audience

would ritually respond "God help you as well" (Bog ti pomogao). In the aforementioned meeting, Ivan Ivanović of Naši said:

> None of us here or in any other patriotic organization advocates going
> to fight against the regime like some anarchists or I don't know what. We
> simply fight for our state, we fight for all the holy Serbs who lived before us,
> and we fight for all the Serbs who will come, for our future, our children.
> That is our responsibility before God.

This shows that the nationalists often constructed their own actions as guided
by religious duty toward their "ancestors" and "children." Here kinship served as
a model for both past- and future-oriented responsibility that collectively and
metaphysically obliged Serb contemporaries to their ancestors, including very
distant ones, and descendants.

   As any populist politics, the nationalists' project ostensibly addressed the
interests of broad popular masses. But their emphasis on family, coupled with
silence on the issues of class and social policy, seems to have been actually
appealing to individuals with a particular configuration of personal aspirations and position in the life cycle. It had little to offer the elderly or those
younger people uninterested in having an idealized heteronormative family.
But it was bound to appeal to the many young and productive-age people frustrated by their inability to start a family, or those who already did and struggled
to make ends meet. Young people in Serbia are hit particularly hard by unemployment, and many are forced to live with their parents. The talk about a
"patriarchal" family addressed especially those young men whose breadwinner
self-image clashed with their poverty. The nationalists endeavored to articulate
and channel their anger. For instance, Serbian Action, a lesser-known organization, posted the following stickers throughout Belgrade in 2011: "Youth without
hope / Work's waiting / And the regime walks faggots through Belgrade / Now
that's enough!"

   Dveri's participation in the general elections of May 2012 also hinted at
whom the nationalists were addressing. In their Letters to the Voters, Dveri
pledged to "speak in the name of small and medium entrepreneurs, family com-
panies, household production, the village, agriculture and all socially threatened categories" (Dveri 2012). Their Economic Manifesto presented a mer-
cantilist vision of national capitalism and avoided, in line with the assump-
tion of national unity, any mention of labor unions, worker rights or workers
themselves (Dveri 2011). Dveri's electoral performance was respectable for a
newcomer—they narrowly missed the 5% threshold for entering the national
parliament but secured seats in 12 city and municipal assemblies. The charac-

teristics of these municipalities suggest a predominantly urban and middle-class electorate. Dveri captured more than 15% of votes in Čačak, the fifth largest Serbian city from which one of the Dveri leaders comes and which is known for an economy based on small and medium private enterprises (SMEs). They further passed the electoral threshold in one Belgrade municipality, in the City of Novi Sad (the second largest in the country), two municipalities in Niš (the third largest), two relatively wealthy Vojvodinian municipalities (Sremski Karlovci and Bačka Palanka), and Arilje, another town with a proliferation of SMEs. They failed to pass the census in the biggest industrial centers, such as Kragujevac, Bor, Pančevo, Šabac or Smederevo. It thus seems likely that Dveri mobilized, alongside the aforementioned demographic groups, especially the many small entrepreneurs hard hit by the crisis. One should further consider that the leaders of nationalist organizations were mostly highly educated middle-class urbanites—university students and professors, journalists, lawyers, teachers, professors, entrepreneurs, IT specialists, and even an odd official of the Milošević regime. Some of the organizations had been established and/or enjoyed significant memberships and institutional support in institutions of higher education, especially the Faculties of Law (Nomokanon), Mechanical Engineering and Philology (Dveri) and Philosophy and Theology (Obraz) of the University of Belgrade. All of this suggests that the working class was probably not the only or even the principal group attracted by the nationalist movements.

### Conclusion

In this chapter, I described the pivotal role of religious nationalism in the sustained resistance to the Pride Parade and, more broadly, LGBT rights in Serbia. I argued that the social and political ideology of religious nationalism calls for the full sovereignty and autonomy of the Serbian ethnic nation, desecularization of the public sphere and retraditionalization of social relationships, while marking LGBT rights as antithetical to all these goals. The long historical continuity of religious nationalist thought and practice contributes to its legitimacy with a part of the society. However, a more complete understanding of the role of religious nationalism at the present historical juncture necessitates setting the relevant cultural and identitarian discourses in a material context of sociopolitical struggles, and identifying the actors who use them, their strate gies, objectives and achievements.

The analysis presented above shows that the Pride Parade has become one of the main lines of confrontation between liberal civil society and the "Europeanizing" state, on the one hand, and nationalist organizations and movements, on the other. The latter found the Pride Parade an efficient way of mobilizing support for their own political project, which responded to a much broader set of issues related to Serbia's integration into the transnational order. Identitarian fears, a sense of national subjugation, and socioeconomic frustrations coalesce into a nationalist-populist narrative whose construction is in many ways reminiscent of Milošević's rise to power in the late 1980s. In terms of more immediate and instrumental political goals, anti-Pride mobilizations have been a central element of the nationalist NGOs' attempted expansion into institutional politics, as the example of Dveri illustrates.

However, the overall achievements of the nationalist organizations have been limited. They did achieve some partial victories: the Ministry of the Interior banned the Prides in 2011–2013, and the 2014 Pride was again accompanied by extensive security measures and EU integration rhetoric, both of which reaffirmed a sense that LGBT rights are an issue imposed from the outside and against the will of Serbian society. This, together with some of the earlier sympathetic critiques that I mentioned, raises complex questions about whether the Pride, however legitimate in principle, is a correct political strategy for LGBT rights in the current Serbian context. Nevertheless, it also bears mentioning that there was little physical resistance to the 2014 Pride, which might suggest that the support for the nationalists' violent tactics, at least, is on the wane. Some of the nationalist organizations became participants in local institutional politics, but only Dveri proved that they have a relatively stable electorate at the national level, and even this has been insufficient to enter the parliament. The government that took power in 2012 has successfully appropriated populist rhetoric in a manner that supports its own ascendancy, thus squeezing out nationalist movements from that part of political space. In sum, then, the nationalists have failed to build a strong social and political coalition to challenge the advance of Serbia's globalization and liberalization.

### References

Asad, Talal. 2003. *Formations of the Secular: Christianity, Islam, Modernity*. Stanford, CA: Stanford University Press.

Barr, Michael D. 2010. "Religious Nationalism and Nation-Building in Asia: An Introduction." *Australian Journal of International Affairs* 64: 255–261.

Blagojević, Mirko. 2006. "Current Religious Changes in Serbia and Desecularization." *Filozofija i društvo* 31: 239–253.

Brubaker, Rogers. 2012. "Religion and Nationalism: Four Approaches." *Nation and Nationalism* 18: 2–20.

Comaroff, Jean. 2011. "Populism and Late Liberalism: A Special Affinity?" *The Annals of the American Academy of Political and Social Science* 637: 99–111.

Drezgić, Rada. 2010. "Religion, Politics and Gender in the Context of Nation-State Formation: The Case of Serbia." *Third World Quarterly* 31: 955–970.

Dveri. 2011. *Ekonomski manifest Dveri.* Retrieved April 30, 2012, from http://www .dverisrpske.com/sr-CS/nasa-politika/izborni-program/ekonomski-manifest-dveri .php.

———. 2012. *Pisma biračima.* Retrieved April 30, 2012, from http://www.dverisrpske .com/sr-CS/nasapolitika/pisma-biracima/.

Falina, Maria. 2007. "Svetosavlje. A Case Study in the Nationalization of Religion." *Schweizerische Zeitschrift für Religions- und Kulturgeschichte* 101: 505–527.

Fraser, Nancy. 1990. "Rethinking the Public Sphere: A Contribution to the Critique of Actually Existing Democracy." *Social Text* 25/26: 58–80.

Gay Straight Alliance. 2010. *Prejudices Exposed: Homophobia in Serbia 2010.* Retrieved September 29, 2014, from http://en.gsa.org.rs/wp-content/uploads/2012/08/ Research-Prejudices-Exposed-2010-GSA.pdf.

Ghodsee, Kristen. 2009. "Symphonic Secularism: Eastern Orthodoxy, Ethnic Identity and Religious Freedoms in Contemporary Bulgaria." *Anthropology of East Europe Review* 27: 227–252.

Greenberg, Jessica. 2006. "Nationalism, Masculinity and Multicultural Citizenship in Serbia." *Nationalities Papers* 34: 321–341.

Grigoriadis, Ioannis N. 2013. *Instilling Religion in Greek and Turkish Nationalism: A "Sacred Synthesis."* New York: Palgrave Macmillan.

Ilić, Angela. 2009. "Serbia: The Role of Religion in Society from 1990 to the Present." Pp. 237–252 in I.A. Murzaku (ed.), *Quo Vadis Eastern Europe? Religion, State and Society after Communism.* Ravenna: Longo.

Jansen, Stef. 2001. "The Streets of Beograd: Urban Space and Protest Identities in Serbia." *Political Geography* 20: 35–55.

Juergensmeyer, Mark. 1993. *The New Cold War? Religious Nationalism Confronts the Secular State.* Berkeley: University of California Press.

———. 2006. "Nationalism and Religion." Pp. 357–367 in A.R. Segal (ed.), *The Blackwell Companion to the Study of Religion.* Malden, MA: Blackwell.

———. 2008. *Global Rebellion: Religious Challenges to the Secular State, from Christian Militias to al Qaeda.* Berkeley: University of California Press.

Kahlina, Katja. 2014. "Local Histories, European LGBT Designs: Sexual Citizenship, Nationalism, and 'Europeanisation' in Post-Yugoslav Croatia and Serbia." *Women's Studies International Forum* http://www.sciencedirect.com/science/article/pii/ S0277539514001204.

Kostovicova, Denisa. 2006. "Civil Society and Post-Communist Democratization: Facing a Double Challenge in Post-Milošević Serbia." *Journal of Civil Society* 2: 21–37.

Mikuš, Marek. 2011. "'State Pride': Politics of LGBT Rights and Democratisation in 'European Serbia'." *East European Politics and Societies* 25: 834–851.

Mudde, Cas. 2000. "In the Name of the Peasantry, the Proletariat, and the People: Populisms in Eastern Europe." *East European Politics and Societies* 15: 33–53.

Nedeljković, Violeta. 2010. *Porodičnom šetnjom protiv Parade ponosa*. Retrieved from: http://www.pressonline.rs/sr/vesti/vesti_dana/story/136016/Porodi%C4%8Dnom+%C5%A1etnjom+protiv+Parade+ponosa.html.

Nielsen, Christian Axboe. 2013. "Stronger than the State? Football Hooliganism, Political Extremism and the Gay Pride Parades in Serbia." *Sport in Society: Cultures, Commerce, Media, Politics* 16: 1038–1053.

Perica, Vjekoslav. 2002. *Balkan Idols: Religion and Nationalism in Yugoslav States*. Oxford: Oxford University Press.

Perica, Vjekoslav. 2006. "The politics of Ambivalence: Europeanization and the Serbian Orthodox Church." Pp. 176–203 in T.A. Byrnes and P.J. Katzenstein (eds.), *Religion in an Expanding Europe*. Cambridge: Cambridge University Press.

Stakić, Isidora. 2011. "Homophobia and Hate Speech in Serbian Public Discourse: How Nationalist Myths and Stereotypes Influence Prejudices against the LGBT Minority." *Equal Rights Review* 7: 44–65.

Van den Berg, Mariecke, Bos, David J., Derks, Marco, Ganzevoort, R. Ruard, Jovanović, Miloš, Korte, Anne-Marie, and Sremac, Srdjan. 2014. "Religion, Homosexuality, and Contested Social Orders in the Netherlands, the Western Balkans, and Sweden." Pp. 116–134 in G. Ganiel, H. Winkel and C. Monnot (eds.), *Religion in Times of Crisis*. Leiden: Brill.

Van der Veer, Peter. 1994. *Religious Nationalism: Hindus and Muslims in India*. Berkeley, CA: University of California Press.

Verdery, Katherine. 1996. *What was Socialism, and What Comes Next?* Princeton, NJ: Princeton University Press.

Vukomanović, Milan. 2005. *What the Church Can(not) be Asked About: The Serbian Orthodox Church, State and Society in Serbia*. Belgrade: Helsinki Committee for Human Rights in Serbia.

CHAPTER 2

# European Culture Wars: Sexual Nationalism between Euro-Christian and Euro-Secular Civil Religion in Poland and Romania

*Mihai Tarta*

In a highly secular Europe, Romania and Poland are exceptional cases provided that they are counted as European. From the time when Eurobarometer surveys included both Poland and Romania, it was clear that there are few countries in Europe that show such robust positive feelings towards the European Union (EU) and such high levels of religious belief. Even after the 2008 crisis, the majority population in both countries displays a positive attitude towards the EU. The World Value Survey shows that the importance of religion has gone up spectacularly immediately after 1990. Church attendance remained constant or had an insignificant decrease in Poland while it increased in Romania.[1] Romania is one of the most religious countries in Europe, with 92% of people saying that they believe in God, followed closely by Poland with a little less than 80%. In addition, Romania had the largest percentage of people who became affiliated with the church soon after communism, a trend that gradually stabilized by 1997 (Voicu 2007). After 2000, in terms of religious participation, 22% of Romanians attend church once a week, up from 15% a decade earlier. The World Values Survey found church attendance to be around 46% in Poland down from 49% in the earlier decade. Romania was nevertheless the champion of post-communist religious revitalization with a 15% increase in participation (Voicu 2007). Given these numbers, it seems fairly easy to read the religious and the European enthusiasm as signs of backwardness where the EU's cohesion funds and God represent some compensators for post-communist economic dismay.

Some inconsistencies about these numbers remain, however, since high religious belief contrasts with relatively low religious participation as in Romania, or with what nationalism scholar Zdzisław Mach (2000) observed regarding the relaxed sexual mores in Poland. I argue that the difference between belief and professed belief comes from the existence of a civil religion based on tradi-

---

1   See Tables 1 and 2.

© KONINKLIJKE BRILL NV, LEIDEN, 2015 | DOI: 10.1163/9789004297791_004

TABLE 1

| Country | Importance of religion | Period | Period | Period | Period |
|---|---|---|---|---|---|
| Poland | | 1989–1993 | 1994–1998 | 2005–2009 | 2010–2014 |
| | Very important | 33% | 46% | 47% | 46% |
| | Rather important | 23% | 36% | 39% | 34% |
| | Not very important | 5% | 13% | 10% | 15% |
| Romania | | | | | |
| | Very important | | 38% | 57% | 50% |
| | Rather important | | 38% | 32% | 33% |
| | Not very important | | 18% | 7% | 13% |

Source: World Values Survey 1994–2014, http://www.worldvaluessurvey.org/WVSOnline.jsp

tional religion, and on the particular historical context where both countries traditionally see the Church as a carrier of national identity. In the following pages I will show the historical context in which Churches gained a central role in politics, especially in connection with national identity, and I will show how they nowadays feel threatened by the EU's demands concerning homosexuality. I will analyze a series of works on religious and sexual nationalism related to Poland and Romania to demonstrate that there is a discernable "culture war" happening in these countries whose shape and content depends on two competing visions of identity which I call Euro-Christian civil religion and Euro-secular civil religion.

Both countries exited the so-called "Godless Communism" period with a functional religious sector, apparently hardly affected by state policies of secularization. During communist rule both the Polish Roman Catholic Church (PRCC) and the Romanian Orthodox Church (ROC), have gone through continuous negotiations with the communists and managed to maintain an influential position within society. In Poland, for example, the communists attempted to control and mitigate the PRCC through various tactics including a Catholic group (PAX) close to the Communists, while on the opposite side, political dissidents (even notorious atheists) also stayed close to the PRCC and even attended service, as the prestige of the PRCC was highest during the time of open resistance to communists. Similarly, in Romania the communists seized the opportunity from the beginning to influence the ROC through controlling the Patriarch (Leustean 2009), through mutual formal and informal support, either by the continuing use of the church for traditional rituals like weddings, burials and baptisms, or through supporting priests' salaries, church building

TABLE 2

| Country | Church attendance | Period | Period | Period |
|---------|-------------------|--------|--------|--------|
| Poland  |                   | 1994–1998 | 2005–2009 | 2010–2014 |
|         | More than once a week | 7% | 9% | 4% |
|         | Once a week | 49% | 48% | 46% |
|         | Once a month | 18% | 18% | 17% |
|         | Only on special holy days | 14% | 14% | 15% |
| Romania |                   |        |        |        |
|         | More than once a week | 6% | 4% | 4% |
|         | Once a week | 15% | 23% | 22% |
|         | Once a month | 18% | 19% | 17% |
|         | Only on special holy days | 28% | 31% | 28% |

Source: World Values Survey 1994–2014, http://www.worldvaluessurvey.org/
WVSOnline.jsp

or reconstruction, and the like. Communist governments and Church leaders decided that it is better to cooperate for the sake of the nation, and in both countries the Church was recognized for its historical role in defending and preserving the nation in times of trial.

The bond between Church and nation helped the Romanian communists in the nationalist comeback of the 1960s when Romania was distancing itself from the Soviet Union, and when the communists encouraged a revival of the *Ortho-doxist* doctrine from the interwar period, which posited that a true Romanian must be Orthodox (Gillet 2001). Traditionally the PRCC was seen as the guardian of the Polish nation and the "Christ" of the nations which sacrificed its territory for its ideals. When Poland was partitioned among the empires of Europe, the nation had one common denominator, the Church. This image was sustained by powerful national symbols such as the "Cross," the "Black Madonna," and by places of pilgrimage such as Czestochowa. This idealized image of PRCC was outlined in the *Polak-Katolic* doctrine which posited that a true Pole is neces-sarily a Catholic. During the communist period the PRCC used this dangerous ethno religious nationalism to show opposition to a different kind of invader, typically the Soviets or the Godless Polish Communist regime.

The ROC was in a similar position, however in a different context, since they ousted the Greek Catholics from the dominant discourse about "national church" even though this group contributed most to the Romanian national revival. Occasioned by the destruction of the Greek Catholic Church in the

Ukraine after the Second World War, the Romanian Greek Catholic Church was also dismantled, hence the ROC remained the only large competitor fighting for the souls of Romanians. If the "social apostolate" (the doctrine that justified ROC's collaboration with the Communists) appears to be the continuation of the typical Orthodox submission to political authority reminiscent of its Byzantine history, a more attentive look at it seems that the State and the Church did not cooperate past their common national project of national unity founded on a mythical past. These monopoly Churches used a combination of traditional faith and nationalistic discourse to function as virtual civil religions in the vicinity of the nation-state (Tarta 2012; Gentile 2006).

In the period following the fall of Communism the PRCC and the ROC came across new ideas about modernization and liberalization, but as I pointed out above, this did not translate into a radical loss of faith. Quite to the contrary, in Romania church attendance had the highest increase in all of Europe (Voicu 2007). At the opposite end, the number of atheists, non-believers or agnostics, appeared to be insignificantly increasing from 2% to 5% in Poland and shrinking in Romania, at least when compared to an increase in belief from 85 to 89% (WIN Gallup International 2012). The WIN Gallup International Poll found that only one percent of Romanians and five percent of Poles fall into the atheist category. A 2011 Open Society Foundation empirical study described the atheists in Romania in its very title as "few, young, educated, right-wing and intolerant" distinguishing themselves by a less negative attitude toward gays (Fundatia Pentru o Societate Deschisă 2011). However, if atheism seems insignificant and the importance of religion is relatively stable, critical attitudes toward the Church and especially toward the Churches' un-modern standpoint have become fashionable. In the absence of the traditional enemies—Germany, the Soviet Union or Jews—and with the comfortable prospect of EU integration, Churches were left without clear objectives for the immediate future and started to look for other enemies. Historian John Pollard (2007) argued that minority clerical fascist groups like *Narodowe Odrodzenie Polski* (National Polish Rebirth, NOP) reignite anti-Semitism, anti-Roma and homophobic discourses. The Churches' views on minorities in general appear increasingly obsolete, and both Churches fear that a continuation of their influential role in society depends on their reorientation from identity politics toward the idea of Church as an ethical paradigm and toward public morality and family life (Bănică 2007, Mach 2000: 114, Zubrzycki 2010: 614).

Culture Wars and Orientalism

Not all the conservative camps inside the Churches, however, were yet ready to abandon their national mission, and they repositioned the national fight on a new level, this time against Western modernity. When the conservative camps entered in direct conflict with modernity, the modernist elements in society started to associate the whole Church with anti-modernity, and the fiercest of modernizers adopted a conservative orientalist discourse to define their opponents. Many of the formatting elite's pressures to modernize came along with this orientalist discourse. Edward Said (1979) defined *orientalism* as a set of discourses and practices which the West employed when dealing with what they thought is the East, ranging from the political to the scientific and cultural domains. Larry Wolff (1994) and Maria Todorova (2009) extended Said's work with Eastern Europeanism and Balkanism, mental areas which appear to adopt European civilizational elements imperfectly. Michał Bukowski (2006: 466) also noticed that these Western mental maps also work by ideologically separating citizens within a country. Therefore, the spatial Occident-Orient distinctions translated into tensions between different understandings of modernity, usually as confrontations between capitalism and communism, civility and primitivism, elites and plebs, or traditionalists and modernists. For example in Poland, *culture wars* became first palpable in the conflict between the "two Polands" as early as the 1995 elections, depicting the losers and the winners of the transition period—one based in central Poland and the western territories, Kwaśniewski's Poland, and one located in Galicia, Silesia, and Pomerania/West-Prussia, Wałęsa's Poland (Bjork 2010: 140). These battles coexist with other fault lines within the Polish society regarding the past: de-communization (lustration) versus reconciliation, a welfare state versus a market economy, and secularism/liberalism versus Christian values (Wyrozumska 2007: 317). These symbolic fault lines are also valid for Romania. Left-wing political activist and writer Vasie Ernu (2014) analyzed this phenomenon as manifested during the most recent presidential elections, when mainstream media depicted the voters' profile in the same orientalist terms: the social-democrat candidate, Victor Ponta, got votes from the poor, religious, uneducated, and rural Romanians from the southeast, while the current president, Klaus Iohannis, got the votes of the richer, urban, more educated Romanians from the Transylvania region.

Culture wars are less a social phenomenon where opposing sides confront ideologically, since ideological subtleties escape most of the people involved in these confrontations. Culture wars are instead the rhetorical result of these types of ideological tensions vis-à-vis images of the "other" within the fabric of society. The term culture wars was introduced by James Davison Hunter (1991) who argued that from the 1970s onwards American society increasingly polarized over issues of culture, crossing older alliances and building new ones corresponding to traditionalist and progressivist views over religious, social and political issues such as family, children, education, and abortion. Hunter specifies that participants at the bottom of these culture wars are less significant and less divided than the opinion-forming elites, which include policy analysts, commentators and clergy, and which are more prone to polarization (Uecker and Lucke 2011). In countries like Poland and Romania the polarization is potentially stronger, since there are no visible progressive religious groups that would include a green or gay assimilationist agenda (Graff 2010: 599), and there are no progressive groups that would be open to dialogue with religious groups, therefore reifying the progressive-traditional polarization into a secular-religious polarization. In these conditions atheists, LGBT activists, politicians from the Left, greens and anarchists, ultimately fight against religious people, right-wing politicians and the de-privatization of religion. Once conflicts do occur, as in the right-wing political mobilization against the LGBT marches in Poland, it encourages more polarization and recruitment of people who were likely to be neutral *vis-a-vis* LGBT (Graff 2010: 588) or *vis-a-vis* the Church's influence in society. The stake of these conflicts is a national identity that redefines along sexual lines. For PRCC and ROC to be gay is to be outside the Church and outside the nation, while for their alleged opponents it implies secularism and assumptions about secularization as modernization.

### EU Civil Religion

Sociologist Robert Bellah (1967) defined civil religion as a common set of beliefs, myths, symbols, values and practices based on the bond between nation and religion. In the monopoly religious markets of Poland and Romania, the traditional Churches function as virtual civil religions (Gentile 2006). At the EU level these civil religions become less relevant, as the EU and globalization processes reduce the significance of both the Church and the nation-state. Therefore local civil religions have to adapt to address both local (morality-focused) and transnational concerns (European secularity). This behavior indicates that transnational "moral" alliances do occur (Payne and Kent 2011), especially against Euro-secularism (Berger et al. 2008). Overall a little more than half of European citizens claim some kind of European identity and adopt a civic understanding of this identity irrespective of language, religion or ethnicity, while right-wing groups support an ethnic and exclusionary European identity, often seen as Christian (Fligstein, Polyakova and Sandholtz 2012: 117, 119). Anthony Smith (1992) argued that Europe does not share myths, symbols and values like a nation state, and nation-state structures are not going to disappear soon. However, there are common symbols that have the potential to form a European civil religion regardless of its eventual position vis-à-vis institutional religion. Despite many differences, several common symbols of the Brussels bureaucracy have already entered the *psyche* of European citizens who have their own flag, national anthem, national day and currency. Europeanization also entails sharing some beliefs and norms, and EU membership requires respecting minority rights, including those of sexual minorities, stipulated in the European Directive 2000/78 (O'Dwyer 2012: 334). In Poland and Romania, respecting these rights brought the greatest challenge to what citizens perceive as the true European identity, which is one of the two forms of European civil religion.

I argue that there are more versions of European Civil Religion based on different local understandings of European identity. In *The Broken Covenant* Robert Bellah (1975) also spoke about dissensions in American society which he called "times of trial" in America's civil religion, conflicts which overlap with the cleavages described in the culture wars thesis (Haberski 2012). If Bellah discerned a morally superior American Civil Religion challenged occasionally by slavery, the war in Vietnam or by celebratory and self-serving forms of civil religion (priestly), I separate civil religion into competing versions that follow different community dynamics in a given national territory and which are not necessarily moral or referring to a deity. Civil religion is thus a religion or a tradition legitimizing politics which can take many shapes. To give a few notorious examples: it can be a secular faith or faith in secularism as in France's *laicité* model (Asad 2004), or a hybrid of religious tradition and national symbols, as it is the case in Poland and Romania (Tarta 2012). The culture wars rhetoric is very useful to both traditionalist and modernist elites who separate intensely over these issues of European identity.

Countries at the periphery of the EU like Poland and Romania intensify the dispute of European identity vis-à-vis religion by adding their own ideas of westernization and modernization into this equation. These wars occur when either one identity or the other is challenged, and the two competing civil religions have already started to polarize Polish and Romanians in two camps debating the very core of the European identity. I will now discuss how discourses about sexuality, education and family became very important issues in the definition and the reproduction of the traditional view on national identity in Poland and Romania. Because religious faith was for almost a century a vital national identity component, it was very difficult for the Churches to respond to the EU's views and demands regarding a third gender, homosexuals, since they perceived any identity dilution as a direct attack on the Church and on the nation.

## Homosexuality

### Romania

After 1989, opinions about homosexuality, abortion and prostitution became a litmus test for Europeanness and indicated deep divisions in Romanian society (Stan and Turcescu 2007: 171). Romania had a full ban on homosexual relations (article 200) and the Council of Europe pressured Romania early on to remove the article, which the Council deemed to be incompatible with European standards (Năstase 2004: 316). The battle was carried on for over a decade by unenthusiastic politicians with irrelevant law amendments in 1996, 1998, only finally removing the article 200 in January 2002. While the whole society including the Church was eventually committed to Westernization in the sense of a symbolic and economic integration in the West, there was long-lasting resistance to human rights laws, homosexuality and the separation of church and state (Năstase 2004: 317). The ROC interprets homosexuality as an extreme form of adultery, a disease affecting both the body and human nature, but the Church was mostly affected by the consequences it had in terms of national pride and cultural identity (Conovici 2010: 658).

In 1993, when the Constitutional Court decided not to authorize the application of article 200 for homosexual acts between consenting adults conducted in private, the Court's decision was influenced not only by the Church but also by human rights associations. These associations included the local *Romanian Institute for Human Rights*, the *Association for Defending Human Rights in Romania-Helsinki Committee* (APADOR- CH), the *League for Defending Human Rights*, and international associations like *Amnesty International* and the Human Rights Commission of the *Homosexuals and Lesbians International Federation*. By 1996 the former *Bucharest Acceptance Group* became ACCEPT, an NGO dedicated only to LGBT issues and which became more and more successful as Romania gradually implemented the EU's recommendations. Interestingly enough, the Court's decision was also based on the Health Ministry's opinion, an institution which could not offer clear answers regarding the alleged deviant character of homosexuality (Conovici 2010: 661).

As soon as there were rumors about the removal of article 200, the vocal Association of Christian Orthodox Students (ASCOR) petitioned ROC's Patriarch Teoctist to sway the politicians and initiated various intimidation campaigns (Stan and Turcescu 2007: 177). When article 200 was removed it was done by an extraordinary government ordinance, circumventing the Parliament, as deputies of the lower Parliament chamber joined forces to reject the modification, saying that they "want to join Europe, not Sodom and Gomorrah" (Stan and Turcescu 2007:174; Năstase 2004: 320). ROC's traditional close relation with political power translates into quick access in mobilizing politicians according to its interests (Năstase 2004: 323), but it would be an exaggeration to conclude that this is an effortless routine, since most politicians only pay lip-service to the Church. Some politicians openly assumed an anti-Church attitude, becoming advocates of Europeanness, like Cristian Radulescu, a Democrat Party MP, who stated that the Parliament's attitude is anti-European and isolates Romania from its EU neighbors (Năstase 2004: 317). While most political parties finally adopted the goal of European integration, the Church ceased to see Europe as an absolute enemy. Nonetheless, some conservative groups inside the Church remained Eurosceptic. While the ROC acknowledged the importance of European integration, its verbal confrontation with LGBT supporters remained unchanged.

Field data also suggested that Romanians explicitly oppose homosexuality and are not "Europeans" by this measure. A 1993 opinion poll showed that 4 out of 5 Romanians disapprove of homosexuals and approve their suppression. In 2001 another poll revealed that 86% do not want gay neighbors, and three years later 43% still believed that homosexuality is something of a treatable disease (Stan and Turcescu 2007: 172–173). At the societal level, besides the local LGBT groups, some unexpected allies of Romanian homosexuals appeared in Milan where a group of Italian gay and lesbians protested in front of the *Romanian Italian Chamber of Commerce* joined by representatives of trade unions and Green and Communist parties (Năstase 2004: 320). In May 2005 Romania had its first weeklong gay festival which finished with a parade through Bucharest, organized by ACCEPT. Even though the event was opposed by the mayor, it was endorsed by Romania's President and by the Justice Minister. The parade met the fury of the neo-Nazi group *Noua Dreaptă* (New-Right) which tried to intimidate the participants. Another group organized by the Conservative Party held a parallel meeting where several dozen participants listened to a priest who ignored the Patriarchy's advice to pay no attention to the manifestation.

### Poland

In Poland homosexuality was not prohibited by law. Therefore compared with Romania, Polish LGBT groups had a head start in defining their identity, their goals and raising their voices. Natural alliances among left-wing politics and

LGBT groups were thwarted, however, by the neoliberalization of older waves of the cultural and political Left (O'Dwyer 2012: 341, Sikora and Majika 2010:89). While the political Left used a Marxist discourse with regard to the economy, it left the sexual identity (cultural Left) issue under the influence of conservative discourse, as an eccentricity of the caviar left (Sikora and Majika 2010: 95). Only after Poland's accession to the EU, did groups formed by feminists, ecologists, anticlerical and anarchist movements join and start to cooperate more intimately with LGBT organizations (Graff 2006; Chetaille 2013: 138).

At the beginning of the 1990s, Polish society and political elites were not fully alert to the potential polarization regarding sexual identity. Opposition to LGBT in early 1990s was actually more "local, informal and apolitical," with small protests around AIDS care centers that were actually supported and run by the PRCC (O'Dwyer 2012: 341). With the prospect of joining the EU, the groups which opposed homosexuality gradually became affiliated to parties and coalesced against the sexual libertinism that was seen as threatening the *Polak-Katolik* identity doctrine (Graff 2010). The closer Poland was to the EU, the more the PRCC had to accept the presence and the voice of homosexuals. Paradoxically, LGBT marches generated a "double coming-out"—of homosexuals and their fiercest enemies (Gruszczynska in Shibata 2009: 257).

After Poland's EU accession this polarization became ever more visible and attracted more members on both sides. The *International Lesbian and Gay Association* (ILGA) which lobbied in the EU since 1992 influenced the mobilization of local NGOs like *The International Lesbian and Gay Cultural Network Polska* (ILGCNP) which organized the first equality march in 2001 in Warsaw (Chetaille 2013: 126, 129, Graff 2006: 442). International networks also influenced *Kampania Przeciw Homofobii* (Anti-Homophobia Campaign-KPH) (O'Dwyer 2012: 333, Chetaille 2013:131). In 2004 the march in Krakow was attacked, and in 2005 marches in Warsaw and Poznan were prohibited but ended with protests and almost 70 arrests, an occasion at which the mainstream media tipped the balance to the side of the protesters (Graff 2006: 438, 441, Binnie 2014: 246, Keinz 2011: 111, Gruszczynska in O'Dwyer 2012: 346). The *Equality Foundation* (Fundacja Rownosci) alliance between KPH, ILGCNP and Lambda Warszawa overturned the Warsaw ban on marches at the *European Court of Human Rights* (ECHR), establishing a compulsory legal precedent against future bans in Europe. Additional professional NGOs like the *Polish Society of Anti-Discrimination Law* as well as the *Zieloni 2004* (Greens 2004 Party) came to meet the different expectations of Polish society. In 2010 Poland hosted the famous Euro Pride with participants from all Europe, which was followed by an exhibition called "Ars Homo Erotica" at the National Museum in Warsaw, a place that typically celebrates the nation (O'Dwyer 2012: 347). In November the same year

Kristian Legierski became the first openly gay elected politician in Poland, and more recently gay politician Robert Biedron was elected mayor of Slupsk.

In the mid-2000s Poland's right-wing Law and Justice Party (PiS) characterized by xenophobic, nationalist, masculinist and homophobic discourse, campaigned using the population's opposition to neoliberalism following the economic "shock therapy" (Binnie 2014: 247, Shields 2007). In fact PiS did not follow up on their promise of "social solidarity" (Wyrozumska 2007: 334), and actually worked to consolidate neoliberalism by turning peoples' attention from social issues to morality issues (Binnie 2014: 247); specifically by regulating sex life with the Constitution's 18th article "imposing heterosexual marriages" (Miezilinska in Shibata 2009: 257). After the 2003 poster campaign "Let them see us" faced violent replies and vandalizing of billboards, the ultra-Catholic League of Polish Families (LPR) Party encouraged a discourse about losing national sovereignty in the EU, thus making homophobia "the new patriotic discourse" (Graff in Chetaille 2013: 134). The mainstream media also insisted on the loss of tradition, and the loss of traditional gender roles in Europe was described as a crisis of masculinity and perversity (Graff 2010: 585). President Lech Kaczynski appeared on a TV show saying that European laws seek to violate the integrity of Poland. In this show he used video footage from a homosexual wedding, suggesting that normality works in the nation's interest and cohesion. The New York gay couple in the video, Brendan Fay and Thomas Moulton, were active members of a Catholic LGBT group (Graff 2010: 59–87). To Kaczynski's surprise the two Americans traveled to Poland and appeared on a private TV show which took the culture wars to a totally new level since there are no known LGBT religious persons in Poland. Their presence "shocked" both society's religious conservatism and the secular moralism of the European-styled sexual modernity supporters (Graff 2010: 602, Tvn24 2008).

Yasuko Shibata argues that homosexuality seemed a contentious issue even for scientists in Poland, while studies show that only around 18% of the Poles accept homosexuals compared to the average of 41% of EU citizens. Also 66% do not approve public expressions of homosexuals, and 90% do not approve of child adoption in gay families (Shibata 2009: 245, 256). The Council of Europe decided to emit a warning resolution for countries like Poland, and in 2006 and 2007 the EU Parliament voted two more resolutions which specifically mentioned Poland (Graff 2010: 589). These resolutions were seen as an attempt to impose deviant and foreign norms on Poland and on its culture, and were interpreted as a "pink international" against the "85% Polish (who) don't accept homosexual partnerships" (Chetaille 2013: 135). The language of these resolutions was perceived as a direct attack on the Polish nation since it made 19 references to the Polish authorities (http://www.europarl.europa.eu 2007).

### Education, Family, Gender and Reproduction

*Romania*

Civil religion is also sustained by the banal nationalism of religious symbols present in schools and other state institutions. After the loss of most confessional schools during communism, the ROC returned to promote religious education in public schools. This has stirred lots of debates, especially concerning the problem of captive audiences for those who did not want to participate, but who were basically forced to stay in class, even though the law specifies that religion is an optional subject. Another problem was the presence of icons, crosses and other religious symbols, potentially incompatible with those of a different religion or with children who receive an atheist education at home (Stan and Turcescu 2007). Lately the mainstream media are more vocal in attacking the clergy and the Church for interfering with education and education funding. For example, the right-wing daily *Gândul* started an anti-Church campaign called Godporația (Godporation), with an allusion to both the power and the tax exempt status of the ROC. The campaign starts with a quote inspired from the Secular Humanist Association in Romania (ASUR): "In Romania after the Revolution, for every new school there were five new churches opened. This fact tells us a lot about the Church's influence in Romanian society" (Campanii.gandul.info 2014).[2]

After it lost the fight on criminalizing homosexual acts, the ROC tried to prohibit organizations and public manifestations favoring homosexuals, since it viewed homosexuality as infringing on the idea of family and as a treatable disease. Legal acceptance of homosexuality made it socially acceptable. However, in the eyes of the Church all homosexuality is pederasty and pedophilia, and the youth are possible victims of this new normalcy standard for the family (Conovici 2010: 666). Moreover its acceptance not only could change traditional morality but also weaken the national vigor (Conovici 2010: 667). In this logic especially in the early 1990s the ROC opposed "the West" generally as a morally corrupt entity which could spread its influence in Romania.

In Romania abortion was legalized in 1989 after the removal of a draconian law prohibiting it under Ceausescu's plan to increase both Romania's workforce and economic potential. The legalization of abortion meant that in a few years Romania had the highest abortion rates in Europe! This caused fears about the preservation of the Romanian nation, which helped form an alliance between all the religious groups, where the Orthodox and Greek-Catholics became the most vocal supporters of pro-life campaigns (Miroiu and Popescu 2004: 303;

---

2  All translations from Romanian and French language in the text belong to the author.

Stan and Turcescu 2007: 181). The ROC and the minority Romanian Roman-Catholic Church cooperated to organize a congress "Family and Life at the Beginning of a New Christian Millenium," condemning abortion and homosexuality. Talks about genocide, the mass murder of fetuses and "the maiming of Romanian womanhood" were not uncommon, while sexist stereotypes were also frequent in the mainstream media and even in academia which was suspicious of "politically correct language" in general and considered it a utopia of the Left (Antohi 2007), a confusion which resulted in lumping together homosexuality, feminism and ecology (Miroiu and Popescu 2004: 309). Political initiatives such as the one to prohibit abortion proposed by Ioan Moisin, a Greek-Catholic MP, were abandoned after only a few debates. A new amendment proposed in 2003 stipulated that women must undergo a psychological assessment before an abortion (Stan and Turecscu 2007: 183). During this time neo-Nazi groups which were more and more troubled by both homosexuality and abortion, protested on the streets, and in December 2005 the *Noua Dreaptă* (New Right) picketed abortion clinics in Bucharest and Timisoara with slogans stating "abortion, a crime against the Romanian nation." In 2012, Romanian Deputy Marius Dugulescu, of the Democrat Liberal Party, the son of a Baptist pastor, proposed the adoption of an anti-abortion law as well as pro-life counseling and mandatory film watching sessions for those who decide to have abortion (Dan 2012). Earlier, in 2007 Romania director Cristi Mungiu won the Palme d' Or film festival with his "4 months, 3 weeks and 2 days" which became educational material telling about the tribulations and risks of having and restricting abortion.

### Poland

The PRCC strengthened its role after 1989 by first reinstating religious instruction in schools in 1991. A 1992 directive stated that "Christian values" must be respected by radio and TV stations, and a new Concordat with Rome was signed in 1997 (O'Dwyer 2012: 340). In 2007 the European Parliament was especially concerned about Poland's intention to draft a law punishing homosexual propaganda in schools, which also mentioned the dismissal, fines and imprisonment for those school employees and students responsible for LGBT rights activism. Also there was concern about the Deputy Minister of Education who declared that "teachers who reveal their homosexuality will be fired from work" while he was also declaring that he intends to propose similar laws at EU level (www.europarl.europa.eu 2007).

Occasioned by discussions around education and family, in 2005 Polish European MP Wojciech Wierzejski wrote an article in the weekly *Myśl Polska* titled "Going to War for the Polish Family," using the culture wars toolkit in line with the conservative policies which would reverse the declining birthrate in Poland (Graff 2006: 445, Shibata 2009: 262). Conservatives reacted against "European permissiveness" and condemned homosexuals for the misfortunes of Polish families, while progressive forces fought for free-speech, freedom of assembly and the right to privacy as "European standards" (Graff 2006: 445, 2010: 584). By this time the analogies between Europe and Sodom, as those between homophobia and anti-Semtism became increasingly salient. Both groups pointed to the legalization of homosexual marriages in Spain, and the "liberal" circles that wanted the same thing for Poland were portrayed as deviants who disseminate a disease that permeates the fabric of the Polish society: "War against the deviants, peace to the family" (Shibata 2009: 263). Conservative politicians were ultimately fighting anti-Christian Europe and international extreme Leftism (connected with the Jewish conspiracy, an older nationalist issue in Poland) and proposed the death penalty for pedophiles who, according to them, are mostly homosexuals (Keinz 2011: 109, Graff 2006: 436, Shibata 2009: 264).

Attacks on sexual minorities in Poland increased between 2005 and 2007 when the LPR entered a coalition with PiS and with Samoobrona (Self-Defense) (Graff 2006: 436). The ultra-Catholic LPR used its bureaucratic pressure in the administration to intervene against the activities of sexual minorities and atheists. LPR openly used street pressure through the organization All Polish Youth (MW) and the media group Radio Maryia (Shibata 2009: 257–258). The MW youth organized parallel normality marches using anti-EU slogans such as "Euro-Sodom." Reporting of sexual minorities in the weekly *Nasz Dziennik* reminded readers of the pre-war characterizations of the Jews and pointed to the "Jew" status of LGBT persons (Graff 2006: 444, 2010: 592, Shibata 2009: 251–252).[3] After the 2007 elections the LPR and PiS failed to mobilize the voters on morality issues in the midst of corruption scandals. In the fall of 2013 the rainbow monument in downtown Warsaw, a symbol of tolerance and openness, was attacked and set on fire by the *All Polish Youth* on the occasion of the LGBT parade (Kozlowska 2013, Ciobanu 2013). Very recently a whole new war reissued around the premiere of *Golgota Picnic* in Warsaw by Argentinian Rodrigo Garcia, a theater performance which attracted criticism from religious conservatives all over Europe (Sierakowski 2014).

In Poland women lost some of the social and economic rights they previously had during communism, among which the most important were repro-

---

3   Agnieszka Graff mentions the graffiti inscription on a Warsaw bus: "It's not a myth, it's very true—you see a gay, you see a Jew."

ductive rights in 1993, when abortion was prohibited (Keinz 2011: 97). Gender equality and women's political rights were perceived as imported, or as a glamorous artefact of the communist legacy even though the only other countries prohibiting abortion are Malta, Northern Ireland and Ireland (Keinz 2011: 103). For women, the EU integration also meant the creation of a supra-national contesting frame where they could find new alliances and ultimately protection in the EU political structures (Chetaille 2013: 129).

## Conclusions

EU's pressures toward new member states transformed the EU from a rather reluctant supporter of minority and LGBT rights into a powerful symbolic opponent of the Christian Churches, a "bastion of modernity, in sexual terms" (Chetaille 2013: 139). These obstacles and the debates caused by the clashes of Church and state created a symbolic civilizational frontier along sexual lines, which continues the reproduction of the old East-West ideological divide. EU does not have a formal religious agenda, and different Church and state models coexist inside it. Euro-Christian civil religion counts on religious tradition and conservative politics to propose religious faith at the center of European identity, even though the conflict initiated in connection with national and cultural identity and not with sexual views or public morality (Graff 2010: 584). This conflict automatically reifies support for sexual rights into Euro-secular civil religion—in short into a secular version of Europeanism, Europeanization and EU norms.

Religious conservatives from Poland and Romania did not search for cross-country alliances, and they relied exclusively on a theoretical Christian heritage, even though their goals and programs showed a lot of similarities. There are fault lines within the Churches themselves, and the official Church position is more moderate while culture-war discourse increasingly polarizes religious people:

> In the Polish case, this struggle is taking place not only between liberal, civic, and secular actors and conservative ethno-nationalist religious elites, but also between two great camps within the Church: that of post-Vatican II "open Catholics" and "purists," who argue for a de-politicization of religion and a deepening of faith, and that of "traditionalists" and "integrists" who maintain that Catholicism is primordially linked with Polishness and that the Church's mission is necessarily political.
>
> ZUBRZYCKI 2010: 615

The culture wars rhetoric is more preeminent in Poland which carries a fiercer fight to reclaim the old status of a powerful and influential European country. In Romania the same debate did not produce an intense mobilization around the "traditional" values versus the "liberal" values, but this dispute is gaining more and more potential supporters since Poland and Romania share the same religious doctrinal elements vis à vis the nation despite different political evolutions. A larger Euro-Christian Civil Religion as the one based on the Catholic-Orthodox alliance to counter the "dictatorship of relativism and liberalism," as was suggested by the Russian Orthodox Bishop of Vienna and Austria, Hilarion (Bănică 2007: 134), seems unlikely to formalize very soon because of the multiple church-state models in the EU. However, certain steps to fight secularism in Europe have been taken in this direction both by the Orthodox Churches and the Catholic Church (Payne and Kent 2011, Makrides 2013: 263, 265). So far the international media have reported only on the European culture wars between left-wing progressivists and conservatives (Weigel 2006) and on the increasingly popular theme opposing the public-sector and trade union culture versus the private-sector culture, the social Europe versus the entrepreneurial one, or the core versus periphery (Nixon 2014).

In the case of Poland and Romania the interplay of sexuality, nationalism and religion materialized in civil religion as a form of religious nationalist discourse. After 1989 when religion de-privatized, the traditional Churches attempted to take a symbolic central place in national politics. When EU accession became a national goal and the conservative's camp could not stop the decriminalizing of homosexuality, the Churches unsuccessfully claimed the European Christian heritage and unsuccessfully claimed that deviant sexuality and sexual libertinism pose the greatest threat to the nation—to the nation's continuity, moral health, and survival. Since there was no credible external threat to the nation and since the language used was full of abstract notions about sexual nationalism, this strategy failed to stir the interest of that majority of Romanian and Polish citizens who claimed to be believers. Instead, by using opposing ideologies and an essentialist discourse about national identity, the conservatives antagonized a segment of the population which was inclined to believe in the inopportune influence of the Church on their country's socio-political development. Hence, culture wars rhetoric took precedence over other means of communication between these opposing groups. I have explained the culture wars rhetoric in the shape of competing civil religions, or totalizing views about the state, church and nation. These culture wars offer a new insight into the potential nationalist developments in relation to a shared European identity and into the possibility of conceiving a single European civil religion.

### References

Antohi, Sorin. 2007. *Razboaie culturale. Idei, Intelectuali, Spirit Public*. Iassy: Polirom.

Asad, Talal. 2004. Reflections on Laicité and the Public Sphere. Retrieved 26 March 2009 from: http://www.islamamerica.org/ArticleLibrary/tabid/55/articleType/ArticleView/articleId/94/Default.aspx.

Bănică, Mirel. 2007. *Biserca Ortodoxă Română: Stat Şi Societate În Anii '30*. Iaşi: Polirom.

Bellah, Robert N. 1967. Civil Religion in America. *Daedalus* 134(4): 40–55.

———. 1975. *The Broken Covenant*. New York: Seabury Press.

Berger, Peter, and Grace Davie (eds.). 2008. *Religious America, Secular Europe?: A Theme and Variations*. Aldershot, England: Ashgate.

Binnie, Jon. 2014. "Neoliberalism, Class, Gender and Lesbian, Gay, Bisexual, Transgender and Queer Politics in Poland." *International Journal of Politics, Culture & Society* 27: 241–257.

Bjork, Jim. 2010. "Bulwark or Patchwork? Religious Exceptionalism and Regional Diversity in Postwar Poland." Pp. 129–158 in B. Porter-Szűcs and B. Berglund (eds.), *Christianity and Modernity in Eastern Europe*. Budapest: Central European UP.

Buchowski, Michał. 2006. "The Specter of Orientalism in Europe: From Exotic Other to Stigmatized Brother." *Anthropological Quarterly* 79: 463–482.

*Campanii.gandul.info*. 2014. Godporaţia. Retrieved 14 July 2014 from: http://campanii.gandul.info /godporatia/#slide-01.

Chetaille, Agnès. 2013. "Une «Autre Europe» Homophobe? L'Union Européenne, le Nationalisme Polonais et la Sexualisation de la «Division Est/Ouest»." *Raisons Politiques* 49: 119–140.

Ciobanu, Claudia. 2013. "Burning Down a Rainbow in Poland." *Al Jazeera*, Retrieved 2 July 2014 from: http://www.aljazeera.com/indepth/opinion/2013/11/cloneofburning -down-rainbow-poland-2013111293719-2013111343533605488.html.

Conovici, Iuliana. 2009. *Ortodoxia în România Postcomunistă*. Cluj-Napoca: Eikon.

Dan, Oana. Neo-Decreţeii. *România de la Zero*. Retrieved 12 July 2014 from: http://www .delao.ro/pdl-initiativa-legislativa-consiliere-avort.

Ernu, Vasile. 2014. "Alegeri Prezidenţiale ca un Război Civil." *Criticatac*, Retrieved November 25 2014 from: http://www.criticatac.ro/26846/alegerile-prezideniale-ca -rzboi-civil-sau-limba-roman-pragul-unei-crize-de-nervi/.

Fligstein, Neil, Alina Polyakova and Wayne Sandholtz. 2012. "European Integration, Nationalism and European Identity." *Journal of Common Market Studies* 50: 106–122.

Fundaţia Pentru O societate Deschisă. 2011. *Ateii din Romania: puţini, tineri, educaţi, de dreapta şi intoleranţi*, Retrieved 14 July 2014 from: http://www.fundatia.ro/ateii-din -rom%C3%A2nia-putini-tineri-educati-de-dreapta-%C8%99i-intoleranti.

Gentile, Emilio. 2006. *Politics as Religion*. Princeton: Princeton University Press.

Gillet, Olivier. 2001. *Religie Şi Naţionalism: Ideologia Bisericii Ortodoxe Române Sub Regimul Comunist*. Bucharest: Compania.

Graff, Agnieszka. 2006. "We Are (Not All) Homophobes: A Report from Poland." *Feminist Studies* 32: 434–449.

————. 2010. "Looking at Pictures of Gay Men: Political Uses of Homophobia in Contemporary Poland." *Public Culture* 22: 583–603.

Haberski, Ray. 2012. "Civil Religion and Culture Wars." *u.s. Intellectual History Blog*. Retrieved 10 July 2014 from: http://s-usih.org/2012/06/civil-religion-and-culture-wars _30.html.

Hunter, James D. 1991. *Culture Wars*. New York: BasicBooks. Tvn24. 2008. *Nie straszcie nami ludzi*. Retrieved 12 July 2014 from: http://www.tvn24.pl/wiadomosci-z-kraju,3/ nie-straszcie-nami-ludzi,53774.html.

Keinz, Anika. 2011. "European Desires and National Bedrooms? Negotiating "Normalcy" in Postsocialist Poland." *Central European History* 44: 92–117.

Kimmelman, Michael. 2010. "When Fear Turns Graphic." *The New York Times*, Retrieved 15 February 2012 from: http://www.nytimes.com/2010/01/17/arts/design/17abroad .html?pagewanted=all.

Kozlowska, Hanna. 2013. "Passport: Why Poland's Right-Wing Thugs Keep Burning Rainbows." *Foreign Policy*, Retrieved 15 May 2014 from: http://foreignpolicy.com/ 2013/11/12/why-polands-right-wing-thugs-keep-burning-rainbows/.

Leuştean, Lucian. 2009. *Orthodoxy and the Cold War: Religion and Political Power in Romania, 1947–65*. Michigan: Palgrave Macmillan.

Mach, Zdzislaw. 2000. "The Roman Catholic Church in Poland and the Dynamics of Social Identity in Polish Society." Pp. 113–128 in T. Inglis, Z. Mach, and R. Mazanek (eds.), *Religion and Politics. East-West Contrasts from Contemporary Europe*. Dublin: University College Dublin Press.

Makrides, Vasilios. 2012. "Orthodox Christianity, Modernity and Postmodernity: Overview, Analysis and Assessment." *Religion, State and Society* 40: 248–285.

Miroiu, Mihaela and Liliana Popescu. 2004. "Post-Totalitarian Pre-Feminism." Pp. 297–314 in H. Carey (ed), *Romania since 1989: Politics, Economics, and Society*. Lanham: Lexington.

Năstase, Mihnea I. 2004. "Gay and Lesbian Rights." Pp. 315–334 in H. Carey (ed), *Romania since 1989: Politics, Economics, and Society*. Lanham: Lexington.

Nixon, Simon. 2014. "The Danger in Europe's Culture War." *The Wall Street Journal*, Retrieved 14 August 2014 from: http://online.wsj.com/articles/the-danger-in -europes-culture-war-1402260966.

O'Dwyer, Conor. 2012. "Does the EU Help or Hinder Gay-Rights Movements in Post-Communist Europe? The Case of Poland." *East European Politics* 28: 332–352. *http:// www.europarl.europa.eu*. 2007. European Parliament resolution of 26 April 2007 on homophobia in Europe. Retrieved 1 December 2014 from: http://www.europarl

.europa.eu /sides/getDoc.do?pubRef=-//EP//TEXT+TA+P6-TA-2007-0167+0+DOC+ XML+Vo//EN.

Payne, Daniel P. and Jennifer M. Kent. 2011. "An Alliance of the Sacred: Prospects for a Catholic-Orthodox Partnership against Secularism in Europe." *Journal of Ecumenical Studies* 46: 41–66.

Pollard, John. 2007. "'Clerical Fascism': Context, Overview and Conclusion." *Totalitarian Movements and Political Religions* 8: 433–446.

Said, Edward. 1979. *Orientalism*. New York: Vintage Books.

Shields, Stuart. 2007. "Too Much Shock, Not Enough Therapy: Transnational Capital and the Social Implications of Poland's Ongoing Transition to a Market." *Competition & Change* 11: 155–178.

Sierakowski, Slawomir. 2014. "Poland's Culture War Rages On." *The New York Times*, Retrieved July 2014 from: http://www.nytimes.com/2014/07/04/opinion/slawomir -sierakowski-polands-culture-war-rages-on.html?module=Search&mabReward= relbias%3Ar.

Sikora, Thomasz and Rafał Majka. 2010. "Not-so-Strange Bedfellows: Considering Queer and Left Alliances in Poland." *Dialogue and Universalism* 20: 89–100.

Smith, Anthony D. 1992. National Identity and the Idea of European Unity. *International Affairs* 68: 55–76.

Stan, Lavinia, and Lucian Turcescu. 2007. *Religion and Politics in Post-communist Romania*. Oxford: Oxford University Press.

Tarta, Mihai. 2012. *Dynamic Civil Religion and Religious Nationalism: The Roman Catholic Church in Poland and the Orthodox Church in Romania, 1990–2010*. Ph.D. dissertation, Baylor University.

Todorova, Maria. 2009. *Imagining the Balkans*. Oxford: Oxford University Press.

Voicu, Mălina. 2007. *România Religioasă: Pe valul European sau în urma lui?* Iassy: Institutul European.

Weigel, George. 2006. "Europe's Two Culture Wars." *Discovery Insitute*, Retrieved 14 July 2014 from: http://www.discovery.org/a/3460. *WIN—Gallup International*. 2012. *Global Index of Religiosity and Atheism*, Retrieved 13 July 2014 from: http://www .wingia.com/web/files/news/14/file/14.pdf.

Wolff, Larry. 1994. *Inventing Eastern Europe*. Stanford: Stanford University Press.

Wyrozumska, Aleksandra. 2007. "Who is Willing to Die for the Constitution? The National Debate on the Constitutional Treaty in Poland." *Perspectives on European Politics and Society* 8 (3), 314–341.

Zubrzycki, Geneviève. 2010. "Religion and Nationalism: A Critical Re-examination." Pp. 606–625 in B. Turner (ed.), *The New Blackwell Companion to the Sociology of Religion*. Chichester: Wiley-Blackwell.

# CHAPTER 3

# For the Sake of the Nations: Media, Homosexuality and Religio-Sexual Nationalisms in the Post-Yugoslav Space*

*Srdjan Sremac, Zlatiborka Popov Momčinović,
Martina Topić, and Miloš Jovanović*

During the last decade, the public perception of religion and (homo)sexuality has undergone fundamental change in the countries of the former Yugoslavia. The rights and liberties of lesbian, gay, bisexual and transexual (LGBT) people are still marginalized in the societies of the post-Yugoslav space.[1] The ethnic construct, specifically ethno-nationalism, as the attendant ideology of the states newly established after the breakup of Yugoslavia, is inherently based on principles of exclusion.[2] The vacancies in its cultural and social semantic are performatively filled with rhetorical claims and constructs in order to establish "universality" (Butler 2000: 35). LGBT issues are included in this, and radical separation is sought for them. For this to be achieved, however, they must be recognized as a troublesome factor in relation to the ideal of all that is ideal in the false universality and substantiality of ethno-nationalism. Thus the practice resorted to is one of translating opposing concepts into one's own terms using Žižek's (2000: 103) syntagm of "false disidentification" for the purposes of hegemonistic policy. In doing so, the supposedly radically 'Other' and different is integrated into one's own symbolic network and order of things with the use of oppressor-imposed designations, which have ontological force since they give rise to subordination. This performativity, as Butler notes (2006: xv), is never an individual act; rather it is a ritual repetition which achieves its impact by way of naturalization in the context of the body, which has a temporal aspect and cultural support.

---

* Prepared as a part of the project *Sustainability of the Identity of Serbs and National Minorities in the Border Municipalities of Eastern and South-Eastern Serbia* (179013), conducted at the University of Niš—Faculty of Mechanical Engineering, and supported by the Ministry of Science and Technological Development of the Republic of Serbia.
1   In this chapter we focus on Serbia, Croatia, and Bosnia and Herzegovina.
2   As Bjelić (2011: 1) notes that ethno-nationalism in the post-Yugoslav space "became the master narrative, presenting itself both as a consciousness of national liberation and a psychic cure for the social pathology of Communist totalitarianism."

In such a context, the nations of the former Yugoslavia need religion in order to transcend the post-transitional reality symbolically and ritually. Religion is the prime mover that sets all that is national in motion, yet at the same time it sets its ultimata, as traditional religious values are presented as the height of morality (Juergensmeyer 2006, 2008, Brubaker 2012, Grigoriadis 2013). Such religion and religiosity is of necessity ideologized, though declaring and presuming itself to be universal, transcendent and uncontaminated. It is presented as universal despite seeking to define key aspects of the ethnopolitical narrative (Mujkić 2010: 102). Or as Bourdieu (1977: 167) has noted, every established order has a tendency to portray its arbitrariness as something natural.

In the context of Serbia, Croatia, and Bosnia and Herzegovina, both religion and diversity relating to sexual orientation and/or gender identities have taken on public significance. Public statements by religious officials and political leaders have displayed a high degree of homonegative attitudes, including hate speech and strong discriminatory positions. Of course there are also positive and affirmative examples that do not get much media coverage, especially not at times when Pride Parades or other occasions involving LGBT issues come under the media spotlight. For example, the political and religious discourse in Serbia rejects the explicit acceptance of the LGBT community. As a result of the patriarchal tradition and homonegative attitudes, 67% of those surveyed in Serbia, male and female, have said that homosexuality is an illness, while 53% believe that the government needs to act to suppress homosexuality (Prejudices exposed 2010). Similar results have become evident from research recently conducted by the Centre for Civic Education, according to which two thirds of Montenegrins believe that homosexuality is an illness, while 80% believe that it should remain a private matter. Other data from Central and Eastern Europe and South-Eastern Europe show that homophobia is far more pervasive than in other parts of Europe (Andreescu 2011, Takács and Szalma 2011).

As we will see later in this chapter, the background to these attitudes lies in the interpretation of homosexuality as a threat from the West against the traditional values of national and religious identity. The tone, intensity and ideological oversaturation of these accusations is situated within today's traditionalist discourse in the post-Yugoslav space, which is opposed to processes of modernization, postulating conservatism as the answer to social crisis, insecurity and the devastating consequences of transition (Jovanović 2013, Van der Berg et al. 2014).

This study is based on a constructivist approach that tackles issues of the representation of symbolic systems capable of expressing meaning and power

systems connected with specific relational forces. Using a combination of theoretical insights, this approach proposes an analysis of representation (Hall
1997) as a source of the production of social constructs regarding the LGBT
community (including hate speech), taking into consideration who constructs
these representations and how, through a variety of discursive practices. In this
way, public discourse or what Ahmed (2004) calls the "effective economies"
(hate speech, disgust, fear, shame) has power and is able to dictate modes of
behavior. Therefore, in the context of this study, the social power of discourse
is exhibited through the hate speech of religious actors and politicians, in order
to exclude and marginalize the LGBT community, to the extent that it can even
create national identities through the debate. Our aim is to understand how
hate speech functions in public discourse, as well as how the relationships and
effects of these discourses of marginalization, social exclusion and violence are
named against sexual minorities. Thus, the research aims to contribute to a better understanding of the power of the discourse and its effect on social exclusion, which has important ramifications for nation-state building and national
preservation and/or defense.

In this chapter the key research issues that will be addressed are as follows:

1) Investigation of the connection between ethno-nationalism, religion and
   homosexuality in current public discourse in Serbia, Croatia, and Bosnia and
   Herzegovina;
2) Investigation of the relationship between these discourses and the religious-
   political configuration in different national and media contexts;
3) Analysis of the consequences of these discourses on marginalization, social
   exclusion and violence.

### The Example of Serbia: "Clenched Fists of the Humiliated and Offended"

Until recently the Serbian Orthodox Church was completely indifferent and
mute on the issue of homosexuality. With the increased visibility of the LGBT
population that began with the fall of the Milošević regime in 2000 and the
(unsuccessful) attempt to organize the first Pride Parade in 2001 (now remem-
bered as the "massacre pride"), the Church has felt provoked, and open hostility has followed, permeated by moralist and nationalist discourse (Jovanović,
2011). Generally speaking, the emergence of homosexuality as a topic of debate
has been interpreted in Church circles as an imposition of the "decadent West"
(Tucić 2011: 45) and as foreign to "our history, tradition and culture" (Irinej,

2011).³ The syntagm "non-traditional sexual orientation," used to indicate this variant of human sexuality, is somewhat indicative.

We also encounter publicists who, inflamed with the ardor of self-victimization, speak of "LGBT dictatorship" (Informativna služba Srpskog sabora Dveri 2010), the "gay Inquisition" (Dimitrijević 2011), and "terror of the minority." Or we might quote Živković (2007: 22): "Who gave them the right to 'tolerate' and respect the right of so-called 'marginal groups' while at the same time meting out totalitarian and fascistoid treatment of the rights of the 'majority' (including the faithful of the SPC [Serbian Orthodox Church])?"

The Pride Parade is seen as an offense—"a humiliation and a fulfillment of foreign desires: These marches insult the morals of the absolute majority, not just those of Christians but those of members of the other great religions, and they should not be allowed. I respect individual liberty, but not liberty that leads to anarchy" (Spaić and Popović 2012: 18). Patriarch Irinej demonstrated a similar attitude when he sent a memorandum to Prime Minister Ivica Dačić demanding a ban on an exhibition of photographs called *Ecce Homo* by Swedish artist Elisabeth Ohlson Wahllin that opened in Belgrade on 3 October 2012, which he described as "shameful," "horrific" and "scandalous." At one point Patriarch Irinej (2012) declared the following:

> This deeply insulting exhibition has been promoted by homosexuals, the organizers of the Pride Parade, planned for 3 October this year [2012]. We likewise request and demand that the planned tragicomedy known as the Pride Parade—which really ought to be called the "Shame Parade," and which casts a dark moral shadow over our city, our centuries of Christian culture and the dignity of the family as the basic cell of the human race—be prevented from taking place.

The negative attitude toward the LGBT issue reached its pinnacle in a statement by the Patriarch in which he claimed that the rains that had caused catastrophic flooding in Serbia in 2014 were a warning from God and a call to repentance regarding preparations for a gathering which "represents great lawlessness and a despicable vice, in which they declare pride and assert their dignity and democracy, yet which entirely opposes god and the law of life" (Tanjug 2014a). This was an allusion to the Pride Parade to be held in Belgrade, which in a second statement published on the same day (15 May) he called "the tip of an iceberg of immorality, a gathering of all flaw and vice" (Tanjug 2014b). In the

---

3 All translations from foreign language sources are the authors' own unless otherwise stated.

same spirit, four days later Metropolitan Amfilohije joined the blaming game, declaring that the flooding which had befallen the nation was "a sign that the Lord loves us," that he was testing us so that we might "return to the true path," and that it was no coincidence that the disaster had come in the wake of the victory by Austrian drag artiste Conchita Wurst at the 2014 Eurovision Song Contest, explaining that the extreme weather was a sign that people must reject this "Jesus-like figure" (Internet portal 021: 2014).

The Church is mounting an antimodernist defense against the assault from the Western "ideology of homosexualism" (*sic*) whereby the issue is being relocated from the field of human rights to the sphere of moralism. Leading the way in this is Metropolitan Amfilohije, who speaks of "violence against the moral order of things" (2010: 6–7). The list of pejoratives, already lengthy, aimed at homosexuals and homosexuality, is constantly being expanded: "mental illness," "grave disorder of the human personality," "abomination before God," "persons almost entirely lacking in physical and human virtue," "conscious or unconscious impulse to self-destruction," and "desecration and misuse of human nature and its God-given drives."

An indicative example of such discourse is the article by Nebojša Bakarec in the newspaper *Печат*, an egregious example of conspiratorial anti-Western discourse in the context of the public debate on the 2013 Pride Parade. Bakarec, vice-chair of the executive board of the DSS (the Democratic Party of Serbia [Demokratska Stranka Srbije]), a center-right party with a conservative agenda and open support for the Serbian Orthodox Church, wrote the article under the title "I won't forgive you for the children" (*Decu vam neću oprostiti*) as a response to an exhibition called *Our Queer Childhood*, held in Belgrade as part of the Pride Parade event in 2013. It is worth noting that in 2012 Bakarec was found guilty of discrimination against LGBT people and of hate speech when he claimed in his article titled *Drugi oktobar 2011* that homosexuality was a pathology that should be treated medically. In "I won't forgive you for the children," Bakarec (2013: 36) "exposes" the gay lobby with the following claims:

> It is obvious that foreign patrons have footed the bill for everything— either that or the self-proclaimed associations of fags,[4] lesbians and oth-

---

4  Serbo and Croatian—*peder*. *Peder* and *pederluk* are terms which once had a "technical" meaning and are frequently used by opponents of LGBT issues, even in print, but can today hardly be construed as anything other than derogatory. They are loosely translated herein as "fag" and "faggery."

ers have got lots of money. Either way the money originated abroad. What I am getting at is that it is clear that the EU and USA have invested significant funds in the Parade itself—the Week of Shame—and every year this funding clearly increases, as does the political support, pressure and blackmail.

According to Bakarec (2013: 37), Serbia needs to protect juveniles by way of a law similar to that in Russia. Even more interesting is the apocalyptic undertone of the article as a whole, and of the subtitle "The end of the world is nigh" (*Biće skoro propast sveta*), with Bakarec developing a discourse on eschatological technocracy, predicting:

> ... a brave new world, in which children will be conceived and born by purely artificial means, in surrogate wombs. Children will be brought up by homosexually conditioned robots and artificially generated e-personas. Only same-sex sexuality will be permitted ... What remains of the human race will ultimately die out, extinguish itself. Apocalypse. The Day of Judgment.

Through these and similar statements, Bakarec is explicitly agitating for and promoting an anti-Western discourse with the mission of saving Serbia from the morally ruined West.

An even more banal example of sexual and religious nationalism can be found in statements by Borislav Pelević (2013) in the television program *Revolucija* broadcast on TV Happy. Pelević, once better known as the general of Arkan's Tigers[5] had the following to say:

> I wonder if the parents [of the organizers of Pride] are proud of their children who are homosexuals. Who are abnormal, who are perverted, who are sick and who war against normal life in Serbia. Against our Orthodox faith, against our glorious Serbian tradition. I see no reason; nobody is preventing them from engaging in their perverse and debauched acts in their own homes ... But why do they poison our children? Why do the media devote so much attention to those sick, perverted, abnormal people? Why do they want to poison our children with that?

---

5   Željko Ražnatović Arkan was a Serbian criminal and commander of a paramilitary force in the Yugoslav wars. He was accused by the UN of crimes against humanity for his role during the war in Croatia.

Pelević's homonegative statement is a classic example of the perception of homosexuals as sick, sinful and deviant, and his invocation of tradition and Christianity in the struggle against homosexuality is a well-established discursive strategy. As a rule, the debate is waged on the level of religion, ethics and morals, while neglecting the issues of human rights, discrimination and tolerance. General lack of moderation coupled with moralistic zeal in the rhetoric of both Bakarec and Pelević actually attests to their marginal position in the political life of contemporary Serbia, as that rhetoric's main function is in drawing public attention and securing some space under the political sun.

It seems that church officials would prefer to ignore and gloss over same-sex attraction as a subject of no importance: "Given the current spiritual, social and political condition of our nation and state we believe that certain media and certain non-governmental organizations, out of their own base, if not subterranean interests, have imposed this disagreeable topic on our entire society, a topic which is in essence irrelevant to us" (Irinej, 2010: 5). Calls can also be heard from certain secular circles, to "prohibit homosexual propaganda and its promotion among juveniles" (Vukadinović et al. 2012; regarding the debate which this sparked, see Antonić 2012 and Gligorijević 2012), a wording which is very reminiscent of the legislation on "the prohibition of homosexual propaganda," enacted in Russia in June 2013 at the same session of the Duma at which the law prohibiting "offense against believers" was passed.

The proposed Law Against Discrimination in 2009 "forced" the Church to react and to end its "policy of silence." Two articles of this law were a particular focus of attention. First was Article 18, which in the draft law prohibited the denial of the right to accept, maintain, express and change faith or convictions, to which, at the initiative of the seven "traditional religious communities," headed by the Serbian Orthodox Church, a paragraph was added which absolved priests and religious ministers of responsibility for discriminatory action if their behavior was in accordance with the religious doctrine they advocated. Article 21 of the draft law prohibited discrimination on the basis of sexual orientation and gender identity, with specific mention of transsexuality in the third paragraph. In the final, enacted version of the law, the third paragraph was left out, as was all mention of gender identity (Jovanović 2013: 89–91). Condemnation of homosexuality from a position of religiously colored nationalism is done by juxtaposing the Pride Parade with the problem of Kosovo and Metohija, thus situating homosexuality in the position of the "Other," among the opposition according to which "the national" is constituted. The patriarch himself employs this discursive strategy (cf. Irinej 2011).

A thorn in the side of the church remains in the form of homosexuality (including homosexual pedophilia), which is dealt with by way of deafening silence. Examples of this have been accusations against Bishop Pahomije of Vranje, the homosexual scandal concerning the Bishop of Zvornik-Tuzla, Vasilije Kačavenda, which ended in his early retirement, as well as the case of Abbot Ilarion of Novo Hopovo monastery who was accused of "prohibited sexual acts with juveniles."[6] Any mention of the topic that there may be is couched in denial.

### The Example of Bosnia and Herzegovina: "It Should be Kept Within Four Walls"

Bosnia and Herzegovina is another striking example of the relationship between religion, nationalism and (homo)sexuality. As in other areas of the post-Yugoslav space, religious institutions have been the main incubators of nationalism (Mujkić 2010: 120). However, nowhere has this been more apparent than in Bosnia and Herzegovina, in view of the fact that this is the only Republic of the former Yugoslavia which did not have a titular nation and to this day no official definition of the Bosniac nationality has been adopted (Mujkić 2010: 129). Religion "sprang to assist" in the "nativization" and "indigenization" of the three "leading," so-called constitutive nationalities in Bosnia and Herzegovina: Bosniacs, Croats and Serbs. Within such a context, LGBT issues are, seemingly of some kind of historical necessity, set within ethno-confessional frameworks and subject to their rule and measure. In Bosnia and Herzegovina, gay pride parades have not been organized to date.

Since in Bosnia and Herzegovina there is a constant manufacturing of the national, which as such remains incomplete, the role of various elites in these discourses is of special significance. As regards the political elite, political parties in the country have no official stance, either positive or negative, toward this subject, except that there is a particular tendency toward the expression of homonegative attitudes on the part of politicians from parties on the political right, who not infrequently invoke God's laws and traditional values, and in that context directly or indirectly condemn the LGBT community. Thus, for example, Bakir Izetbegović, currently a member of the country's Presidency

---

6   In a response to the 2014 Pride Parade, Patriarch Irinej glossed over the pedophilia scandal among the bishops. Using the well-established anti-Western discourse, the patriarch declared the following: "If the gay sexual orientation is justified and should be propagated, then why is the same not true for pedophilia, widespread in the Western world, as well as incest [...] Why is their right less important than the so-called right of your sexual (dis)orientation." (B92 2014).

and vice-president of the Party of Democratic Action (Stranka Demokratske Akcije—SDA), once said: "I am not in the least pleased with the holding of the Queer Festival. This reminder of Sodom and Gomorrah on the day of the 27th night [of Ramadan], a noble night which Muslims look forward to—I am not at all pleased by that" (Nurkić 2012). Izetbegović also said around the time of the Queer Festival that, "They [LGBT people] have a right to their sexual orientation, or rather disorientation, but we will employ all moral means to fight the influence of homosexuality on youth ... It's something that will spread if you let it. It should be kept between four walls ..." (Čaušević and Gavrić 2012: 317). Statements like these can be perceived by ultra-nationalist organizations as a call to violence against LGBT people, which serves to solidify further the stereotypes and prejudices that homosexuality is an illness and is to be weeded out. As chairman of the BiH Presidency, Izetbegović also stated, in *Gracija* magazine of October 2010, "we must fight with all moral means against those who seek to pervert a highly moral society. Everybody has the right to live their life as they please, but not the right to present the perverted as normal to young people and to call them to join in" (Barreiro and Vasić 2012: 24). Member of the Federation of Bosnia and Herzegovina Parliament, Amila Alikadić-Husović deemed it inappropriate that "something like that" was being held in the month of Ramadan, adding, "[h]omosexuality is condemned by every religion. Who are we to approve of something that God forbids?" (cf. Vučetić, Rašević and Popov-Momčinović 2013: 15). From this and similar quotes one can see the intermingling of the ethno-nationalist, religious and homonegative, as well as the way in which such statements circulate practically unhindered in public discourse, the primary mediators of which are the mass-media. With their lack of critical distance from the source of the "information," they further contribute to the circulation of hate speech against LGBT people and lend support to constructs which reflect certain power relationships, social fracturing and hierarchy.

The most homonegative statements by religious officials could be read in the magazine SAFF, which has a narrow readership oriented towards radical Islam, though it should be noted that this magazine also has an online edition accessible by the broader public. In this magazine, LGBT people are depicted as having fallen into the trap of Shaytan, concealing obvious sin by calling it by another name while invoking human rights and liberties (Durkalić 2012a:147). The most egregious example of "anti-gay propaganda", as cited by Durkalić, could be read in the same magazine in the editorial "Fagland" (*Pederland*) (Alispahić 2008: 18), headlined "Struggle for Survival" (*'Borba za opstanak'*) with the opening sentence of the editorial: "The goal of the festival of fags in the month of Ramadan was not just meant as an affirmation of faggery but as a provocation and intimidation of Muslims, with the ultimate ambition of having the Bosniacs accept faggery as a lesser evil than their own tradition" (Durkalić 2012b: 176). What is especially striking is that ethnic distancing from the "aggressor" (read: the Serbs[7]) has, by use of discursive sophistry in one article in this magazine, been depicted in a positive light as regards the treatment of LGBT issues, with the goal of mobilizing Bosniacs and Muslims against LGBT people and, more generally, awakening their patriotic sentiment. So we read the words of Milanko Mihaljica, leader of the Serbian Radical Party of the Republic of Srpska, who declared that Sarajevo was just the place for the Queer Festival, since "[the Republic of] Srpska will never allow debauchery and perversion in its streets, nor lend support to unnatural tendencies" (Durkalić 2012a: 99).

This well-established discourse does not end here however. It also produces and reproduces moral panic and social confusion. Thus the largest daily newspaper in BiH, Dnevni Avaz, ran a front page headline on August 28, 2008 which inquired in huge letters: "Who is trying to trick the Bosniacs by holding the gay gathering during Ramadan?" (*Ko Bošnjacima podvaljuje gay okupljanje u Ramazanu?*). This linking of Ramadan with the festival served to depict the festival as an attack on religion, even though the festival program did not touch on religious themes. Dnevni Avaz used less inflammatory language than SAFF, "ideologization in 'so many words' ... but the 'job' was done for them by numerous public figures, their statements serving to indoctrinate the readership in the idea that queer people are sick and that the festival was deliberately timed to coincide with Ramadan and hence they were disrespecting Islam and its fundamental values" (Durkalić 2012b: 181–182).

It should also be noted that the supposedly more politically correct media do not always respect the code of professional reporting ethics where LGBT topics are concerned. For example, they constantly interview the same people, they place no critical distance between themselves and the source of the (dis)information, and so on, thereby contributing to the creation of a homonegative social climate. The fact that the great majority of members of the public, both male and female, consider homosexuality to be an illness and have a high degree of social distance toward the LGBT population, would seem to support this theory (Popov-Momčinović 2013), while the media are just there to show "things as they are" (see Milojević 2012).

As the guardians and proponents of the national interests of the constitutive nationalities, politicians have also not been immune to moral panic. These

---

7   The Bosniacs tend to regard the 1990s war in BiH as an act of aggression by the Serbs and reject the term "civil war."

interests which they mystify in various ways in view of the fact that the Constitution does not specify which issues come under the category of national
interests, even though under this guise and through the so-called House of
Peoples in which the representatives of the constitutive nationalities sit, they
can block laws and decisions taken by the representative parliamentary bodies. From such statements we can clearly see the intermingling of the national
and the religious, and this intermingling is not infrequently mediated by LGBT
issues. This discursive negotiation is thus a place of agreement and common
ground irrespective of the national and religious affiliations of the politicians
and of whether or not this topic is discussed or glossed over. And when it is
discussed, using the mechanisms of restrained, mute and hypocritical sexuality (Foucault 1978: 3), it is declared taboo through the attribution of imposed
meanings which correspond to local symbolic orders and the ethno-national
*status quo*, within which it is perpetuated by way of the narrative of one's own
victimhood and the need to ensure survival through biological multiplication.
Fear of assimilation or extermination is constantly manufactured through the
repetition of stories and ethnic narratives which, although incongruous, have
the same internal logic (Vlaisavljević 2009: 78). The war in Bosnia produced a
replacement for the vacant position of the enemy in the form of the "domestic enemy" (Vlaisavljević 2009: 81). Although the domestic enemy is usually a
member of another ethnic group or indeed the group itself, sometimes, and
in certain circumstances and depending on political expediency, it can be the
other and the different in the non-ethnic sense too: those of different ideology
provenance or of other sexual orientation.

We can say that, although homophobia is very much present in BiH and
that the re-patriarchalization and re-traditionalization of society seeks to set
everyone in his or her proper place in accordance with a binary understanding of gender roles, it is also somewhat "loose," being intersected by *ad hoc*
media, religious and ethno-national constructs. Thus, for example, although
religious institutions have a hardline attitude toward this topic, one survey conducted on a representative sample of the population of BiH did not find that
religiosity was a major determinant of homonegative attitudes. Specifically,
even though religious people showed a slightly greater degree of social distance
toward LGBT people and somewhat more homonegative attitudes, statistically
significant differences were not found for any of the questions between the
attitudes of religious and non-religious interviewees, both male and female
(Popov-Momčinović 2013: 10). Religious institutions continue to resort to certain ploys with regard to LGBT rights. They frequently use the syntagm of the
so-called separation of the "sin from the man" and the "state from the act." They
frequently address the subject *ad hoc* and through mechanisms of decontextu-

alization. Thus, for example, religious institutions in BiH sometimes make public statements regarding Pride Parades to be held in countries of the region or
further abroad, or on the referendum recently held in Croatia, without deeper
reflection on the BiH context. This points to subtle mechanisms of Foucauldian
control and punishment (and pastoral power is one form of power) on the
part of local religious institutions in regard to the topic of LGBT. This power,
exercised through discipline as an "ensemble of minute technical inventions"
(Foucault 1995: 220), gives rise to a variety of discursive plays which obscure
and conceal the limitation of the public arena (Žižek 2000: 100).

### The Example of Croatia: "In the Name of the Family"

Croatia presents an interesting example of a country that has strong relations
with the dominant religion (Perica 2002), but at the same time also gives the
greatest rights to its LGBT population in comparison to the rest of the region.
From one point, the Catholic Church as the main religion in the country has
great influence over state affairs (e.g. history textbooks and a strong position in
enforcing identification based on an interplay between religion and ethnicity
[cf. Topić 2012, Topić and Vasiljević 2011a, 2011b]). On the other hand, the LGBT
population is able to organize gay prides (albeit not always without problems)
and has recently won its long struggle to obtain the right to civil partnership
and equalization of status with heterosexual marriages. However, the LGBT
population has been the subject in 2013 in which one conservative NGO—as
will be discussed below—called for a referendum to insert the definition of
marriage as a "biological union between a man and a woman" into the country's
Constitution. At the same time, Croatia is also the only country that has a
football fan group fighting against homophobia in football stadia and where
the media stand up against every attempt to violate the rights of the LGBT
population (Jutarnji list, Novi List, Index.hr, Slobodna Dalmacija), while those
media that belong to the conservative side and are traditionally more affiliated
with the Catholic Church (Večernji List) still cannot be called hate preachers.

Even though the rights of the LGBT population are greater than in other
countries of the region, the group has emphasized a few points that still need to
be addressed. Namely, LGBT activists believe they are still discriminated against
because the legislative system inadequately addresses issues of the legal protection of LGBT people. Besides the anti-discrimination law, the Constitution
of the Republic of Croatia does not address the matter of the protection of the
rights of its LGBT citizens. Indeed, LGBT rights organizations called for provisions to be included in the Constitution regarding the protection of the rights of

gender minorities (Izvještaj o stanju ljudskih prava seksualnih i rodnih manjina u 2010. godini), however, these demands were not met, and in 2013 a referendum was held seeking the addition of a provision in the Constitution according to which marriage would be defined as a "biological union between a woman and a man." This was the initiative of the "In the Name of the Family" (*U ime obitelji*) association (2014), which invokes democracy in its campaigning and criticizes the media and the government for undemocratically prohibiting the expression of opinion, and for the "terrorization" of the silent majority by the so-called aggressive minority. In doing so, this association is effectively distorting the fundamental tenets of democracy, advancing the idea that the majority has the absolute right to decide, something which the President of Croatia himself, Ivo Josipović, pointed out, saying that democracy was not a "vote-ocracy" and that democracy did not mean that the majority could trample on the rights of the minority (Jutarnji 2013). Such insistence on the absolute right of the majority was characterized by more left-leaning media and individuals as fascist and discriminatory.

In Croatia the media are not complicit in discriminating against minority rights as is the case in Bosnia and Herzegovina where the media do not adopt a firm stance with regard to discrimination. Indeed, some media openly position themselves as "guardians of democracy," exposing themselves to insult and accusations. The difference in verbal discrimination in relation to other former Yugoslav republics is that the LGBT community in Croatia is perceived as representing a threat to the family (which was the focal point of the referendum on marriage in December 2013), and less as an illness. The reason for this probably lies in the fact that Croatia and Slovenia removed homosexuality from the list of mental illnesses as early as 1973, and in 1977 the criminal law of the Socialist Republic of Croatia decriminalized homosexual relations. Slovenia, Montenegro and Vojvodina did the same, while the other republics did not. However, the official teaching of the Roman Catholic Church to students of religious catechism is that homosexuality is an illness (Jutarnji 2013a).

As regards Pride events, despite discrimination against the LGBT community, Croatia is the only former Yugoslav republic in which these events are held regularly, albeit amidst heavy security. The first Zagreb Gay Pride was held in 2002, accompanied by verbal abuse from the public and violence against marchers, but also enjoying significant support from the media, which called the event a test of democracy (Jurčić 2012). After the first event a campaign was launched called "Love is Love" (*Ljubav je ljubav*), and further publicity was given to LGBT rights by the film "Fine Dead Girls" (*Fine mrtve djevojke*) by director Dalibor Matanić. However, participants in the 2007 event in Zagreb had a petrol bomb thrown at them, leading to the first ever hate crimes conviction for the perpetrator. The year 2007 was marked by large-scale attacks on people of LGBT orientation in all public places, as well as in their offices and their own homes. Until 2011, these events were held only in Zagreb, often accompanied by a parallel gathering organized by the HČSP (Izvještaj o stanju ljudskih prava seksualnih i rodnih manjina u 2010), an ultra-right wing political party which has hitherto failed to meet the election threshold and enter the Croatian parliament, but which systematically seeks to garner publicity and support for its beliefs, including glorification of the Ustasha regime. Such parallel events have often involved discriminatory aspects, in view of the offensive placards they feature (Topić 2013).

Although the Gay Pride events in Zagreb have mostly occurred peacefully (with the exception of 2007), a Pride Parade in Split in 2011 led to a wave of violence in which event participants had stones thrown at them and were verbally abused. Nazi salutes were also in evidence. The media reported that 10,000 protesters wanted to "tear apart the 400 participants of the event" (Jutarnji 2011). On that occasion the police halted the event. The following year the event went ahead, and the LGBT population was able to express its views—but it should also be noted that the event was held amid a heavy police presence, with all approaches blocked to streets through which the parade was to pass. In other words, this outcome does not mean that there would not have been incidents had they not been physically prevented by shutting down the entire center of Split. It was not until the 2013 event that things passed without incident and without a complete shutdown of the city (Bačić 2013). However, the events that followed, with the referendum initiative regarding the definition of marriage, showed that an end to the discrimination toward the LGBT community was not a social reality.

Nevertheless, the greatest discrimination comes in verbal form, where those of LGBT orientation are abused at football stadia and by Catholic associations which are not officially part of the Catholic Church but are affiliated with it. Thus the aforementioned referendum initiative on the definition of marriage from 2013 got the fervent support of the Church, which on the day of the referendum (traditionally held on Sundays) called on citizens to come out and vote "yes" (Laudato 2013). The leader of the referendum initiative, Željka Markić, personally admitted after the referendum was over that the referendum was her way of ensuring that the LGBT community would never gain the right to marriage, which belonged only to "normal people" (Jutarnji 2013b). After the referendum, the government continued drafting the Life Partnership Act which it had earlier begun (this separate law serving as proof that there had been no intention to give the LGBT community the right to marriage, hence that the referendum had been unnecessary), and which would permit LGBT citizens a status equivalent to marriage, albeit under the official term "life partnership" (*životno partnerstvo*) (Index 2013).

This draft law (Ministarstvo uprave RH 2013) provoked protest from the referendum initiative, which protested against the Act claiming that it was evading the referendum decision regarding the status of marriage in Croatia (Jutarnji 2013c). Nonetheless the law was passed on 1 September 2014 without triggering major protests, and on 5 September 2014 two men in Zagreb committed to life partnership, which gave them all the same rights as in a heterosexual marriage except in name, and there is no possibility of adopting children (Law on Life Partnership of Same Sex Persons NN 92/14 [Jutarnji 2014a]). The media called this event the "first gay marriage," which triggered complaints from the For the Family group that filed a complaint to the Council for Electronic Media asking the Council to punish and warn all national media that life partnership cannot be called marriage (Večernji 2014). The request was rejected by the Council which stated that the Council could not violate freedom of speech and order the media how to interpret certain laws and terms (Jutarnji 2014b).

As regards the activities of the Roman Catholic Church and the rights of the LGBT community, the Church has traditionally opposed the recognition of LGBT rights to marriage and the adoption of children, being equally opposed to medically facilitated fertilization and any form of sexual awareness education. After the governing coalition led by the Social Democratic Party introduced a health education curriculum that included a fourth module on sexuality, the Catholic Church took up an opposition stance and called for the government to be brought down by use of arms (Jutarnji 2013d, 2013e). This example shows that the Catholic Church in Croatia does not have quite as much public support as was previously thought, despite its strong relations with politics. When the national media came out in support of the secularization of the state and when public opinion surveys showed that citizens were opposed to the interference of the Church in health education (Jutarnji 2013f), Catholic associations suddenly thrust themselves into the public arena, taking over the task of campaigning against health education.

Considering the public opposition to church interference in matters of state and the arrival of moderate Pope Francis at the helm of the Catholic Church, who after the referendum on marriage even announced that four extreme right-wingers among the Croatian bishops would be sent into retirement (Jutarnji 2014), it is clear that the Church did not dare wage the battle over the marriage referendum personally, and the "In the Name of the Family" association appeared instead, run mostly by people affiliated either with the Church itself or with organizations affiliated to it. Evidence of this includes the writing of *Glas Koncila*, the official mouthpiece of the Catholic Church. This journal openly campaigned for the marriage referendum, using arguments rather similar to those coming from the In the Name of the Family association. For example, the January 9, 2014 issue carried a report on an interview with Cardinal Bozanić conducted by Croatian Catholic Radio (Hrvatski Katolički Radio) in which the media and government were criticized for their bias and tendentiousness (Glas Koncila 2014), arguments which echoed those of the association which initiated the referendum.

It is clear, therefore, that in Croatia the LGBT community is treated as a threat to the family even though it is not explicitly verbally abused as in other states of the former Yugoslavia, and especially not in the media, which have stood in defense of the rights of people of LGBT orientation.

## Conclusion

From the foregoing we can see that in Serbia and Bosnia-Herzegovina the media, with their lack of critical distance, contributed further to the circulation of hate speech, lending support to well-established power structures and hierarchies or giving excessive voice to hate speech even when not advocating problematic attitudes themselves. A well-established relationship between ethno-national, religious and homonegative attitudes can be seen at work, where hate speech and similar forms of expression circulate almost unhindered in public discourse, mediated primarily by the mass media. The connection between ethno-nationalism, religion, and especially (homo)sexuality in post-conflict societies explains the functioning of religious nationalism, conferring privilege on heteronormativity and stirring up and supporting an intolerant culture. Open homonegativity is cunningly concealed using what Švab and Kuhar (2005) call the "transparent closet" and the reduction of homosexuality to a personal preference or lifestyle choice, for which there is in fact no place in the public identitary politics of this region. For the only identity which is possible—i.e., that which has an ontologically elevated status—is an ethno-confessional one in these societies in which the principles of justice and right have been ethno-nationalized.

Croatia presents a different case where the media do not openly agitate toward discrimination of LGBT groups and where Gay Pride manifestations are regularly held more-or-less without incident. However, Croatia has the general problem of the enormously influential Roman Catholic Church which interferes in all aspects of state politics. The LGBT community in Croatia has managed to secure the right to life partnership, which is what they have been seeking for more than a decade. The overall continuing influence of the Catholic Church should not be underestimated, and the fact that the LGBT community managed to obtain this right does not mean they will not become targets of significant verbal abuse if Church-related groups manage to gain more political power, which is currently happening with a new referendum initiative led by the For the Family group to change electoral law so as to allow smaller parties to enter Parliament again.

## References

Ahmed, Sara. 2004. *The Cultural Politics of Emotion*. New York: Routledge.

Alispahić, Famir. 2008. "Pederland." *SAFF. Islamist Magazine* 10:18–19.

Amfilohije, Mitropolit crnogorsko-primorski. 2010. "Kolo smrti na ulicama Beograda." *Pravoslavlje—Novine srpske patrijaršije* 1046: 6–8.

Andrescu, Viviana. 2011. "From Legal Tolerance to Social Acceptance: Predictors of Heterosexism in Romania." *Revista Romana De Sociologie* 22: 209–231.

Antonić, Slobodan. 2012. "Ko je rekao 'zabraniti'." *Vreme* 1113. Retrieved 5 January 2014 from: http://www.vreme.rs/cms/view.php?id=1050110.

Bakarec, Nebojša. 2013. "Decu vam neću oprostiti." *Печат* 288: 34–37.

*Balkan Insight*. 2013. Retrieved 27 July 2013 from: http://www.balkaninsight.com/en/ article/montegrin-cleric-consecrates-budva-after-pride-parade.

Barreiro, Marinha and Vladana Vasić. 2012. *Praćenje provedbe Preporuke Vijeća Evrope o mjerama za borbu protiv diskriminacije zasnovane na seksualnoj orijentaciji ili rodnom identitetu. Izvještaj za Bosnu i Hercegovinu*. Sarajevo: Sarajevski otvoreni centar.

Bačić, Mašenka. 2013. "Relaksirajući Gay Pride u Splitu." Retrieved 12 January 2014 from: http://www.h-alter.org/vijesti/ljudska-prava/relaksirajuci-gay-pride-u-splitu -fotogalerija.

Bjelić, Dušan I. 2011. *Normalizing the Balkans: Geopolitics of Psychoanalysis and Psychiatry*. Burlington: Ashgate.

Blažević, Jozo, Bobić Feđa, Saša Gavrić, and Jasmina Čaušević (eds.). 2013. *18 +: Knjiga o nešto drugačijim muškarcima*. Sarajevo: Sarajevski otvoreni centar.

Brubaker, Rogers. 2012. "Religion and Nationalism: Four Approaches." *Nation and Nationalism* 18: 2–20.

Butler, Judith. 2000. "Restaging the Universal: Hegemony and the Limits of Formalism." Pp. 11–43 in J. Butler, E. Laclau and S. Žižek (eds.) *Contingency, Hegemony, Universality: Contemporary Dialogues on the Left*. London: Verso.

———. 2006. *Gender Trouble: Feminism and the Subversion of Identity*. New York: Routledge.

B92. Net. 2013. "Violence during Montenegro's First Gay Parade." Retrieved 23 January 2013 from: www.b92.net/eng/news/region.php?yyyy=2013&mm=07&dd=24& nav_id=87056.

———. 2014. "Serbian Orthodox Church: Make a Parade but use your own money." Retrieved 24 September 2014 from: http://www.b92.net/eng/news/society.php?yyyy =2014&mm=09&dd=23&nav_id=91690.

Čaušević, Jasmina and Saša Gavrić (eds.) 2012. *Pojmovnik LGBT kulture*. Sarajevo: Sarajevski otvoreni centar and Fondacija Heinrich Böll.

Čustović, Mia and Zlatiborka Popov-Momčinović. 2013. *Prava LGBT osoba u Bosni i Hercegovini: unutrašnji poslovi*. Sarajevo: Fondacija Heinrich Böll, Fondacija CURE, Sarajevski otvoreni centar.

Dimitrijević, Vladimir. 2011. "Jedna nakaradna knjiga, manifest nakaradne budućnosti porodice u Srbiji." Retrieved 12 November 2013 from: http://www.dverisrpske.com/ sr/za-dveri-pisu/saradnici/114-vladimir-dimitrijevic/4125-manifest-smrti-porodice .html.

Foucault, Michel. 1978. *The History of Sexuality—Volume I: An Introduction*. New York: Pantheon Books.

———. 1995. *Discipline and Punish: The Birth of the Prison*. New York: Vintage.

Gavrić, Saša. 2012. "LGBT aktivizam u Bosni i Hercegovini". Pp. 111–117 in A. Spahić and S. Gavrić (eds.) *Čitanka LGBT ljudskih prava*. Sarajevo: Sarajevski otvoreni centar & Heinrich Böll Stiftung.

*Glas koncila*. 2014. "Referendum o braku poticaj i za neke nove inicijative." Retrieved 13 January 2014 from: http://www.glas-koncila.hr/portal.html?catID=2&conID=35172& act=view.

Gligorijević, Jovana. 2012. "Ecce homo(seksualnost)." *Vreme* 1112, Retrieved 5 January 2014 from: http://www.vreme.rs/cms/view.php?id=1048739.

Grigoriadis, Ioannis N. 2013. *Instilling Religion in Greek and Turkish Nationalism: A "Sacred Synthesis."* New York: Palgrave Macmillan.

Hall, Stuart. 1997. "The Work of Pepresentation." Pp. 15–64 in S. Hall (ed.) *Representation: Cultural Representations and Signifying Practices*. London: Sage.

Huremović, Lejla. 2012. "Najmlađi homoseksualac u BiH ima 12 godina. Analiza sadržaja izvještavanja printanih medija o LGBT temama u drugoj polovini 2011." Pp. 188–195 in A. Spahić and S. Gavrić (eds.) *Čitanka LGBT ljudskih prava*. Sarajevo: Sarajevski otvoreni centar & Heinrich Böll Stiftung.

*Index*. 2013. "Završava javna rasprava o Zakonu o životnom partnerstvu." Retrieved 12 January 2014 from: http://www.index.hr/vijesti/clanak/zavrsava-javna-rasprava-o -zakonu-o-zivotnom-partnerstvu/715051.aspx.

Informativna služba Srpskog sabora Dveri. 2010. "Država gori, a režim gejeva se češka." Retrieved 5 January 2014 from: http://dverisrpske.com/sr/dveri-na-delu/1286drzava -gori.html.

*Internet portal 021.* 2014. "Amfilohije: Poplave su znak da Bog voli Srbiju i BiH." Retrieved 25 May 2014 from: http://www.021.rs/info/svet/101460-amfilohije-poplave-su-znak -da-bog-voli-srbiju-i-bih.html.

Irinej, Episkop bački. 2010. "Saopštenje Svetog Arhijerejskog Sinoda povodom najavâ gej-parade u Beogradu: Protiv javnog reklamiranja seksualne orijentacije." *Pravoslavlje Novine srpske patrijaršije* 1046: 5.

Irinej, Patrijarh srpski. 2011a. "Poruka Njegove Svetosti Patrijarha srpskog G. Irineja." Retrieved 19 November 2011 from: http://www.spc.rs/sr/poruka_njegove_svetosti_ patrijarha_srpskog_g_irineja.

————. 2012b. "Pismo Patrijarha srpskog g. Irineja predsedniku Vlade R. Srbije g. Ivici Dačiću." Retrieved 7 June 2013 from: http://www.spc.rs/sr/pismo_patrijarha_srpskog _g_irineja_predseniku_vlade_r_srbije_g_ivic_dachitshu.

*Izvještaj o stanju ljudskih prava seksualnih i rodnih manjina u 2010. godini.* 2010. Zagreb: Iskorak.

Jovanović, Miloš. 2011. "Moralistička osuda homoseksualnosti u pravoslavlju." *TEME— Časopis za društvene nauke* 35: 705–744.

————. 2013. "Silence or Condemnation: The Orthodox Church on Homosexuality in Serbia." *Družboslovne razprave* 29: 79–95.

Juergensmeyer, Mark. 2006. "Nationalism and Religion." Pp. 357–367 in A.R. Segal (ed.) *The Blackwell Companion to the Study of Religion.* Malden, Mass.: Blackwell Publishing.

————. 2008. *Global Rebellion: Religious Challenges to the Secular State, from Christian Militias to al Qaeda.* Berkeley: University of California Press.

Jurčić, Marko. 2012. "Povijest LGBT aktivizma u Hrvatskoj." Pp. 89–100 in S. Gavrić (ed.) *Čitanka LGBT ljudskih prava.* Sarajevo: Sarajevski Otvoreni Centar and Heinrich Böll Stiftung.

*Jutarnji.* 2011. "Sramota u Splitu: 10.000 homofoba htjelo rastrgati 400 sudionika gay parade." Retrieved 12 January 2014 from: http://www.jutarnji.hr/gay-pride-split-10 -000-homofoba-htjelo-rastrgati-400-sudionika-gay-parade/952694/.

————. 2013a. "'Zakonom bih odmah izjednačio tradicionalni i istopolni brak' Predsjednik Josipović u Magazinu Jutarnjeg." Retrieved 12 January 2014 from: http://www .jutarnji.hr/template/article/article-print.jsp?id=1108708.

————. 2013b. "Vlada čisti udžbenike. Ekskluzivno: 'Djecu u školi više nećemo učiti da je homoseksualnost nastrana bolest'." Retrieved 13 January 2014 from: http://www .jutarnji.hr/-djecu-u-skoli-vise-necemo-uciti-da-je-homoseksualnost-nastrana -bolest-/1019932/.

————. 2013c. "Željka Markić 'Želimo da *gay* parovi nikada ne dobiju ista prava kao normalni ljudi'." Retrieved 12 January 2014 from: http://www.jutarnji.hr/zeljka -markic-zelimo-zacementirati-to-da-gay-lezbijski-parovi-nikada-ne-dobiju-ista -prava-kao-normalni-parovi-/1143293/.

————. 2013d. "Protiv zakona o životnom partnerstvu. Markić 'Povucite zakon koji gay parovima dopušta posvajanje djece' Vlada 'Nema šanse!'." Retrieved 12 January 2014 from: http://www.jutarnji.hr/markic-protiv-zakona-o-zivotnom-partnerstvu-to-je -zaobilazni-nacin-da-im-se-dozvoli-posvajanje-djece-/1144202/.

————. 2013e. "Biskup pozvao na oružano rušenje vlasti. Vlada: Iz Crkve dolazi govor mržnje! KAPTOL: Nitko nas neće zaustaviti u pobuni protiv vlasti!" Retrieved 13 January 2014 from: http://www.jutarnji.hr/vlada-iz-crkve-dolazi-govor-mrznje-kaptol -nitko-nas-nece-zaustaviti-u-pobuni-protiv-sdp-ove-vlasti-/1077724/.

————. 2013f. "Video, skandalozan istup! Biskup usporedio vladu s nacistima: 'Treba nam nova Oluja za svrgavanje vlasti!'" Retrieved 13 January 2014 from: http://www .jutarnji.hr/biskup-usporedio-vladu-s-nacistima/1077502/.

————. 2013g. "Istraživanje pokazalo: Čak 56,2% građana protiv miješanja Crkve u zdravstveni odgoj!" Retrieved 13 January 2014 from: http://www.jutarnji.hr/ istrazivanje-cak-56-2-gradana-hrvatske-protiv-mijesanja-crkve-u-zdravstveni -odgoj-/1077233/.

————. 2014. "Rošade u vrhu Katoličke crkve u RH. Odreknuće: Papa će do Uskrsa umiroviti četvoricu najdesnijih hrvatskih biskupa." Retrieved 13 January 2014 from: http://www.jutarnji.hr/papa-ce-do-uskrsa-umiroviti-cetvoricu-najdesnijih -biskupa/1151567/.

*Laudato.* 2013. "Biskupi pozivaju vjernike da izađu na referendum o braku i zaokruže 'ZA'." Retrieved 12 January 2014 from: http://www.laudato.hr/Novosti/Hrvatska/ Biskupi-pozivaju-vjernike-da-izađu-na-referendum-0.aspx.

Milojević, Snježana. 2012. "Zašto je različitost važna?" Pp. 161–168 In A. Spahić and S. Gavrić (eds.) *Čitanka LGBT ljudskih prava.* Sarajevo: Sarajevski otvoreni centar & Heinrich Böll Stiftung.

Ministarstvo uprave RH. 2013. *Nacrt prijedloga Zakona o životnom partnerstvu.* Retrieved 12 January 2014 from: http://www.uprava.hr/default.aspx?id=13946.

Nurkić, Edina. 2012. *"Queer Sarajevo Festival: Kolaps sistema."* Retrieved 14 December 2012 from: http://www.diskriminacija.ba/node/72.

Perica, Vjekoslav. 2002. *Balkan Idols: Religion and Nationalism in Yugoslav States.* New York: Oxford University Press.

Pikić, Aleksandra and Ivana Jugović. 2006. *Nasilje nad lezbijkama, gejevima i biseksual- nim osobama u Hrvatskoj: Izvještaj istraživanja.* Zagreb: Kontra.

Popov-Momčinović, Zlatiborka. 2013. *Ko smo mi da sudimo drugima? Ispitivanje javnog mnjenja o stavovima prema homoseksualnosti i transrodnosti u Bosni i Hercegovini,* Sarajevo: Fondacija Heinrich Böll, Fondacija CURE & Sarajevski otvoreni centar.

Prejudices Exposed: Homophobia in Serbia. 2010. *Research and Analysis of: Public Opinion, Views of LGBT Population, Discrimination in the Workplace.* Belgrade: Gay Straight Alliance & CeSID. Retrieved 15 September 2013 from: http://gsa.org.rs/wp -content/uploads/2012/04/Research-Prejudices-Exposed-2010-GSA.pdf.

Rašević, Dragana, Vuk Vučetić, and Zlatiborka Popov-Momčinović. 2013. *Prava LGBT osoba u Bosni i Hercegovini: Političke partije.* Sarajevo: Fondacija Heinrich Böll— Ured za BiH, Fondacija CURE, Sarajevski otvoreni centar.

Spaić, Nebojša and Vasilije Popović. 2012. "Patrijarh Irinej—Intervju—Prvi deo." *NIN,* 3233: 16–22.

Švab, Alenka, and Roman Kuhar. 2005. *The Unbearable Comfort of Privacy: The Everyday Life of Gays and Lesbians.* Ljubljana: Peace Institute.

Takács, Judith and Ivett Szalma. 2011. "Homophobia and same-sex partnership legalization in Europe." *Equality, Diversity and Inclusion: An International Journal* 30: 356–378.

*Tanjug.* 2014a. "Patrijarh Irinej: Ovo je Božja opomena zbog pripreme skupa bezakonja i mrskog poroka." Retrieved 25 May 2014 from: http://www.pressonline.rs/info/drustvo/311579/patrijarh-irinej-ova-kisa-nije-kazna-vec-bozja-opomena-zbog-gej -parade.html.

———. 2014b. "Patrijarh: Gej parada vrh nemoralnog brega." Retrieved 25 May 2014 from: http://www.politika.rs/rubrike/Drustvo/Patrijarh-Gej-parada-vrh -nemoralnog-brega.sr.html.

Topić, Martina. 2012. "Deconstruction of The Religious Narrative: *Antemurale Christianitatis* and the Construction of Difference." Pp. 47–74 in N. Knežević and S. Sremac (eds.) *Demitologizacija religijskih narativa na Balkanu: Uloga religija u (post)konfliktnom društvu i pomirenju.* Novi Sad: Centre for the Study of Religion, Politics and Society.

———. 2013. "European Identity and the Far Right in Central Europe: A New Emerging Concept or a New European 'Other'?" Pp. 229–270 in B. Radeljić (ed.), *Debating European Identity: Bright Ideas, Dim Prospects.* Oxford: Peter Lang.

——— and Snježana Vasiljević. 2011a. *Identity Construction Programs of the State and the EU: Case study Phase III—Citizens and Modernities: Between National and European Paths in Croatia.* Research report to the European Commission in FP7 EC project "Identities and Modernities in Europe."

———. 2011b. *Identity Construction Programs of the State and the EU: Case Study Phase II.* Research report to the European Commission in FP7 EC project "Identities and modernities in Europe."

*Tportal.* 2013. "U nedjelju će hrvatska demokracija biti likvidirana." Retrieved 12 January 2014 from: http://www.tportal.hr/vijesti/komentari/301745/U-nedjelju-ce-hrvatska -demokracija-biti-likvidirana.html.

Tucić, Živica. 2011. "SPC u novom veku (3): Homoseksualnost i pedofilija—Greh pohote." NIN 3137, 42–45.

*U ime obitelji.* 2014. Official site. Retrieved 12 January 2014 from: http://uimeobitelji.net/.

Vlaisavljević, Ugo. 2007. *Rat kao najveći kulturni događaj: Ka semiotici etnonacionalizma.* Sarajevo: Maunagić.

Vukadinović, Đorđe. 2012. "Inicijativa za spas Srbije." Retrieved 5 June 2014 from: http://www.nspm.rs/politicki-zivot/inicijativa-za-spas-srbije.html.

Van den Berg, Mariecke, David J. Boss, Marco Derks, R. Ruard Ganzevoort, Miloš Jovanović, Anne-Marie Korte, and Srdjan Sremac. 2014. "Religion, Homosexuality, and Contested Social Orders in the Netherlands, the Western Balkans, and Sweden." Pp. 116–134 in G. Ganiel, H. Winkel and C. Monnot (eds.) *Religion in Times of Crisis*. Leiden: Brill.

Živković, Gordana. 2007. "Srpski liberali u strahu od fašizacije Srbije." *Pravoslavlje—Novine srpske patrijaršije* 966: 20–22.

Žižek, Slavoj. 2000. "Class Struggle or Postmodernism? Yes, Please!" Pp. 90–135 in J. Butler, E. Laclau and S. Žižek. *Contingency, Hegemony, Universality: Contemporary Dialogues on the Left*. London: Verso.

# CHAPTER 4

# Antagonism in the Making: Religion and Homosexuality in Post-Communist Poland

*Dorota Hall*

In Poland, religious and national ideals have long been strongly intertwined and far from relegated to the private realm. Scholars point in concord to political factors when explaining this situation. The religion–nation symbiosis coalesced during the nineteenth century when Poles, deprived of their own state, built their national identity by referencing the Catholic religion. This was later reinforced during communism, when the Roman Catholic Church served as a representative of the nation and the locus of political resistance to domination by the state. The symbiosis was visible in the public arena: Poles used both religious and national iconography in their protests against the regime (Casanova 1994, Zubrzycki 2006).

The Church came out of communist times as a powerful institution to which nearly 95% of Poland's inhabitants adhered (Hall 2012). In the 1990s, Church officials successfully influenced legislation and policy-making, for instance in the realm of women's reproductive rights, and still acted as if they needed to protect the nation from cultural tendencies hostile to religious values (Gowin 1995). Although the most nationalistically-hued religious expressions became contested by liberal parts of Polish society (Zubrzycki 2006), the religion–nation symbiosis preserved its cultural plausibility (Mandes and Marody 2005–2006). Sticking to the nation-protecting rhetoric, Church hierarchs initially opposed Poland's EU accession, but they changed their standpoint, however, before 2004 in light of Pope John Paul II's support for the political idea. The lack of constitutive Others, such as invasive neighboring countries or the communist state, produced the cultural need to define the nation anew. Homosexual people, surrounded by considerable silence in the public arena before 1989 (Szulc, 2011), appeared as a convenient reference point to achieve this aim in the 2000s. Treated with reluctance within Church rhetoric, they became the target of exclusionary practices exercised especially by those who strove to keep traditional aspects of the nation's definition (Graff 2006).

There is a scholarly consensus suggesting that meanings of religion, nationalism and homosexuality have been dynamically constructed in Poland. This chapter's aim is to expand on this dynamic process by presenting Polish press

© KONINKLIJKE BRILL NV, LEIDEN, 2015 | DOI: 10.1163/9789004297791_006

coverage of religion and homosexuality after the fall of communism. Since competent scholars have already discussed the relationship between nationalism and homosexuality in Poland (e.g. Graff 2006, 2010, Kulpa, 2014, 2015), this chapter deals with nationalism-related issues only in the context of representations of religion and homosexuality. At the descriptive level, it uses press cuts gathered in the Polish Central Archives of Modern Records (1989–2009, collection taken over from the Polish Public Television), in all archive units referencing Poland and labeled with the term homosexuality,[1] as well as materials from the author's press monitoring (2010–2014). Of the numerous press titles subject to analysis, this chapter refers mainly to: (1) *Gazeta Wyborcza* and *Rzeczpospolita*—the most opinion-leading dailies, the former left-liberal, the latter center-right; (2) journals published by "Catholic intelligentsia" (*Tygodnik Powszechny, Znak, Więź*);[2] (3) traditionalist Catholic newspapers and magazines (*Nasz Dziennik, Niedziela, Fronda*); and (4) other nationwide dailies, in particular *Trybuna* (published until 2009, left-wing, associated with post-communist factions), *Słowo* (published until 1997, Catholic), and *Życie* (published 1996–2002 and 2004–2005, conservative).

At the analytical level, the chapter draws on the anti-essentialist conceptual framework established by Ernesto Laclau and Chantal Mouffe (1985). The considerations below show that the antagonism between religion and homosexuality has evolved over time, engaging various discursive components. Articulation practices, i.e. practices "establishing a relation among elements [of the discursive field] such that their identity is modified as a result of the articulatory practice" (Laclau and Mouffe 1985: 105), have stimulated the change. The chapter's leading motif is the analysis of articulation possibilities for "LGBT Christians," i.e., Christians who do not wish to suppress their non-normative sexuality or gender expression. The common Pole's adherence to Catholicism suggests there must be gay-identified people among Catholic believers. Indeed, in 1994 in Warsaw they established the Group of Lesbian and Gay Christians to support individuals in their efforts to integrate religious and sexual aspects of their lives. The Group's name referred to Christianity because both Catholics and Protestants participated in the initiative (Orłowski 2006). In 2010, four years after the Group's dissolution, the Faith and Rainbow nationwide ecumenical community of LGBT Christians was set up. Apart from providing sup-

---

1   This was 1863 cuts, of which 389 came from the years 1990–1999, 97 from the year 2000, 135 from 2001–2002, 200 from 2003, and 1042 from 2004–2009.

2   "Catholic intelligentsia" is a term used in Poland to describe lay Catholic circles associated with Clubs of Catholic Intelligentsia set up in several Polish cities during communism. The Clubs promoted Vatican II decisions among Polish Catholics.

port, it works for the full inclusion of LGBT people in the community of believers (Hall 2015).[3] Now, the question is what chances "LGBT Christians" have had
in the last 25 years to express themselves within a momentous articulation, i.e.
to manifest themselves socially as an important subject position within the layout of antagonistic forces that govern the social field. Hence, the analysis below
focuses on the process of subject position formation. In this context, it is mainly
concerned with the work of the logics of difference, which consist in the demarcation of the antagonistic Other, and the logics of equivalence, which consist
in the construction of a chain of similarities between various articulations and
their symbolic contents.

### 1990s: The Fluidity of Articulations

The fall of communism brought with it a chaotic fluidity of articulations and
stimulated the emergence of new subject positions and new universalist myths.
In this anomic context, the Roman Catholic Church was still an important
actor in political struggles and proved its effectiveness in influencing policy-
making processes. The Vatican actively created tension between religion and
homosexuality: in its documents and hierarchs' statements, it referred to the
"deceitful propaganda" from the "pro-homosexual movement" (Congregation
for the Doctrine of the Faith 1986) and related menaces. In the 1990s, the Polish
press was not especially interested in the issue of homosexuality, yet it reported
on the Vatican's views, particularly the letter to European bishops aimed at
confronting European legislators' attempts to protect homosexual people from
discrimination and recognize same-sex unions (Pontifical Council for the Family 1994), and statements by the Pope and Church hierarchs that followed. The
Pope condemned the idea of allowing homosexual couples to adopt children,
which in his view would "distort the essence of the family." Catholic titles,
including *Tygodnik Powszechny*, a weekly considered liberal, frightened the
public with the vision of political approval for societal phenomena that misrep-
resented the "truth" inscribed in the human condition. The Catholic daily *Słowo*
dichotomized between "violent, hateful sounding homosexuals' reactions" to
Vatican statements abroad and the Pope's words, which were "full of love" (J.S.
1994).

---

3  The vast majority of the Group's participants are Roman Catholics and the group mainly
works for a change in the Catholic Church's teachings. It is worth adding, however, that in
Poland no registered churches or religious associations are open to homosexuality to the
extent that they would bless same-sex unions or ordain openly gay clergy.

Non-Catholic newspapers provided rather short notes on the Church's stance. Still, after the publication of *Some considerations concerning the response to legislative proposals on the non-discrimination of homosexual persons* (Congregation for the Doctrine of the Faith 1992), *Rzeczpospolita* (24.07.1992) managed to publish information about "some gay groups" who had "defined the document as 'racist'."[4] From time to time, the press published comments distanced from Church views. For instance, *Trybuna* referred to works on the 1997 Polish Constitution, when the Polish Episcopate ensured that the definition of marriage would be as a union between a man and a woman. The newspaper quoted the Secretary of the Polish Episcopate, Bishop Tadeusz Pieronek, who explained that "homosexual partnership is against nature," and it suggested that nevertheless it would hardly be possible to keep hiding the problem in the long run (Łuczyńska 1998).

Thus, the Church's position consigned "homosexuals" (the word used by the Church and the media of the 1990s) to the position of the Other and blamed them for problems in building a seamless society. The press supported the religion–homosexuality dichotomy by mentioning foreign gay organizations' opposition to the Vatican. Still, the tone of press comments varied. Additionally, reports were accompanied by a variety of news from abroad that sounded exotic in the Polish context due to a lack of connections with other elements of the discursive field, e.g., news about some Dutch Protestants being open to homosexuality, some priests who had come out as gay, or a gay wedding ceremony secretly performed in Vilnius Cathedral.

The press also published interviews with activists of newly-established gay organizations in Poland. Strikingly, leaders who were distanced from religion were very cautious when criticizing the Church. In turn, those adhering to Christianity argued that homosexuality and religiosity might be able to co-exist harmoniously and that the Catholic Church would eventually recognize the value of same-sex partnerships. Furthermore, press descriptions of Polish gay organizations pointed to the popularity of support groups for believers. *Gazeta Wyborcza* (Fabjański 1998) and *Tygodnik Powszechny* (Makowski and Strzałka 1999) published reportage of the Group of Lesbian and Gay Christians. In an affirmative way, they referred to the informal pastoral care of the Reverend Michał Czajkowski, a professor of the Academy of Catholic Theology, over the community.

The Group of Lesbian and Gay Christians was relatively widely discussed in the press in 1996 after it sent letters to a dozen rectors of Warsaw parishes

---

4   The note bore neither an author or a title.

and the Polish Episcopate. The group asked rectors for pastoral care and the Episcopate for the formal designation of a minister. The rectors did not answer, and the Episcopate declined the request. The same year, upon invitation from the Group, saw the arrival in Poland of Father Robert Nugent, co-founder of New Ways Ministry, an American organization targeting gay people. Its activities would be condemned by the Vatican three years later. *Gazeta Wyborcza* published an interview with Father Nugent, while Dorota Narewska (1996) of the *Słowo* Catholic daily cautioned people not to be "seduced" by Nugent's views and harshly criticized participants of the gay Christians' group for their brazenness in interpreting Christian doctrine. In the same newspaper Jacek Gałuszka (1997), then a Dominican, decidedly reacted to Narewska's publication. He referred to his recent conversation with a distraught mother of a teenager who had fought with his homosexual orientation and committed suicide after a priest had presented him with Vatican views about the "intrinsic disorder." Gałuszka commented: "This is a tragic example of pastoral care that uses Church documents to justify its own phobias and drives those redeemed by Christ to emotional meltdown."

In essence, the media representation of Polish gay and lesbian organizations differed from the representation of adversarial "homosexuals" who opposed the Church abroad. However, since the press undertook the issue only occasionally, the image was rather hazy. In the first decade after the fall of communism, Polish gay and lesbian organizations were created almost from scratch. Their articulation possibilities were restrained not only by the fact that the dominating Church situated homosexual people in the position of the Other, but also by their difficulties in building a chain of equivalence that would validate their importance. The values that representatives of such organizations referred to were the use of freedom of association, the general mission of breaking with the traditionalism of Polish society, and the vision of freedom from discrimination gradually being achieved by homosexual people "in the West." These justifications were important in the period of "transformation" when Poland was to catch up with "the West," thus the press, probably driven by dreams about the successful establishment of a new order comparable to the Western pattern, by and large touched upon the issue of new gay and lesbian initiatives. However, no newspaper clearly and consistently supported the initiatives. As far as "lesbian and gay Christians" were concerned, Father Nugent, Father Czajkowski, and the Dominican Gałuszka were rather meager allies. Moreover, their activity and move to establish a formal ministry for gay people were met with the Episcopate's refusal.

### 2000: Homosexuality Versus the Nation

The year 2000 was essential for the stabilization of the opposition between the Church and related symbolic values on the one hand and homosexuality on the other. Nationalistic values entered the stage. In July, WorldPride 2000 took place in Rome. Its date coincided with the Great National Pilgrimage of Poles to Rome for celebrations of the Great Jubilee of 2000 Years of Christianity. Newspapers undertook the subject as early as in January and reported on Italian controversies surrounding the gay event. The Catholic press was especially meticulous in this regard and in the following months published commentary. The *Niedziela* weekly quoted the Vatican daily *L'Osservatore Romano* and presented a vision of "dozens of thousands of homosexuals employing obscene vocabulary and dressed up in a blasphemous way" who would "march in front of sacred places, symbols of Christianity" (2000, no. 23).[5] The weekly also wrote about gay activists blurring the boundary between norm and deviation, praised the Church for its courage in expressing critical views on homosexuality, pointed to the European Union's lack of respect for Europe's Christian roots, and spread fear about the next likely step which EU countries that had already recognized same-sex civil partnerships would take: the legal approval of adoption by homosexual couples.

In July, all newspapers widely covered Roman events. *Trybuna* distanced itself from the Pope's statement that WorldPride was "an affront to the Great Jubilee of the year 2000 and Christian values of the city" (Rzekanowski 2000). *Rzeczpospolita* and *Kulisy*, in turn, added fuel to the fire, the former by publishing an article dramatically titled "To abuse and defile the city of Popes" (Zubowicz 2000), and the latter by polarizing between the "festival of the homosexuals" and the Great National Pilgrimage of the Great Jubilee formed by the united nation: Poles gathering regardless of whether they were well-off or unemployed, abled or disabled (Skała 2000). Both newspapers presented striking photos of dandified men kissing each other.

After WorldPride, Jan Turnau (2000), a columnist of *Gazeta Wyborcza*, recognized that the Vatican's criticism of the event was too severe, however he presented "homosexuals" as "provocative" and expressed his doubts as to whether respect "can be gained with noise." Similar ambivalence could be found in *Trybuna*: it published an article about the history of homoeroticism written in a gay-friendly tone, but which nevertheless concluded with the author's strong reservation toward gay pride events (Trojanowski 2000). Conservative pub-

---

5   The material bore no author or title.

licists harshly evaluated WorldPride and grieved over contemporary culture saturated by corruption and "devoured by the moral, ethical and intellectual relativism of postmodernity" (Przewoźniak 2000). Piotr Semka (2000a, 2000b) compared the meeting of the International Lesbian and Gay Association, also held in Rome that year, to "generals' military deliberations" and the ILGA's strategies to Bolshevik methods. At the same time, he pointed to the Roman Catholic Church as the last bastion of values in the Western world.

In his publications, Semka did more than build the image of gay troops planning to invade Christian values: he tightly intertwined the issue of homosexuality with Polish politics and political debates. In the run-up to WorldPride, he referred to the appeal by the *Nasz Dziennik* newspaper to send letters to Italian diplomatic institutions calling for WorldPride's cancellation. *Gazeta Wyborcza* labeled this appeal "nonsense of the day," which drove Semka to identify a "deeper problem": the Polish "liberal left's" disdain for the civic activity conducted by traditionalist Catholic circles and the fact that the left usurps for itself the right to understand civic attitudes and democracy in the only proper way (Semka 2000c). In response, Andrzej Osęka (2000) of *Gazeta Wyborcza* reproached the "right" for perceiving WorldPride as an attack on what is most sacred, and specifically Semka for inciting panic by propagating the vision of a gay totalitarian threat to the world.

What was clear within articulations in 2000 was the vision of "homosexuals" as the Other that opposes not only the Church, but also the Polish nation and the values pertaining to its Christian heritage. On one side, the unity of the Polish nation, and on the other side, the image of licentious "homosexuals" who profane "symbols of Christianity" by walking in front of them—this constituted the discursive structure for protests against gay pride parades organized in Poland in the coming years. In 2000, press quotations from the Vatican hierarchs, including the Pope, as well as references to the Church as the last bastion of "European civilization" enhanced the antagonism. Furthermore, chains of equivalence became visible. The support for Poland's EU accession and the optimistic vision of the post-communist cultural change took their place aside the approval for homosexual people's efforts to improve their situation. Criticism of EU policy and the cultivation of national values and the Catholic religion became linked in the disapproval of such efforts. Homosexuality became entangled in the antagonistic struggle between the "liberal left" and the "right." Accordingly, out of the most important dailies, *Trybuna* and *Gazeta Wyborcza* became relatively (and ambiguously) supportive of gay activists' aspirations, while *Rzeczpospolita* and *Życie* spoke out against them. The Catholic press put themselves in line with *Rzeczpospolita* and *Życie*, however *Tygodnik Powszechny* barely raised related issues, and other journals linked to the

"Catholic intelligentsia" (*Znak*, *Więź*) remained silent. The space for "lesbian and gay Christians" rapidly shrank, since in issues related to homosexuality the antagonistic layout of articulations, which involved homosexuality on the one hand and religion on the other, took over the discursive field. Polish gay activists were absent from this picture. "Homosexual" was intensively othered and scandalous photos published by the press confirmed this truth.

### 2002: Homosexuality and Healing

For a whole decade after the fall of communism, the press did not undertake the issue of reparative therapy. Columnists associated with the *Fronda* magazine, which at that time combined countercultural esthetics with traditionalist views and ran a program for youth on public television (1994–2001), emerged as precursors of new trends. In 1999, they published *Homosexuality and Hope* by Gerard van den Aardweg. At the end of the 1990s, a few articles about reparative therapy appeared in traditionalist journals.

In 2002 a scandal involving Archbishop Juliusz Paetz gained significant media coverage: the press presented evidence that he had sexually harassed subordinate seminarians. Representatives of the "Catholic intelligentsia" suggested there was a "homosexual lobby" among the clergy and called for a thorough discussion on the issue. *Tygodnik Powszechny* took up the challenge, although its response to the need for debate was very peculiar. It gave the floor to Adam Fons (2002a), who confessed he had "experienced homosexuality" himself, and after years of grappling with the problem and not being able to identify either with the "victims' trade union," that is, the gay community, or with the Church's strategy to deny the phenomenon or to call for heroism without showing the way to achieve it, he had finally found the perfect solution: the reparative program implemented by the newly-established *Odwaga* [Courage] group based in Lublin, which drew on Richard Cohen's therapeutic methods from the United States.

Fons argued that the program had great potential to prevent scandals like the one involving Paetz, and deplored the lack of Church support for this initiative. In his response, the Jesuit Józef Augustyn (2002), known for his publications about homosexuality and the invitation to chastity, suggested the support would probably be premature if one took into account the social controversies surrounding homosexuality that would make any priest working for *Odwaga* haunted by the irremovable "homosexual shadow." However, the subsequent discussion allowed for the conclusion that the offer based on Cohen's views was really needed, especially since it would entirely comply with Church teachings and, as such, it would resist the alternative proposal from "lesbian and gay Christians" (Fons 2002b). Expressing their care for homosexual people, editors of the *Więź* monthly supported Fons' views in *Tygodnik Powszechny*. They also published the *Więź* monographic issue (2002, no. 7) with reportage on *Odwaga* and various comments praising the therapeutic program aimed at "curing" homosexuality.

By constructing the difference as gay activists on the one hand and the passivity of the Church (as revealed in the Paetz case) on the other, Fons initiated the reparative therapy supporters' articulation. The therapy became intensively propagated by the *Fronda* milieu, the *Nasz Dziennik* daily and other traditionalist journals. Conservative actors contributed to the constitution of the hegemonic formation. Differently from *Tygodnik Powszechny*, however, their articulations did not emphasize the catechetic formula for accepting homosexual people "with respect, compassion, and sensitivity," but rather the vision of homosexuality as corruption, a disease to be healed in order to protect an endangered society. Even *Gazeta Wyborcza* came close to this chain of equivalence by publishing an article on the newest findings by the American psychiatrist Robert L. Spitzer, who provided evidence for the therapy's efficacy (Zagórski 2003).

Moreover, the discussion in *Tygodnik Powszechny* othered the Group of Lesbian and Gay Christians. This allowed for sharpening of the articulation by reparative therapy supporters. Afterwards, however, the press ignored this community. Other factors contributed to the silence: the parallel articulation of LGBT organizations in opposition to the Church and the "right," the declining membership in the Group and the Group's dissolution in 2006, and additionally in 2006 the public stigmatization of the Reverend Czajkowski for his collaboration with the secret services in the communist era.

### 2003: Homosexuality Versus the Church

Polish gay activists began to articulate their demands according to the logic of difference in 2001. They categorically opposed the Church's rhetoric, specifically statements made by Bishop Pieronek, who compared homosexuality to a contagious disease, and claimed that openly gay teachers should not perform their profession but rather suggested that they should be isolated. In response, the International Lesbian and Gay Cultural Network in Poland notified the public prosecutor of the crime. However, the prosecutor refused to initiate proceedings due to a lack of social interest in prosecuting insults against homosexual people *ex officio* and the lack of recognition of homosexual people as a group to be protected by Polish law (Basiuk 2004). Nevertheless, in 2001–2002, few newspapers referred to gay activists' actions. Only the radically anti-clerical (*Nie*) and traditionalist (*Nasz Dziennik*) press noticed efforts to initiate Pieronek's prosecution, and the newly established *Fakty i Mity* anti-clerical weekly interviewed gay leaders, who criticized the Church far more unambiguously than in the 1990s. Additionally, the *Bez Dogmatu* niche periodical published a letter by the film critic Bartosz Żurawiecki, who employed the "just anger" rhetoric to oppose the reparative therapy project.

The mainstream press revisited the issue of homosexuality in 2003. This was for three reasons. First, Campaign Against Homophobia, an organization established in 2001, initiated its first large-scale project—the billboard campaign *Let Them See Us*, which triggered aggressive reactions across Poland despite the project's assimilationist nature. The billboards presented photos of gay couples holding hands. Second, Senator Maria Szyszkowska of the Democratic Left Alliance announced the preparation of a draft act on civil partnerships. The Senate [the Upper House of Parliament] approved the draft in 2004, however the Sejm [the Lower House of Parliament] did not debate the issue before the end of its term and the draft perished. Third, the Vatican published *Considerations regarding proposals to give legal recognition to unions between homosexual persons* that called on Catholic lawmakers to oppose legislative proposals aimed at recognizing homosexual unions clearly and publicly (Congregation for the Doctrine of the Faith, 2003).

The coincidental timing of Szyszkowska's draft act and the Vatican's *Considerations* drove the press to draw again on the homosexuality–religion dichotomy and this time to enhance it. *Trybuna* headlined an article about the draft act entitled 'Szyszkowska versus the Vatican' (Chmielewska 2003). A few other articles mentioned the *Let Them See Us* campaign in this context, suggesting that the project also directly opposed the Vatican. Interestingly, Szyszkowska herself was ambiguous in criticizing the Church, and in one of her comments she declared that her draft did not aim to fight this institution (J.K., 2003). The spokesman of the Democratic Left Alliance provided similar declarations. At the same time, leaders of other important parties (Civic Platform, Law and Justice, League of Polish Families) unambiguously supported the Church's recommendations to oppose any proposal for the statutory regulation of same-sex partnerships (*Gazeta Wyborcza* 2–3.08.2003). This landscape of discursive forces pointed to the hegemony of the Catholic Church, which was not explicitly challenged by any significant articulation. Publicists associated either with traditionalist circles (*Niedziela, Nasz Dziennik*) or "Catholic intelligentsia" (*Tygodnik Powszechny, Więź*) spoke in clear agreement, regardless of whether they referred to the Vatican document, the *Let Them See Us* campaign, or

Szyszkowska's draft. There were only minor differences in how they assessed the situation. While traditionalist circles presented homosexuality as a threat to the family, the "Catholic intelligentsia" underlined compassion in their attitude toward homosexual people and saw homosexuality not as a cause, but rather as a result of the crisis of the family, a phenomenon rooted in the "emotional deficiency" suffered by families of the present day.

Among numerous press interviews with participants of the *Let Them See Us* campaign, there were two in which the interviewees spoke about their devoutness. One of them referred to his previous plans of becoming a monk. The interviewer reacted "Were you in an order?!" by which he suggested that being both gay and religious is unimaginable (Łupak 2003). The other interviewee spoke about his visit to the church in his home city after the campaign had been launched and the ostracism that he experienced from the parish community (Szczygieł 2003). Hence, the press publications of 2003 referring to homosexual people's religiousness did not put into question the discursive polarization between homosexuality and religion. At the same time, statements by gay leaders perfectly resonated with the antagonism. Although Polish activists rarely mentioned the Vatican's *Considerations*, they claimed the Church discriminated against them, and they expressed their resistance in various ways. The president of Campaign Against Homophobia suggested that it was the clergy living in celibacy, thus "against nature," rather than homosexual people who should be subject to healing (J.K. & J.Z. 2003). He also sued a Catholic columnist of *Nasz Dziennik* who had argued against the employment of gay teachers by asserting that homosexuality is a disease that endangers the healthy family.

## 2004–2005: "Catholic Intelligensia" Versus Conservative Catholics

In subsequent years, gay and lesbian organizations, since described with the LGBT abbreviation both by themselves and their supporters, kept producing their articulation within the antagonistic relationship with the Church, religion and the "right." On the other hand, the "right," in particular the "radical right," articulated its concerns more and more eagerly within the antagonistic relationship with "homosexuals" (they continued to use this term, along with notions of even more derogatory connotations, such as "deviants" or "sodomites"). Rainbow flags were met with signs featuring copulating stick figures in a crossed circle bearing the statement "faggotry forbidden" (cf. Graff 2006), and the conflict reached the streets in connection with gay pride parades, their ban and counter-manifestations, mainly in 2004 and 2005. During Law and Justice rulings (2005–2007), the authorities drew on social reluctance toward homosexuality to gain political support, and while recalling "Christian and national values," they radicalized their anti-gay rhetoric. This resulted in an antagonistic split on the issue of homosexuality within Catholic articulations.

After the 2004 gay pride parade in Warsaw, organized in spite of the Mayor's ban, and the 2004 pride parade in Krakow, attacked by an aggressive counter-manifestation, the president of the "Znak" Cristian Culture Foundation established by the "Catholic intelligentsia" added his voice to the fray. He explained that until that day, his foundation had not taken any position on issues linked to homosexuality due to a lack of relevant expertise. However, the manifestations, counter-manifestations and accompanying disputes had forced him to break his silence. Refraining from suggestions about the need to provide merciful help to those suffering from the alleged deficiencies inscribed in the "homosexual condition," he called for the exchange of views and experiences within the gay and lesbian community (Wilkanowicz 2004). Soon after, other Catholic commentators expressed their friendliness to LGBT people. The editor-in-chief of *Tygodnik Powszechny* categorically condemned aggressive counter-manifestations to gay pride parades and emphasized that the principles of the Christian faith could not justify them (Boniecki 2005). In 2005, when the Mayor of Warsaw banned the Warsaw gay pride parade again, Tadeusz Bartoś, then a Dominican, presented his views in *Gazeta Wyborcza*: in the name of civil rights, he opposed the Mayor's decision. In addition, he decidedly condemned reparative therapy and stated that the Church should stand up for homosexual people suffering social averseness (Lizut, 2005). Bartoś' statements triggered a decisive reaction from traditionalist media.

At about the same time, *Gazeta Wyborcza* published an article by the Reverend Dariusz Oko (2005), who harshly criticized any instances of homosexuality and suggested their connection, among others, with incest, pedophilia, zoophilia and necrophilia. *Gazeta Wyborcza* columnists protested against the publication of texts like the one by Oko in the newspaper, and the well-known Catholic commentator Halina Bortnowska (2005) decidedly opposed the disdain contained in the priest's article. Additionally, the Jesuit Jacek Prusak (2005) critically assessed Oko's views in *Tygodnik Powszechny*. *Nasz Dziennik*, in turn, opposed the whole discussion, pointing in particular to the "fictitious division within the Church" around the issue of homosexuality that it exhibited (Rola, 2005). Paradoxically, by publishing such comments, *Nasz Dziennik* proved the division was becoming increasingly real rather than fictitious.

Additionally, in 2005 the Vatican published a document stipulating that the Church "cannot admit to the seminary or to holy orders those who practice homosexuality, present deep-seated homosexual tendencies or support the so-called 'gay culture'" (Congregation for Catholic Education 2005). This became another point of dissent related to homosexuality within Catholic circles. While *Nasz Dziennik* uncritically welcomed the Vatican instruction, the Jesuit Prusak (2006) underlined doubts that it raised, in particular the fact that it did not answer the question on how the Church understood "deep-seated homosexual tendencies" and who was in a position to judge them.

Furthermore, the growth in antagonism between the "liberal left" and the "right" resulted in a break within the coalition supporting reparative therapy. Politicians from the right-wing party League of Polish Families argued for the necessity to "treat homosexuals," and in 2004 they invited Richard Cohen to a conference on parliamentary premises. This harmonized with the party's policy—its leaders campaigned to make the teaching profession inaccessible to both homosexual people and those supporting same-sex civil unions, and proposed amendments to the Criminal Code so that it penalized public statements in favor of such unions. In 2005, when the party was about to enter a governmental coalition with Law and Justice, the press reported on its proposal for reparative therapy to be state-funded. In this situation, any articulation produced in opposition to the therapy was at the same time an articulation opposing the League. Various media, in particular *Gazeta Wyborcza*, used the emergent discursive opportunity and reported on the shortcomings of the reparative approach, specifically its inconsistency with the views of professional organizations of psychologists. Since that point, building on the atmosphere of the scandal, *Gazeta Wyborcza* has also reported on conferences on reparative therapy in which foreign "experts" participated, especially when the conferences were organized by state-funded institutions. The editor-in-chief of *Więź* distanced himself from the therapy after having cooperated with *Odwaga* for two years and realizing that participants of the program had chosen various lifestyles, including happy self-fulfillment within a sexually active same-sex relationship (Gawryś, 2007). Publicists associated with *Tygodnik Powszechny* also disapproved of the reparative treatment. The articulation by Catholic commentators who distanced themselves from the reparative approach opened up a space for articulation by "LGBT Christians" to emerge.

## 2010: Homosexuality and Christianity

After the 2007 parliamentary elections, which were won by Civic Platform, a moderate party, LGBT organizations kept fighting for political recognition by articulating their demands in opposition to religion and the Church. The government revealed its complete passivity in counteracting discrimination of sexual orientation, hence LGBT communities recognized the work of the government's Plenipotentiary for Equal Treatment as a hindrance. In 2011, during the next electoral campaign, Robert Biedroń, the co-founder and the first president of Campaign Against Homophobia, as well as Anna Grodzka, the president of the Trans-Fusion Foundation established by transgender people, joined the Palikot Movement, a party employing anti-clerical rhetoric, and stood for Parliament. Their electoral success, followed by the subsequent initiatives of their party, such as an effort to remove a cross from parliamentary premises, preserved the discursive polarization between homosexuality and religion and created a sister dichotomy between trans issues and religion. From their hegemonic position, LGBT activists' opponents vigorously worked to uphold the hostility.

Within the antagonistic layout of discursive forces that separate LGBT issues from religion, "LGBT Christians," since 2010 represented by the Faith and Rainbow group, have had weak articulation possibilities. The difficulty is in building chains of difference: neither do Faith and Rainbow members want to challenge the broader LGBT community with whom they identify, nor do they wish to act against the religion to which they adhere. The difficulty is also in building chains of equivalence: Faith and Rainbow participants do not feel close to LGBT organizations' articulation that opposes religion, nor do they accept official views on homosexuality presented by religious institutions, in particular the Catholic Church. Nevertheless, some possibilities have emerged, at least at the level of finding allies.

*Tygodnik Powszechny*, *Gazeta Wyborcza* and opinion-leading magazines (*Wprost*, *Newsweek*) referred to Faith and Rainbow with sympathy. *Znak* published an interview with a Catholic priest who provides an informal ministry to the group, wherein he suggested drawing on the principle of the primacy of conscience to assess homosexual activity individually and supported the legal approval of same-sex partnerships (Kozłowska and Zdanowska 2013). *Więź* editors also seem supportive in their public comments. By establishing this alliance with subject positions that are quite well-situated within the discursive field and aligning themselves with the "Catholic intelligentsia," the group is acquiring articulation abilities. Whether the allies are ready to uphold the alliance and to what extent "LGBT Christians" are able to broaden the chain of equivalence is open to debate. What does not bode well for the future is that "LGBT Christians" are constructing themselves as a reformatory religious movement in the absence of any other radically reformatory religious current in Poland. Another problem is that in 2013–2014 the "Catholic intelligentsia" articulation has been dimmed by a more powerful articulation, involving the Polish Episcopate (and the Reverend Oko), from opponents of the so-called "gender ideology," who posit feminist and LGBT activists as the Other.

   Meanwhile, LGBT organizations continue to implement their identity politics underpinned by opposition to religion and the Church. At the same time, however, they draw on the "queer" approach and seek to recognize their internal diversity by embracing homosexual parenting, monogamous and polygamous relationships, numerous variants of trans expressions, as well as various non-heteronormative identities that hardly fall under the "LGBT" abbreviation. It seems that "LGBT Christians" are becoming an equivalent element of the diversified community. Nevertheless, until now this diversification has become visible only within community events and the *Replika* LGBT periodical. The mainstream press suggests the discourse has not been subject to any reconfiguration: In 2013, after *Gazeta Wyborcza* had organized the *Judgment over homophobia* debate, which involved a Faith and Rainbow participant on the panel, newspaper comments neglected the Christian's voice, focusing instead on the quarrel which involved LGBT rights' supporters and their opponents adhering to the political "right" (Suchecka 2013). Perhaps new developments will come forward within public discussions on Catholicism and homosexuality, which will most likely take place before the Synod of Bishops of the Catholic Church devoted to family issues that is scheduled for 2015.


   ## Conclusion

The press analysis shows that in post-communist Poland, antagonistic struggles involving issues of religion and homosexuality have formed and transformed subject positions such as "Catholic intelligentsia," the political "right," "the liberal left," and "the LGBT community." Articulations by these public actors have produced the opposition between religion and homosexuality. The symbolic content of this opposition was changing according to what forms the chains of equivalence and difference took and how these chains operated in the historical moment. At the beginning of the 1990s, the homosexuality–religion dichotomy was built on the Catholic vision of homosexuality as an unnatural phenomenon and a threat to "family values." Since religion had long functioned in Poland within a symbiosis engaging the nation, the nationalistic potential of anti-gay articulations was already there, however it was not until 2000 that this potential was activated. On the eve of Poland's EU accession, homosexuality emerged as a threat to Poles' values and Poland's sovereignty. The fiercest struggles between protectors of the coherent nation and LGBT rights' advocates took place in 2004 and 2005—that is, at the time when Poland was joining the EU and Polish LGBT organizations had already entered the discursive field as a subject position articulating its demands in opposition to the Church. Subsequently, right-wing anti-gay radicalism produced a split engaging the issue of homosexuality within Catholic articulations. "Catholic intelligentsia" and "conservative Catholics" took opposite positions, the former by aligning themselves with liberal political currents and the latter by continuing the anti-gay articulation and aligning themselves with the political "right."

This history, when seen through the lens of the "LGBT Christians'" subject position formation, reveals its un-linearism. In the 1990s, there was a space in the landscape of discursive forces for "LGBT Christians," then referred to as "lesbian and gay Christians." Afterwards, however, this space rapidly shrank in connection with WorldPride 2000 in Rome and the sexual harassment scandal involving Archbishop Paetz in 2002. "LGBT Christians" temporarily lost their articulation possibilities in the face of the discursive field's domination by the reparative therapy project and strong antagonism between LGBT organizations and the Church. In recent years, they have regained the chance to manifest themselves as an important subject position. The chance is even greater than in the 1990s. Today, "LGBT Christians" have the opportunity to enter the chain of equivalence with both "Catholic intelligentsia" and LGBT organizations, the latter playing a much more significant political role than it did two decades ago.

Whether and to what extent "LGBT Christians" will use the emergent articulation possibilities depends on many factors, including, in particular, future transformations of the discursive field. Poles are still conservative regarding LGBT issues, yet they are becoming increasingly accepting of sexual difference (CBOS 2013), which in some ways enhances "LGBT Christians." At the same time, however, although sociological indicators suggest that the trend of secularization has recently reached Poland (Hall 2012), the strength of conservative Catholics' articulation has not diminished, which is perhaps closely related to the declining trend in Poles' religiousness. If anything is to be envisaged, "LGBT Christians" will most likely enter into power struggles with antagonistic forces. However, the result of these struggles cannot be foreseen.

### References[6]

Augustyn, Józef. 2002. Brak odwagi. *Tygodnik Powszechny* (June 30).

Basiuk, Tomasz. 2004. "Niech nas usłyszą: słuszny gniew jako strategia zwalczania homofobii w sferze publicznej." Pp. 189–199 in Z. Sypniewski and B. Warkocki (eds.), *Homofobia po polsku*. Warszawa: Wydawnictwo Sic!.

---

6   Press cuts gathered in the Polish Central Archives of Modern Records do not provide information about pages on which articles were published.

Boniecki, Adam. 2005. Po paradzie. *Tygodnik Powszechny* (June 19)

Bortnowska, Halina. 2004. Szacunek, nie litość. *Gazeta Wyborcza* (June 4).

Casanova, José. 1994. *Public Religions in the Modern World*. Chicago: University of Chicago Press.

CBOS [Public Opinion Research Center]. 2013. *Stosunek do praw gejów i lesbijek oraz związków partnerskich*. Retrieved from http://cbos.pl/SPISKOM.POL/2013/K_024_13 .PDF.

Chmielewska, Karolina. 2003. Szyszkowska kontra Watykan. *Trybuna* (September 3).

Congregation for Catholic Education. 2005. *Instruction Concerning the Criteria for the Discernment of Vocations with regard to Persons with Homosexual Tendencies in View of their Admission to the Seminary and to Holy Orders*. The Vatican.

Congregation for the Doctrine of the Faith. 1986. *Letter to the Bishops of the Catholic Church on the Pastoral Care of Homosexual Persons*. The Vatican.

————. 1992. *Some Considerations Concerning the Response to Legislative Proposals on the Non-discrimination of Homosexual Persons*. The Vatican.

————. 2003. *Considerations Regarding Proposals to Give Legal Recognition to Unions Between Homosexual Persons*. The Vatican.

Fabjański, Marcin. 1998. W końcu stworzył mnie Bóg. *Gazeta Wyborcza* (September 7).

Fons, Adam. 2002a. Odwaga "Odwagi". *Tygodnik Powszechny* (June 30).

————. 2002b. Kozetka i kamienna twarz. *Tygodnik Powszechny* (July 14).

Gałuszka, Jacek. 1997. Echa naszych publikacji. Homoseksualizm: dar czy grzech. *Słowo* (July 14).

Gawryś, Cezary. 2007. "Homoseksualizm i 'uzdrawianie'." *Znak* 650(11): 61–72.

Gowin, Jarosław. 1995. *Kościół po komunizmie*. Kraków: Znak.

Graff, Agnieszka. 2006. "We are (not all) homophobes: A report from Poland." *Feminist Studies* 32(2): 434–449.

————. 2010. "Looking at pictures of gay men: Political uses of homophobia in contemporary Poland." *Public Culture* 22(3): 583–603.

Hall, Dorota. 2012. "Questioning Secularization? Church and Religion in Poland." Pp. 121–142 in D. Pollack, O. Müller, G. Pickel (eds.), *The Social Significance of Religion in the Enlarged Europe: Secularization, Individualization, and Pluralization*. Farnham, UK: Ashgate.

————. 2015. "Individual choices revisited: Non-heterosexual Christians in Poland." *Social Compass* 62(2) (in print).

J.K. 2003. Model dla wszystkich. *Trybuna* (August 8).

————. & J.Z. 2003. Homofobia pobłogosławiona. *Trybuna* (October 23).

J.S. 1994. Po niedzielnej wypowiedzi Papieża. Echa prasy włoskiej. *Słowo* (February 22).

Kozłowska, Dominika, and Marzena Zdanowska. 2013. "Nie błądzi ten, kto nie wyruszył w drogę. Z duszpasterzem osób homoseksualnych rozmawiają Dominika Kozłowska i Marzena Zdanowska." *Znak* 695(4): 11–17.

Kulpa, Robert. 2014. "On Attachment and Be*longing*: Or Why Queers Mourn Homophobic President?" *Sexualities* 17: 781–801.

———. 2015. "Unlikely Analogies: Homophobia, Anti-Semitism, and Polish National Identity." *Nations and Nationalism* (in print).

Laclau, Ernesto, and Chantal Mouffe. 1985. *Hegemony and Socialist Strategy: Towards a Radical Democratic Politics*. London: Verso.

Lizut, Mikołaj. (2005). Kościół gejów nie odrzuca. Z Tadeuszem Bartosiem rozmawiał Mikołaj Lizut. *Gazeta Wyborcza* (June 11).

Łuczyńska, Renata. (1998). Trójkąt gejowski. *Trybuna* (July 7).

Łupak, Sebastian. (2003). Niech mnie wszyscy zobaczą (wywiad z Marcinem Królem, który pozował do zdjęcia w akcji *Niech nas zobaczą*). *Gazeta Wyborcza—Trójmiasto* (May 16).

Makowski, Jarosław, and Jan Strzałka. (1999). O homoseksualizmie. *Tygodnik Powszechny*, (November 21).

Mandes, Sławomir, and Mirosława Marody. 2005–2006. "On Functions of Religion in Molding the National Identity of Poles." *International Journal of Sociology* 35(4): 49–68.

Narewska, Dorota. 1996. Homoseksualizm: dar czy grzech? *Słowo* (December 9).

Oko, Dariusz. 2005. Dziesięć argumentów przeciw. *Gazeta Wyborcza* (May 28).

Orłowski, Kamil. 2006. "Świątynie sodomy, albo w kim się objawia boża miłość." Pp. 73–87 in T. Basiuk (ed.), *Parametry pożądania: kultura odmieńców wobec homofobii*. Kraków: Universitas.

Osęka, Andrzej. 2000. Sodoma wszędzie. *Gazeta Wyborcza* (September 30).

Pontifical Council for the Family. 1994. *Letter to the Presidents of the Bishops' Conferences of Europe on the Resolution of the European Parliament Regarding Homosexual Couples*. The Vatican.

Prusak, Jacek. 2005. Inni inaczej. *Tygodnik Powszechny* (June 19).

———. 2006. "Tertium non datur?" *W Drodze* 389: 56–96.

Przewoźniak, Marcin. 2000. Homoinwazja. *Tygodnik Solidarność* (July 14).

Rola, Paweł. 2005. Równo idą? *Nasz Dziennik* (June 11).

Rzekanowski, Jakub. 2000. Starszy niż chrześcijaństwo. *Trybuna* (July 4).

Semka, Piotr. 2000a. Szkoła rzymska. *Życie* (July 8–9).

———. 2000b. Idzie homoparada po Rzymie. *Życie* (July 17).

———. 2000c. Polscy Murzyni z Radia Maryja. *Życie* (June 16).

Skała, Jan. 2000. Utrudniona pielgrzymka. *Kulisy* (July 6).

Suchecka, Justyna. 2013. Debata "GW" i KPH o homofobii: "Więcej osób cierpi z powodu otyłości". *Gazeta Wyborcza* (October 12).

Szczygieł, Mariusz. 2003. Nazajutrz po billboardzie. *Duży Format* [supplement to *Gazeta Wyborcza* (April 10)].

Szulc, Łukasz. 2011. "Queer in Poland: Under construction." Pp. 159–172 in L. Downing and R. Gillett (eds.), *Queer in Europe: Contemporary Case Studies*. Farnham, UK: Ashgate.

Trojanowski, Jan. 2000. Kim są geje? *Trybuna* (July 12).

Turnau, Jan. 2000. Wolę ciszę. *Gazeta Wyborcza*.

Wilkanowicz, Stefan. 2004. Trudne wychodzenie z podziemia. *Gazeta Wyborcza* (October 30).

Zagórski, Sławomir. 2003. Gej? Kiedyś nim byłem. *Gazeta Wyborcza* (October 29).

Zubowicz, Beata. 2000. Zelżyć i zbezcześcić miasto papieży. *Rzeczpospolita* (July 1–2).

Zubrzycki, Geneviève. 2006. *The Crosses of Auschwitz: Nationalism and Religion in Post-Communist Poland*. Chicago: University of Chicago Press.

## Funding

This research received funding from the author's project *The institutional and individual dimension of LGBT people's religiosity in Poland* (2011–2014) financed by the National Research Centre in Poland based on decision No. DEC-2011/01/D/HS6/03877.

# CHAPTER 5

# Echoes from the Margin: Responses to the Pope's Statements on Homosexuality in Bosnia & Herzegovina and Sweden

*Mariecke van den Berg and Zlatiborka Popov Momčinović*

Bosnia and Herzegovina and Sweden may be viewed as each other's opposites when the rights and representations of sexual minorities are concerned. At first glance, religion seems to be a factor of importance mainly in the former, where the views of Eastern Orthodox Serbs, Roman Catholic Croats and Muslim Bosniak appear very much in agreement in their public and political rejection of homosexuality. In post state-church Sweden, the dominant political frame is one of secular liberal views and a broad acceptance of LGBT-rights. What both countries do have in common, however, is the fact that the combination of religion and homosexuality in public debate seems to be a recipe for "moral panic" (Weeks 1991): A conflict over identity and moral behavior arises as soon as the two are mentioned in relation to each other. Moreover, the public framing of religion and sexuality often conflates in various ways with nationalism: not only the *right* sexuality is at stake, but also a *Bosnian* or *Swedish* mode of sexual acceptance. In this chapter we see nationalism as a process of public identity-formation, and following Peterson (2010: 35), we define nationalism as "the territorially based *subset* of political identity." Peterson further distinguishes two main forms of nationalism: *state-led*, where citizens assimilate with cultural forms set by the state, and *state-seeking*, where the goal is to obtain a recognized state through group mobilization.

Here we discuss both an example of state-led nationalism (Sweden) and state-seeking nationalism (Bosnia and Herzegovina), which is a recognized state but also has a strong commitment to confirming its own legitimacy. Discussing religious and sexual nationalism, we argue, is not merely a matter of taking nationalism and then "add religion and sexuality and stir," as though there were a "pure" form of nationalism which is then blended with religious beliefs and practices and/or ideologies of sexuality. Many nations have a long history of merging nationalist discourse with religion and even nations which built on secular ideologies, such as communism, have done so in part by disidentifying with religion. God is therefore not so much "once again" present in the public sphere (Friedland 2002: 381), but rather in a different shape. Religious

© KONINKLIJKE BRILL NV, LEIDEN, 2015 | DOI: 10.1163/9789004297791_007

nationalism, moreover, has the organization of sexuality at its center (Friedland 2001: 134). As Pryke (1998) explains, sexuality has figured in nation-building in two important ways: as a *quest for purity* in which an acceptable mode of sexual behavior is outlined, and as the *regulation of human reproduction*. We will focus on the way in which the first strategy, the expression of accepted sexuality, is present in public discourse.

Religious and sexual nationalism, in our definition, means the simultaneous formation of national, religious and sexual identities in a particular geographical context (that of the state). Whether nation-led or nation-seeking, religious and sexual nationalism have as their main goal an investment in the "imagined community" (Anderson 1991), where supposedly fixed cultural codes or frames emphasize the "oneness" of the group (Hall 1990). This community-building, however, comes at a price, namely the exclusion of "[t]hose within the nation who share least in élite privilege and political representation, especially those whose identity is at odds with the projected image of homogenous national identity" (Peterson 2002: 35). In this chapter we will be looking precisely for these perspectives, i.e., on those whose religion or sexuality do not fit within the dominant frames of reference. We shall bring to the fore the marginal voices of those who have no stake in emulating the grand narrative of the nation. In doing so, we shall take as our point of focus the interplay between nationalism, religion and sexuality.

Subjects for research will be responses to Papal statements on homosexuality (both the "pastoral" statements of present Pope Francis and the more "dogmatic" statements by his predecessor Benedict), these being in print and online media in the two national contexts of each of the two states. We pose the following question: What can sexually or religiously marginal perspectives tell us about the way in which religious and sexual nationalism inform each other? Which alternative framings of religious and/or sexual identity might be imagined when the dominant frames are being challenged by the former, i.e., the ones that they have attempted to shut out or misrepresent? What counts as "marginal" in these questions will depend on what, in both contexts, counts as "mainstream," which in Bosnia and Herzegovina is the rejection of "abnormal" sexuality most notably by religious and political leaders. In Sweden it is the dominant liberal attitude toward homosexuality advocated by both the government and the Lutheran Church of Sweden.

To do this, we will first give a concise overview of the ways in which nationalism, religion and sexuality have in recent history become entwined in both countries. We shall then reflect more in depth on the "echoes from the margin" as both an empirical and epistemological choice. By studying responses to the Pope in both contexts, we then hope to gain more insight into the complex ways in which sexual, national and religious identity-formation takes place within different national frameworks. Finally, in our conclusion we will present some common analytical remarks regarding the study of nationalism, religion and sexuality as markers of identity-formation in different European contexts.

### Religion, Nationalism and Sexuality in Bosnia and Herzegovina and Sweden

A post-conflict and post-socialist society, Bosnia and Herzegovina is faced with an increasing presence of religion in the public sphere and the tendency of religious communities to play the role of moral arbitrators. A forced retreat of religion to the private sphere *during* socialism has caused opposite effects *after* socialism's dismantling. It could be said, therefore, that new states, and especially so-called "delayed nations" needed religion to fill voids in newly proclaimed identities—(notably the Bosniak nation which was "formed" and declared at the First Bosniaks' Congress in 1993 during the war).[1] This seems to be especially the case when we take into account that neither language nor ethnicity formed a strong basis for the imagined community of Bosnia. Linguistic differences between Bosniaks, Croats and Serbs are small, and the three groups have the same ethnic origin (Mujkić 2010). What is definite, however, is that the religious hierarchy tries to impose on citizens the national interest as some kind of unchangeable religious constant, albeit in different historical and social circumstances (Cvitković 2012: 99).

As a society of post-socialist confusion and traumatic war experiences, with a complicated political system aiming to safeguard the interests of the three constituent peoples (Bosniaks, Croats and Serbs), however, religion(s) do still have a curative role and help in the "preservation" and articulation of national and state interests. Nonetheless, the political system and political relations in BiH are rather complicated, which leaves plenty of room for different ideological interpellations, interventions and overlap.[2] This creates a rather confusing context regarding myriad "social problems" the new state faces, including LGBT

---

1  The term *Bosniak* was introduced during the war without public discussion and left Bosniak people almost in the same frustrated situation as in previously turbulent historical periods. Their national phantasm can be directed only toward BiH, which must be shared with others (Mujkić 2010: 140). Because of that, they gather mostly around the cultural and political dimensions of Islam which is the non-national religion (Mujkić 2010: 138).

2  Many political parties who are on the Left, for instance, often use nationalist rhetoric.

issues and the way in which religion and homosexuality operate as an opposi-tional pairing.

In contrast to to some Western European states, where the public impor-tance of established religion decreased, in BiH its public role is constantly affirmed and reaffirmed in a variety of ways. To be religious in public has become a new form of social conformism (Mujkić 2007), not unlike being an atheist during socialism. Thus reconstructed religiousness is manifested as collective religiousness, not as individual piety such as church/mosque atten-dance or participation in other activities of the religious community (Cvitković 2013: 84). As the World Values Survey shows, among the post-socialist countries BiH constantly tends to be the most religious (Norris and Inglehart 2004: 121). This in turn has polarized secularists (among whom are feminists, liberals and LGBT activists) and religious anti-secularists; this is a situation in which more nuanced voices offering alternative understandings of religion and secularism are lost. Moreover, there are tensions between ethnic and civic nationalism, or "old" and "new" nationalism (Stychin 1997: 12). Old nationalism is inward looking, clerically based and emphasizes a traditional, religious perspective on social issues, including LGBT rights. New or civic nationalism is based on so-called abstract citizenship and is still in the process of "coming out" on social issues in a population that has strong ethnic/national affiliations (Mujkić 2007; Wilkes et al. 2013). Therefore, the clash between sexual and religious belonging intersects with that of national and cultural belonging (Van den Berg et al. 2014: 117).

Within this context of shifting national and cultural practices laden with meaning, the struggle over LGBT rights is not an easy one. Hate speech, for instance, is considered undesirable if directed toward different ethnic groups (see Džihana 2009; Turčilo 2013). It is harder to tackle when directed at other minorities such as the Roma population, but especially so to LGBT people who cannot lay claim to an ethnic identity. Public lobbying for rights happens only in a step-by-step manner, but LGBT people are risking allegations of imposing a "perverted" life-style (Banović and Vasić 2013: 32). Around 60 % of the popula-tion claim to have no idea what kinds of problems LGBT have in society (Popov Momčinović 2013: 18–19). This lack of understanding can partly be explained by the media's tactic of "de-contextualization." In BiH, this means undue attention on regional events rather than on national issues such as the Gay Pride in Split and Podgorica, a referendum in Croatia, and the prohibition of Gay Pride in Belgrade due to security reasons. Besides, these issues are often understood in the context of show-biz and life-style and much less from a human rights per-spective (Huremović 2012). Moreover, even using entertainment to frame LGBT issues became more difficult when the LGBT community, after being subjected to violent attacks and hate speech during the first *Queer Festival* in Sarajevo in 2008, changed its tactics and withdrew from the public debate.

In Sweden, religion and national identity have for a long time been intertwined officially in the Lutheranism of the Church of Sweden. It was not, in fact, until the year 2000 that the separation of church and state became official, with Swedish citizens no longer automatically (state) Lutherans at birth. Though membership rates remain high, only 2.7 percent of the Swedes have been attending Sunday services regularly from the 1960s onward (Bruce 2000). This gap has been called the Swedish paradox: the majority of the population have what might be called a "weak belief" in traditional dogmas, but they do value Christian life rituals such as baptism, marriage and funerals (Bäckström et al. 2004; Jänterä-Jareborg 2010). Thus, religion, or at least Lutheranism in Sweden, is viewed by some as mainly *cultural religion*: "a way of being religiously connected without being religiously active" (Demerath 2000: 136). Recent heated public debates in Swedish society, however, urge us to question the role of religion in Sweden as "merely" cultural. In 1998 and the years to follow, photographer Elisabeth Ohlson Wallin's exhibition *Ecce Homo*, which pictured Jesus as a gay man, caused a storm of protest from Swedish Christians. A decade later, the introduction of same-sex marriage led to the formation of the action group Protect Marriage (*Bevara äktenskapet*), consisting of Christian, Muslim, Jewish and secular opponents. In between these events, a national debate was fuelled by the statements of Åke Green, pastor to a Pentecostal congregation. He wanted to put to the test a new law against hate speech, especially regarding sexual orientation (in 2002), by referring in his sermon to homosexuality as "a cancerous tumor in Swedish society." Curiously, then, these debates all revolved around issues of (homo)sexuality.

In various respects, these debates show that religion in Sweden cannot be confined to a highly ritualized, cultural form, one completely detached from citizens' personal convictions and interests. Both proponents and opponents of the controversial art exhibition and same-sex marriage invested a lot of time, energy and emotion in defining what religion is supposed to be, in what ways it should or should not enter the public sphere, and how it is to be understood in relation to what are considered to be basic Swedish values. This shows that religion has a connection with ideologies of sexuality, civil rights, and nationalism, among others. Moreover, these debates show that Sweden no longer can be conceived as a mono-religious country in which the narrative of the Lutheran Church of Sweden has a monopoly on religion in the public sphere. First of all, it becomes clear that there is not one such narrative: despite the fact that the Church of Sweden as a whole has positioned itself as liberal toward LGBT-rights (especially when viewed in a global ecclesiastical context), the debates

on homosexuality showed that there is also an outspoken conservative minority. Moreover, the debates show that the "free churches" (*frikyrkorna*), i.e., those
religions at the margins of the Swedish religious landscape (notably Muslims,
Jews, Evangelicals, Pentecostals and Roman Catholics), do speak as one strong
voice, thus actively taking part in defining religion in Sweden, and what role it
should or might take in the public arena. That the debates could have become
so extended is, we argue, also partly related to the wide-spread notion of Sweden as a liberal nation and a front-runner in LGBT-rights, hence accepting of
sexual difference. It is against this background that the position of religion in
the public sphere is being negotiated.

### Marginal Perspectives and Spaces

From the descriptions above, two more general observations can be made
regarding religion and the public sphere in relation to nationalism and sexuality in BiH and Sweden. They show a process of re-traditionalization which limits the rights and visibility of LGBT citizens in BiH, and an increasingly diversified religious landscape in "queer Sweden" (Kulick 2005). With the latter, where
religion and sexuality are connected, the public space appears less secularized
than one might have initially thought. In this chapter we intend to investigate
the marginal discourses against which dominant framings of religion, sexuality
and national identity take place. Both epistemological and empirical motives
underlie this focus.

Epistemologically, marginal perspectives have been an important source of
knowledge for critical cultural studies such as feminist, queer and post-colonial
studies (Alcoff and Potter 2013, Sedgwick 1993, Ashcroft at al. 1995). While
women, sexual and ethnic minorities, among others, have been the subject of
research themselves, their perspectives have also been seen as a lens on the
workings of gendered, sexual and colonial ideology. More particularly even,
an epistemology of the marginalized has illuminated the dominant mechanisms of power which underlie discourses of—for instance—national identity.
These discourses are relevant since while they have a stake in investing in a
narrative of unity and essential cultural characteristics, at the same time they
have been excluding the identities of "awkward subjects" who do not fit very
well into the story of the nation. We do not wish to claim, however, that an
"epistemology of the margins" necessarily leads to a better or more "true" story
of the nation, nor that minority groups in turn share essential characteristics
allegedly different from those of the majority, but we do suggest that the knowledge that is produced at these social margins may challenge the very narratives

by which they are constructed, which in public discourse are often taken for granted.

Empirically, we look for perspectives that are marginal in the sense that they are not voiced in the center of the public arena, but at its periphery. Seeking out voices from these "shadows" presupposes the researchers' scrutiny and dedication, as alternatives are often hidden from the public eye. Our main material, then, is taken from newspapers or magazines with a limited circulation, from blogs and social media, and from online forum discussions. Our informants come from marginal groups in society. This means we are addressing different perspectives in both countries, since the dominant stance on religion, sexuality and national identity differs in both contexts. In BiH, our informants may be LGBT-supportive religious officials. In Sweden, they may be conservative religious people who have objections to LGBT rights or their extension thereof.

Our case-study from these countries consists of reactions to statements on homosexuality issued by the Pope, both the present Pope Francis and his predecessor Pope Benedict XVI (2005–2013). Public statements by the Pontiff, leader of a church that has over a billion adherents, are often cause for discussion, and in strikingly many occasions are about issues of sexuality. In October 2014, homosexuality was openly debated by bishops at a synod on the family. While many in the Western media responded with disappointment when the bishops rejected a more welcoming attitude to "alternative" relationships, other than traditional marriage, many also pointed out the fact that such an open discussion in itself does indicate progress within the Roman Catholic Church. Indeed, Pope Francis is generally seen as the driving force behind this discussion, being the first Pontiff willing to respond to journalists' questions on the topic, thus displaying a more lenient attitude than his predecessor Benedict.

By the same token, media responses to the Popes give us an impression that they are "coming out" in their attitude to homosexuality: the Popes' image, therefore, is the result of the social interplay between their own public statements and the public interpretations thereof. In this portrayal, however, different sides have different stakes in the end result, and not all sides are likely to be heard equally. In other words, in BiH and Sweden the margins of debates on the Pope are already defined by demographics. In both countries Roman Catholics form a social minority. In BiH, this equated to approximately 15% of the population, in Sweden between 2 and 4%. There is, however, also one important difference: Croats who are predominantly Catholic are recognized as a constituent people in BiH and are explicitly protected by various rights, (such as a veto right in parliament), in order to safeguard their own nationalist interests. On the other hand, Catholics in predominantly Lutheran Sweden are mainly immigrants or "native" converts from the Church of Sweden. In both cases, however, statements by the Pope are interpreted from a context where Catholicism is not the dominant religion, and in these interpretations we hope to shed light on the self-definition of both the Catholic margin and the Orthodox, Muslim, Lutheran or secular majority.

### Responses to the Pope in BIH

In order to investigate responses to Pope Francis in BiH, we have selected a number of "a-typical" examples from printed and online media. They are a-typical in the sense that, as will become clear, many media did not discuss the Pope's statements on homosexuality or did so only in a very brief manner. We have conducted additional interviews with people whom we argue represent a marginal perspective in BiH: clergy who argue for more tolerance for LGBT people. In cases where these churchmen have asked to remain anonymous this has been respected.

We would like to start with responses to the inauguration of Pope Francis, which was held on 19 March 2013. This event drew significant public attention, for he was perceived as a "fresh" Pope to replace Benedict XVI, who was seen as more conservative. Francis was described as open toward atheists and LGBT people, his views on the family were seen as more flexible, and his criticism of capitalism was more profound and not just a random declaration (advance.hr 2014). Some of his statements quoted in the BiH media were seen as the promise of a turn-around in the Roman Catholic Church (Radio Sarajevo 2014; Dani 2014). For instance, in an interview cited by Croatian Jesuits, Francis had argued that the Church should not be perceived as an institution purely there for the transmission and imposition of doctrine while ignoring social contexts in which people find themselves (Spadaro 2014).

Understandably, attention for the Pope was more pronounced in Croatian media, such as the newspaper *Večernji list*. If *Večernji list* with much more scrutiny and dedication communicated the Pope's messages, accompanied by colorful photographs, Bosniak and Serbian media,[3] both secular and religious, mostly reported them as a brief statement, in that way staying aloof from possible progressive change in the Catholic Church by remaining "neutral"—if they reported on the Pope at all. According to some liberal voices, the new Pope

---

3  Although media in BiH do not have a national prefix, it is well known that some media are oriented towards an audience with a specific ethnic / national belonging.

is met with silence, both in BiH and neighboring Croatia. The most influential Catholic magazine *Glas Koncila* is, according to the webportal *Žurnalisti*,
ignoring the Pope's messages, because they are not in accordance with the attitude of Croatian Catholic clerical circles (Kulјiš 2014). It is claimed at the same
portal that while in the Catholic Church there may be some kind of silent revolution going on, for the "Church among Croats" the response to this revolution
is nationalistic and reactionary, with *Glas Koncila* as its driving force. Paradoxically, then, against the backdrop of an overwhelming silence and indifference,
in the context of BiH the Pope's statements could be perceived as a voice from
the margins—being the opinion of the leader of the largest church in the world.

Yet, what should also be noted is that the Pope, while professing acceptance
of gay persons, during a press conference was opposed to the so-called gay
lobby. Statements like these did provoke some reactions from more independent and liberal Catholic portals, such as *Križ života*. Moreover, in an interview
published at the portal, Dr. Norbert Reck, a German Catholic theologian who
is very often a guest at different conferences in the region, explained that the
Catholic Church was bound by its own tradition. He argues that the Catholic
Church operates by imposing chains of obedience on its own believers. He
claims that there are no such things as gay lobbies in the Catholic Church and
that many gay priests live in fear. In his opinion, though, being gay is not a sin,
for sin is, in the Christian tradition, a specific way of living without responsibility toward other human beings, without empathy and without conscience.
According to Reck, God has given people the blessing to take delight in other
human beings, and because of that they should not punish one another (Horvat
2013).

The Pope's messages, however, are not easily labeled as "pro" or "anti" homosexuality. Rather, Pope Francis seems to try to find a balance between tradition and new challenges coming from the modern world. His careful grasp of
nuance, however, is not picked up by magazines like *Glas koncila*. In many texts
the magazine urges readers to accept the *Other*. One article even has the title "A
human being without the Other cannot be what he is" ("Pogled u svoje odnose"
dr. Pavla Brajše 2014: 27). Yet, the abstract notion of *Otherness* is never defined,
and provides space to maneuver around different "Others," including LGBT people. As Slavoj Žižek would say, this kind of approach leaves open the possibility
of accepting the *Other* in a way that is acceptable from "my" perspective—in
this case the "liberal-conservative" perspective on cultural heritage, thus self-
confirming ingrained supremacies in the process (2006: 193).

Remarkably, the Pope's statements did not draw much attention from the
LGBT community in BiH, which mostly expresses itself online. On the webfo-
rum *queer.ba* there were no posts and discussions on this issue. At the only

LGBT portal that exists in BiH (*lgbt.ba*) there was only one article about the Pope's statements. It seems that the LGBT community in BiH is aware that the Pope's statements are actually de-contextualized: though they appear as a message for the World, they seem to address the Western world only. The question remains, however, whether the Pope's attempt to re-open the Church to new perspectives on homosexuality will have any effect on the everyday life of LGBT people who are facing everyday discrimination in BiH. On the other hand, as a Catholic theologian we interviewed argued, the new Pope feels that it is wrong to be openly committed to any ideological side. "He rather wants to create an open space for dialogue for different opinions which are all in a way necessarily partial. This will introduce a new dynamic into the Church and will make it more vivid and spacious. Ambivalence could be seen as an advantage, not a deficiency." Taking into account the homophobic environment in BiH, though, the question arises as to whether this is enough to provide a sufficiently normalizing space for the discussion of homosexuality. Rather limited media coverage confirms this doubt. If the media may not want to follow Francis in creating this open space, some believers see good reason: at the *Herceg-Bosna* web-forum, for instance, it is argued that the new Pope "... must be careful not to spoil that which has held that institution together for almost 2000 years," for otherwise "the Catholic Church will be in the same bad situation as the Protestants and the Church of England" (Forum Herceg-Bosna 2013).[4]

In both mainstream and new social media, then, positive responses to "pro-homo" statements by the Pope are limited, and remain marginal in their discursive scope. A few attempts have been made to introduce him into mainstream discourse as a spokesperson for a Catholicism which accepts homosexuality— thereby arguing for the legitimation and protection of marginal sexualities in Bosnia, and by Croat Catholics in particular. These attempts, however, have been obstructed in a number of ways. First, by the power of silence: by ignoring the statements and refusing discussion, national media prevent the Pope's more liberal attitude from becoming a discursive reality in BiH. Second, the Pope's own ambivalent attitude as well as his perceived Western way of expressing himself make it difficult to transpose his views to the local BiH context. Against the overwhelmingly heteronormative (mainstream) discourse, appreciation for the Pope's more nuanced approach seems to be reduced to liberal streams and a small number of theologians in the Catholic Church itself. While

---

4  Herceg-Bosna used to be a self-proclaimed autonomous province in BiH under the control of HVO ("Croatian Council of Defence"). It was abolished in the so-called Washington agreement between Croats and Bosniaks in 1994, under the pressure of the international community and the president of the Republic of Croatia, Franjo Tuđman.

in the future, changes could be imagined—should the Pope continue to speak of homosexuality in a more progressive way—at present his statements do not seriously challenge the heteronormative basis of religious and sexual nationalism in BiH.

### Responses to the Pope in Sweden

In order to analyze the Swedish debate on public statements by the Pope, the search engine *artikelsök.se* was used. It gives access to the digital archive of most of the country's daily newspapers, as well as a Web search for blogs. We searched for all articles related to the terms "Pope" and "homosexuality." Issues most discussed in Swedish media were, apart from Benedict XVI's 2013 resignation, the infamous 2008 Christmas speech in which Benedict XVI allegedly stated that homosexuality is a greater threat to humanity than rain forest destruction. With regard to Pope Francis, what was a popular topic of discussion was the "interview on the jet plane" in 2013, where he was believed to have struck a different, more liberal tone regarding LGBT issues. Following on with these differences, we shall first briefly describe the news from national newspaper coverage to convey an impression of the dominant discourses on the Popes and the Roman Catholic Church in Sweden. We shall then turn to the marginal voices, both of "opponents" of the Roman Catholic Church and those of "defenders," using sources on the Web.

As Pope Benedict resigned in 2013, most Swedish media emphasized conservatism as his main characteristic. *Dagens nyheter*, after citing some biographical facts, states that Benedict has been "criticized heavily for his traditional beliefs" (2013a). The greatest stumbling blocks are "his attitude toward abortion, homosexuality and divorce where he has always supported conservative views." Other media, too, describe Pope Benedict as a leader whose conservative views, statements and thus authority were being questioned. Indeed, *Sweden's Radio* headline stating that the "Disputed Pope quits prematurely," was followed by the subtitle: "Against female priests, married priests, abortion and euthanasia" (Sveriges Radio 2013).

Benedict's successor, Francis, is met with much more enthusiasm, especially after his statements on homosexuality which were generally seen as much more open-minded. The new Pontiff made these statements mostly in an interview with the Jesuit magazine *La Civiltà Cattolica*, and during a press conference when he was flying back from a visit to Brazil in the summer of 2013. From the Swedish media we learn that Francis "stands up for homosexuals" (Sveriges television 2013), "defends homosexuals" (Dagens nyheter 2013b) and "wants to open the church for homosexuals" (Dagens nyheter 2013c). *Svt* (Sweden's Tele-vision) called his statements "historic" (Sveriges television 2013). Many articles quote Francis's by now famous statement that "If a person is gay and seeks God and has good will, who am I to judge him?" However, as discussed in the BiH case, Francis then went on to state that not gay persons, but "the gay lobby" is the problem. Nonetheless, compared to Benedict, a contrast often sketched in Swedish media, Francis seems a much more "acceptable" Pope. While Bene-dict was seen as a scholar, Francis is seen as someone who stands closer to the people. Benedict was seen as stern, conservative, traditional and, ironically, haunted by sex scandals: Francis is now seen as younger, vital, modest, and open for change.

Only *Svenska dagbladet* questions this oppositional pairing of Popes. Göran Hägg, "writer and Pope-expert," was interviewed and stated that Pope Francis did not, in fact, say anything new. "Homosexuality which is acted upon is sinful. This is what the Catholic Church has always been saying." Francis did not change this view. "This is not a change, but rather a definition of the Church's attitude in kinder terms" (Svenska dagbladet 2013). If Hägg is right, one may wonder what causes the overwhelming support for the new Pope in Sweden. The choice of words, the continuous comparison to Benedict and the neglect of what in Sweden might be construed as more "troublesome" remarks—(such as the condemnation of a 'gay lobby', a lobby which in Sweden in fact is institutionalized and funded by the government)—makes one suspect that in the coverage of the new Pope as gay-friendly, Swedish media are constructing a Pope they would like to see: a Pope who strengthens basic Swedish values such as a liberal attitude toward sexual diversity and the importance of protecting the rights of sexual minorities.

In the margins of the Internet, a range of opinions on the Pope and the Roman Catholic Church are voiced. In this space, where the rules of polit-ical correctness are less strictly observed, where ideas about how long an article should be are fluid and where the audience is less certain, there is room both for a more nuanced attitude as well as genuine gossip and slan-der. Nonetheless, some patterns can be distinguished in the way in which the Roman Catholic Church and the Pope in particular, as well as homosexuality, are constructed, i.e., as each other's "opponents." Those who reject Benedict's statements on homosexuality often stress the institutional and political char-acter of the Roman Catholic Church, which they blame for the slow change toward a more accepting attitude. They embed their criticism in historical reflections, but these for the most part are not accompanied by trustworthy historical sources, and are merely colored by previous scandals in the decades and even centuries that have passed. It is no wonder, states Islam-critical website *Dispatch International*, that Martin Luther had found it necessary to end these practices and start the Reformation (Dispatch International 2014).

Besides dredging up such historical "evidence" of the Church's faults and tendency to prefer power over anything else, there are some bloggers who in relation to evil-doers in both the recent and distant past, either establish a link with the Pope (and his views on homosexuality), or distance him from them. With the latter, Bengt, a "medical practitioner and Catholic" from Västergötland who blogs about "church, Christianity, culture and society," calls to mind the 'Catholic' Heinrich Himmler's persecution of homosexual men during World War II. With this comparison Bengt wants to strengthen his argument that the church should avoid homophobia and follow its basic principle that all people are of equal value. On the other hand with the former construct, (that of linking rather than distancing the church from evil), Pope Francis, in being quoted that he objects to the "gay lobby," is compared to Vladimir Putin. This appears in the "traditional social democrat" weblog of Bo Widegren. Widegren sees a clear connection between Francis' "gay lobby" remark and Putin making homosexual "propaganda" illegal in Russia (Bo Widegren 2013).

These constructions of the Pope and Roman Catholicism stand in close relation to how homosexuality is framed. Homosexuality is, for instance, often used as the denominator of a social group, which must be protected from the powerful institution of the Roman Catholic Church. In particular, this goes for LGBT's in Russia, Latin America and Africa, where people, in the bloggers' view, are more prone to follow the church's teachings. Homosexuality can also be used as a rhetorical tool of parody, as the blog *Hänt i Sverige* shows. The blog contains an imaginary conversation between the Pope and Ulf Ekman, a well-known Charismatic pastor in Sweden, who converted to Roman Catholicism. The message of the blog is that while Ekman preferred the Roman Catholic Church for its more conservative view on homosexuality, he is secretly gay and now tries to be part of "gay orgies" which are supposed to be held in the Vatican (Hänt i Sverige 2014). Thus, perhaps, homosexuality here is not an identity or social group that needs to be protected, but rather a secret sexual attraction that all conservatives (Roman Catholics and Evangelicals alike) are trying to suppress.

Indeed, some blogs, and not all of them as might be expected from Roman Catholic bloggers, try to nuance in their views oversimplified readings and unrealistic expectations of Pope Francis's statements on homosexuality. Blogger Mikael Karlendal tries to raise awareness of the fact that decision-making processes and shifts in Catholic church teachings are quite different from those of the much more well-known but nonetheless (also) conservative Christian denomination: the Pentecostal church in Sweden (Mikael Karlendal, för tro och sanningen 2014). Karlendal felt more explanation was needed after Benedict was being compared, on several occasions, to Pentecostal leader Niklas Piensoho, who had made statements that could be interpreted as arguing for a more accepting attitude toward homosexuality in his church. Karlendal argues that several writers who had made this comparison too easily assumed that if one conservative leader could make a change, so could the other. But Roman Catholic teachings, he states, are much more "established" than are Pentecostal, which are developed in local congregations and therefore more responsive to social change. Other bloggers, such as Tor Billgren at *Antigayretorik*, nuance news coverage on Benedict in the same way. As they point out, Benedict was misquoted: not once did he, in his supposedly incriminating Christmas speech, literally mention homosexuality or transsexuality (Antigayretorik 2008). As with blogs that were critical of Benedict's statements, the construction of Roman Catholicism in those that defended the Pope stands in close relation to their construction of homosexuality. In these blogs, for instance, homosexuality is described as a minor ethical issue with which the church needs to grapple. Others point to the fact that while homosexuality is an identity, the legitimacy of which is often touted by those who strive for LGBT equal rights, it is still a relatively new phenomenon. As church teachings far pre-date it, it is no wonder, they seem to argue, that change based on an evolving gay social construction may take some time. From the margins, then, what does arise is a call for nuance, understanding and patience.

In sum, the media debates swirling around Pope Benedict and Pope Francis show that the construction of homosexuality and religion in Sweden are closely connected. The national press, in its general critique of Benedict and support for Francis, shows a clear preference for a liberal, "gay-friendly" Roman Catholicism in Sweden—and the world, for that matter. Yet the Roman Catholic Church for the most part does appear a little "out there"—a historical institution with odd idiosyncrasies from which Sweden distanced itself as early as the Reformation. Its members, understood in the Swedish press mainly as the less articulate inhabitants of Africa and Latin America, are in need of protection by advocates of progress. In the above discussed margins of the internet, however, we also find a more broad discussion of the Pope: Roman Catholic and other perspectives uncover some of the particularly Swedish presuppositions against which statements of the Pope are being assessed. The Church of Sweden, and to a larger extent the Pentecostal and other free churches, are used as the yardstick by which the Pope is measured. In Swedish media, there seems to be a general, overall picture of what "conservative religion" means, and this picture is constructed from experiences with the free churches and the more traditional part of the Church of Sweden, who in their conservatism are still seen as "potentially ethically progressive" when society calls for change. Moreover, the Roman Catholic Church is often being framed in its institutional setting and then compared to values which are seen as characteristic of the Swedish nation state: democracy, freedom of speech, freedom of consciousness and protection against discrimination. Presumably, the Church of Sweden, until recently a state church, has been in close relations with the Swedish government, resulting in an adjustment of both its attitude towards homosexuality and a modernization of its terminology pertaining to the social and political climate. That the Roman Catholic Church functions quite differently is not something picked up on by all journalists.

## Conclusion

What do the margins of BiH and Sweden tell us about the ways in which religion, sexuality and national identity are entwined? And which alternative perspectives do they offer to dominant mainstream framings that exclude awkward subjects from the public debate? Though we are looking at very different social contexts in BiH and Sweden, there is to begin with a striking similarity in the debate. In both countries mainstream media frame (certain forms of) Roman Catholicism largely as something from across the national border. In BiH, this is done by keeping Francis's more liberal statements on homosexuality under wraps. The silence on the Pope's statements, which seemed to stir the globe except for BiH, is perhaps more telling than would have been a more open, extensive national debate. In Sweden, conservative Catholicism is kept at bay by constructing the Catholic faith as something alien to Swedish history, endorsed only by "outside" believers. Elsewhere, both countries use this strategy to negotiate controversial elements of Catholic teaching: in BiH, this concerns the presumably increasing acceptance of homosexuality, in Sweden, the presumed persistence of conservatism. What both contexts have in common, though, is that in the context of a polarized debate, the margins need a broader account of what Catholicism is, and a different terminology, in order to be able to express an alternative version of sexuality, faith and national identity.

In the margins of BiH, we find those who would like to struggle for more acceptance of homosexuality and who find Francis on their side, but do not know how to adapt his views to their own context. In their experience, Francis's "new wind" is expressed in a Western way, to convince Western people. Their attempts to recover from Catholic faith elements which put homosexuality in a different perspective, such as detaching it from sin to see it as a concordance of human desires, are as of yet insufficient to challenge seriously

the "quest for purity" (Pryke 1998) upon which state-seeking nationalism in BiH
is built—whether it be in the form of civic Bosnian nationalism or the religious
nationalisms of Croats, Bosniaks and Serbs. These marginal perspectives show
a need for a toolbox of theological concepts and theories supporting a progressive Catholicism, one that will adequately resonate in the national context of
BiH.

   In Sweden, the margins consist of those who hold a more conservative view
on homosexuality, or those who feel that such a view should at least be tol-
erated in Swedish public debate. The general support there for Francis and
distancing from Benedict suggests that in Sweden the majority, however, would
like to keep these margins intact. Online contributions from the latter reveal
this presumed shared national identity, i.e., one in tandem with the state-led,
secular milieu against which statements of the Pope are being framed. Conservative religious attitudes to sexuality are framed as either from the past or
from across the border, mostly in regions framed as Sweden's opposite: Russia, Latin America and Africa. In the margins of Sweden we find modest voices
who call for a more nuanced perspective on Catholicism, one which does not
take as its point of departure the Swedish history of state-church relationships
and harmless free churches. For the Swedish Catholics themselves, (like their
Bosnian counterparts), what is needed is an investment in terminology that
will make this nuanced version of their faith and convictions comprehensible
to the mainstream. At present, however, the marginal perspective on conservative religion is based on a framing of Catholic attitudes toward homosexuality
as a (minor) ethical problem or, indeed, as a residue from more dogmatic traditions. In mainstream discourse, homosexuality as an accepted social identity
extending to the Church of Sweden, coincides with what is regarded as the basis
for Sweden's liberal national identity.

   We would like to end our chapter with a concluding remark on religious and
sexual nationalism. While we have encountered more or less coherent and consistent narratives of the imagined community of the nation, often the reality of
religious and sexual nationalism appears to be much more complex. Marginal
perspectives show us that besides an obvious and general nationalism, a less
obvious one—specifically religious and sexual—recurs which is harder to pin-
point. As such, those whom this nationalism excludes find it harder to combat. Thus, while nationalism *can* be based on blatant statements, seemingly
unproblematically supported by religious arguments (BiH) or the rejection
thereof (Sweden), more often nationalism seems to be constructed on the basis
of more subtle discursive strategies. In public discourse a direct link between
nationalism, religion and sexuality is not necessarily explicit. Yet a very strong
case for Swedish identity, for instance, can be made through a more indirect

appeal to the public to identify not so much with a restricted definition of "Swedishness," but rather with a certain view on church history, the role of religion in the public sphere or ideology of sexual freedom. Likewise, an appeal to Bosnian (or Serbian, Croatian or Bosniak) identity can be made by assuming that people will want to be complicit in ignoring what in other national contexts, and from marginal voices within the nation, is perceived as a rather revolutionary turn in the attitude of the Pope on homosexuality. The project of understanding religious and sexual nationalism, we therefore argue, will benefit from the perspectives of these margins, which give us important clues in detecting their more subtle forms and hidden mechanisms.

### References

Advance.hr Online list za vanjsku politiku i ekonomiju. 2014. "Papa Franjo- revolucionarni." Retrieved 10 October 2014 from: http://www.advance.hr/vijesti/papa -franjo-revolucionarni-anti-kapitalist-na-celu-vatikana-kojeg-vole-i-ateisti/.

Alcoff, Linda, and Elizabeth Potter (eds.). 2013. *Feminist Epistemologies*. New York: Routledge.

Anderson, Benedict. 1991. *Imagined Communities: Reflections on the Origin and Spread of Nationalism*. London: Verso.

Antigayretorik. 2008. "Påven behöver inte vantolkas for att framstå som hjärtlös." Retrieved 14 August 2014 from: http://antigayretorik.blogspot.nl/2008/12/pven-behver -inte-vantolkas-fr-att.html#links.

Ashcroft, Bill, Gareth Griffiths and Helen Tiffin (eds.). 1995. *The Post-colonial Studies Reader*. New York: Psychology Press.

Bäckström, Anders, Nina Edgardh Beckman and Per Pettersson. 2004. *Religiös förändring i norra Europa: en studie av Sverige: 'från statskyrka till fri folkkyrka', slutrapport*. Uppsala: Diakonivetenskapliga intitutet.

Banović, Damir and Vladana Vasić. 2013. *Seksualna orijentacija i rodni identitet. Pravo i praksa u Bosni i Hercegovini*. Sarajevo: Sarajevski otvoreni centar.

Bengt's Blog. 2013. "Putins Ryssland lagstiftar om att homosexuella skall diskrimineras." Retrieved 14 August 2014 from: http://www.s-info.se/page/blogg.asp?id=1754&blogg =61022.

Bruce, Steve. 2000. "The Supply-Side Model of Religion: The Nordic and Baltic States." *Journal for the Scientific Study of Religion* 39: 32–46.

Cvitković, Ivan. 2012. *Sociološki pogledi na naciju i religiju II*. Sarajevo: Centar za emprijska istraživanja religije u Bosni i Hercegovini.

———. 2013. *Encountering Others: Religious and Confessional Identities in Bosnia and Herzegovina*. Niš: JUNIR.

Dagens nyheter. 2013a. "Påven—konservativ ledare over miljarder själar." Retrieved
14 August 2014 from: http://www.dn.se/nyheter/varlden/paven-konservativ-ledare
-over-miljarder-sjalar/.

————. 2013b. "Påven försvarade homosexuella." Retrieved 14 August 2014 from: http://
www.dn.se/nyheter/varlden/paven-forsvarade-homosexuella/.

————. 2013c. "Påven vill öppna kyrkan för homosexuella." Retrieved 14 August 2014
from: http://www.dn.se/nyheter/varlden/paven-vill-oppna-kyrkan-for
-homosexuella/.

Dani Bosanskohercegovački News magazin. 2014. "Novi stav katoličkog sinoda. Pozi-
tivniji pristup homoseksualizmu." Br. 905, 17.10.2014, p. 10.

Demerath, Nicholas J. 2000. "The Rise of 'Cultural Religion' in European Christianity: Learning from Poland, Northern Ireland, and Sweden." *Social Compass* 47: 127–
139.

Dispatch International. 2014. "Påven föll offer för fraktionsstrider." Retrieved 14 August
2014 from: http://ww.d-intl.com/2013/02/28/paven-foll-offer-for-fraktionsstrider/.

Durkalić, Maša. 2012. "Bosanskohercegovački mediji i Queer Festival Sarajevo." Pp. 97–
100 in L. Huremović (ed.), *Izvan četiri zida. O profesionalnom i etičkom izvještavanju
o LGBT temama.* Sarajevo: Sarajevski otvoreni centar.

Džihana, Amer. 2011. "Mediji u Bosni i Hercegovini". Pp. 359–378 in D. Banović and
S. Gavrić (eds.), *Država, politika i društvo u Bosni i Hercegovini. Analiza postdejton-
skog političkog sistema.* Sarajevo: University Press.

Forum-HercegBosna (2013). "ODBACIVANJE DOGME Papa Franjo: Ateisti koji čine do-
bro iskupljeni su kao i katolici!" Retrieved 20 October from: http://hercegbosna.org/
forum/religija/odbacivanje-dogme-papa-franjo-ateisti-koji-ine-dobro-iskupljeni
-sukao-i-katolici-t10054.html.

Friedland, Roger. 2001. "Religious Nationalism and the Problem of Collective Representation." *Annual Review of Sociology* 27: 125–152.

————. 2002. "Money, Sex, and God: The Erotic Logic of Religious Nationalism." *Sociological Theory* 20: 381–425.

Hall, Stuart. 1990. "Cultural Identity and Diaspora." Pp. 222–237 in J. Rutherford (ed.),
*Identity: Community, Culture, Difference.* London: Lawrence & Wishart.

Hänt i Sverige. 2014. "Ulf Ekman ansluter sig till katolska kyrkan för att ingå i påve Fran-
ciskus homoorgier." Retrieved 14 August 2014 from: http://hantisverige.wordpress
.com/2014/03/10/ulf-ekman-ansluter-sig-till-katolska-kyrkan-for-att-inga-i-pave
-franciskus-homoorgier/.

Huremović, Lejla. 2012. "Najmlađi homoseksualac u BiH ima 12 godina. Analiza sadržaja
izvještavanja printanih medija o LGBT temama u drugoj polovini 2011." Pp. 188–195
in A. Spahić and S. Gavrić (eds.), *Čitanka LGBT ljudskih prava.* Sarajevo: Sarajevski
otvoreni centar, Heinrich Böll Stiftung Bosna i Hercegovina.

Horvat, Nikola. 2013. "Dr. Norbert Reck: Ne postoje homoseksualni lobiji u crkvi, gay svećenici žive u strahu." *Križ života, Vjerski internetski magazin*. Retrieved 25 September from: http://www.kriz-zivota.com/dr-norbert-reck-ne-postoje-homoseksualni -lobiji-u-crkvi-gay-svecenici-zive-u-strahu/.

Jänterä-Jareborg, Maarit. 2010. "Religion and Secular State in Sweden." Pp. 669–686 in X.M. Torrón and W. Cole Durham, Jr. (eds.), *Religion and the Secular State: Interim National Reports issued for the occasion of the xviiith International Congress of Comparative Law*. Provo, Utah: The International center for Law and Religion Studies, Brigham Young University.

Kulick, Don. 2005. *Queersverige*. Stockholm: Natur och Kultur.

Kuljiš, Denis. 2014. "Glas Koncila protiv pape." Retrieved 14 October 2014 from: http:// www.zurnalisti.com/glas-koncila-protiv-pape-franje/.

Mikael Karlendal, för tro och sanningen. 2013. "Påven—med vem kan man likna honom med?". Retrieved 14 August 2014 from: http://www.mikaelkarlendal.se/ uncategorized/paven-med-vem-kan-man-likna-honom-med/.

Mujkić, Asim. 2007. *Mi, građani etnopolisa*. Sarajevo: Šahinpašić.

———. 2010. *Pravda i etnonacionalizam*. Sarajevo: Centar za ljudska prava Univerziteta u Sarajevo i Heinrich Böll Stiftung Bosna i Hercegovina.

Norris, Pippa and Ronald Inglehart. 2004. *Sacred and Secular: Religion and Politics Worldwide*. New York: Cambridge University Press.

Perica, Vjekoslav. 2002. *Balkan Idols: Religion and Nationalism in Yugoslav States*. New York: Oxford University Press.

Peterson, V. Spike. 1999. "Political Identities / Nationalism as Heterosexism." *International Feminist Journal of Politics*, 1: 34–65.

Pogled u svoje odnose dr. Pavla Brajše. 2013. "Čovjek bez drugoga ne mežemo biti ono što jest." *Glas Koncila*, no. 48 (2058): 27.

Popov-Momčinović, Zlatiborka. 2013. *Ko smo mi da sudimo drugima? Ispitivanje javnog mnjenja o stavovima prema homoseksualnosti i transrodnosti u Bosni i Hercegovini*. Sarajevo: Fondacija Heinrich Böll—Ured za BiH, Fondacija cure, Sarajevski otvoreni centar.

Pryke, Sam. 1998. "Nationalism and Sexuality, What Are the Issues?" *Nations and Nationalism*, 4: 529–546.

Radio Sarajevo. 2014. "Papa Franjo o Gay populaciji: Ko sam ja da sudim?" Retrieved 15 October from: http://www.radiosarajevo.ba/novost/120540/papa-franjo-o-gay -populaciji-ko-sam-ja-da-sudim/.

Sedgwick, Eve Kosofsky. 1993. "Epistemology of the Closet." Pp. 45–61 in H. Abelove, M. Aina Barale and D. Halperin (eds.), *The Lesbian and Gay Studies Reader*. New York: Routledge.

Spadaro, Antonio. 2014. "Razgovor s papom Franjom." Retrieved 12 October from: http:// isusovci.hr/datoteke/sadrzaj/PDF/Intervju_s_papom-Obnovljeni_zivot.pdf.

Stychin, Carl F. 1997. "Queer Nations: Nationalism, Sexuality and the Discourse of Rights in Quebec." *Feminist Legal Studies*, 5: 3–34.

Svenska dagbladet. 2013. "Påvens uttalande inget nytt." Retrieved 14 August 2014 from: http://www.svd.se/nyheter/utrikes/paveexpert-uttalandet-ett-skickligt-retoriskt -knep_8383062.svd.

Sveriges radio. 2013. "Ifrågasatt påve slutar I förtid". Retrieved 14 August 2014 from: http:// sverigesradio.se/sida/artikel.aspx?programid=83&artikel=5439870.

Sveriges television. 2013. "Påven tar ställning för homosexuella". Retrieved 14 august 2014 from: http://www.svt.se/nyheter/paven-vill-oppna-kyrkan.

Turčilo, Lejla. 2013. "Monitoring Medija: Govor Mržnje u Predizbornoj Kampanji Av-gust-Decembar 2012". Pp. 44–70 in Lj. Zurovac and B. Rudić (eds.), *Promocija profe-sionalizma i tolerancije u medijima*. Sarajevo: Ured Vijeća/Savjeta Evrope u Sarajevu u partnerstvu sa Vijećem za štampu u BiH i Udruženjem/udrugom BH novinari

Van den Berg, Mariecke, David J. Bos, Marco Derks, R. Ruard Ganzevoort, Miloš Jovano-vič, Anne-Marie Korte, and Srdjan Sremac. 2014. "Religion, Homosexuality and Con-tested Social Orders in The Netherlands, the Western Balkans, and Sweden". Pp. 116–134 in G. Ganiel, H. Winkel, and C. Monnot (eds.), *Religion in Times of Crisis*. Leiden: Brill.

Weeks, Jeffrey. 1991. *Against Nature: Essays on History, Sexuality and Identity*. London: Rivers Oram.

Widegren, Bo. 2013. "Putins Ryssland lagstiftar om att homosexuaella skall diskrimin-eras." Retrieved 14 August 2014 from: http://www.s-info.se/page/blogg.asp?id=1754& blogg=61022.

Wilkes, George R., Ana Zotova, Zorica Kuburić, Gorazd Andrejč, Marko-Antonio Brkić, Muhamed Jusić, Zlatiborka Popov-Momčinović, and Davor Marko. 2013. *Factors in Reconciliation: Religion, Local Conditions, People and Trust. Results from a Survey Conducted in in 13 Cities across Bosnia and Herzegovina in May 2013*. Sarajevo: The University of Edinburgh/Project on Religion and Ethics in the Making of War and Peace, and the Center for Empirical Research on Religion in Bosnia and Herzegovina

Žižek, Slavoj. 2006. *Škakljivi subjekt. Odsutni centar političke ontologije*. Sarajevo: Šahin-pašić.

CHAPTER 6

# Religious Nationalism Blocking the Legal Recognition of Same-Sex Unions in the Baltic States

*Alar Kilp*

The majority of states in the European Union legally recognize same-sex part-nership or same-sex marriage. The family life of same-sex couples is unrec-ognized in all culturally Orthodox countries (Greece, Cyprus, Romania and Bulgaria), in all post-Soviet states (Lithuania, Latvia and Estonia), and in most post-communist member states of the European Union (with the exception of the Czech Republic, Slovenia, Croatia and Hungary).

Despite differences in the scope and strength of religious nationalism (in all indicators, Lithuania is the most and Estonia the least religious), for all of the Baltic States a "religious nationalist" coalition exists as an informal alliance with respect to the dimension of public policy of religious and political actors who disapprove of homosexuality. While the Baltic societies and churches are not supportive of the legal recognition of the family life of same-sex unions, the liberalization of marriage-related laws depends ultimately less on the liberal-ization of social value orientations and on the positions of religious hierarchies than on the support it receives from the political class (government and mem-bers of the parliament). Without the support from the political class, religious nationalism loses its capability to block legal recognition of the sexual citizen-ship rights to family recognition for same-sex couples.

In Lithuania and Latvia, the initiatives to introduce laws recognizing the family life of same-sex couples are likely to fail not because of relatively weak LGBT activism and relatively low social support for the legal recognition of same-sex unions (both of which are also true for Estonia), but because the political class in Lithuania and Latvia supports the protection of the traditional conception of heterosexual family. Members of the Estonian Parliament, how-ever, have recently split over the issue. On March 26, 2014, Social Democrats and the liberal-right Reform Party formed a coalition government determined to adopt a gender-neutral Cohabitation Act. On October 9, 2014, despite sig-nificant social and religious counter-campaigns to this move, the Estonian Parliament ratified a gender-neutral Cohabitation Law with a simple major-ity (40 votes in favor and 38 votes against). The Cohabitation Law enters into force on 1 January 2016, but only when the next Parliament (to be elected on

© KONINKLIJKE BRILL NV, LEIDEN, 2015 | DOI: 10.1163/9789004297791_008

1 March 2015) passes the related implementing Act, which requires the support of an absolute majority of MPs (51 out of 101). Therefore, in order to enter into force, the Cohabitation Law needs wider support by the MPs than it has received so far.

The discourses framing the confrontation over the extension of the rights of same-sex couples in Baltic societies and politics are not markedly different from the ones that exist in Western Europe generally (e.g., in France or Belgium). Those who support changes in morality and the "sex/gender" order frame the equal treatment of hetero- and homosexuals as a democratic responsibility for all member states of the EU as a right associated with Europeanness and European norms. In the Baltic States, religious actors are missing from coalitions supportive of the legislative change.

On the side of the "blocking coalition," both secular and religious actors refrain from considering the rights of homosexuals within the framework of the universal protection of human rights. The dominant churches articulate straightforward antipathy regarding the extension of the rights of homosexuals. For the political actors, opposition to same-sex union serves as a symbol of a broader set of conservative religious, moral and cultural values.

Building on recent scholarship on religious nationalism (Brubaker 2012, Eastwood and Prevalakis 2010, Juergensmeyer 1996, Storm 2011: 830), the relationship between religion and nationalism, which is supportive and complementary, is distinguished from one where religious nationalism as a sub-type of nationalism is in competition and confrontation with secular nationalism (Juergensmeyer 2008: 10–37). In the first type, religion partakes in nationalism as a national religion, which offers a cultural definition of what it is or means to be Lithuanian, Latvian or Estonian. Political leaders can use this type of national religion as a source of political legitimacy, "to develop and unify a national movement or to hold on to or acquire power" (Rieffer 2003: 230), while socially the national religion helps to hold a society together and to unite a population. However, this type of religious nationalism has no explicit religious basis or religious goals for national community. Its public role "is dependent on its willingness to serve directly or indirectly the national interests and the programs of the nation-state" (Wood 1968: 261). On the other hand, as a by-product to the harmonious relationship with nationalism, this type of religious nationalism can be engaged in symbolic confrontation with the ethno-cultural "others" (Merdjanova 2000: 234). Consequently, religious identities operative in "ethnic religious nationalism" can be used for political goals and against ethnically defined enemies (Juergensmeyer 1996: 4).

The second type of religious nationalism aims at the religionization of the nation-state, is "preoccupied with the regulation of sexuality" (Friedland 2011:

66, 85) and seeks to define the basis and goals of the national community religiously (Rieffer 2003: 230). Hence "an ideological religious nationalism" ideologically confronts the secular nationalism within its own cultural (and ethnic) community (Juergensmeyer 1996: 5–7).

This study argues that the first type—ethnic religious nationalism—is present in the Baltic States as it is virtually everywhere in Central-Eastern Europe, where the religious components in national identity have been intensifying and religious traditions have been culturally nationalizing since the Cold War (Spohn 2003: 266, 271, 274). In Lithuania, "ethnic religious nationalism" is the strongest, and religious nationalism is hegemonic over secular nationalism in the policy area of the rights of sexual minorities. In Estonia, "ethnic religious nationalism" is the weakest due to low levels of religiosity, fragmentation of the religious sphere (in contrast to virtual religious homogeneity of the Lithuanian society) and an ambiguous historic relationship between Lutheranism and the Estonian national awakening. In all of the Baltic States, regarding the public recognition of same-sex relationships—their right to family (marriage) and parenthood (adoption)—the religious/secular cleavage has manifested itself in the opposition between religious and secular nationalism. In this dimension, the religious/secular cleavage does not overlap perfectly with ethnic cleavages (although in Estonia, the value orientations of the Russian-speaking minorities are more conservative than the ones of ethnic Estonians). In Estonia, the identifiable confrontation between religious and secular nationalisms has emerged only in the policy area of the rights of sexual minorities.

The chapter proceeds in four parts. The first part argues that the Baltic States have arrived at the stage where public debates over sexual citizenship rights for same-sex couples have concentrated on their legal right to recognized and publicly legitimate forms of family. The practical recognition of the religious rights of homosexuals depends primarily on the religious elites—the leaders of the dominant religious organizations, while the legal changes in family law depend primarily on the political class. The second part identifies the sources of the relative strength of religious nationalism in Lithuania and its relative weakness in Estonia according to the following indicators: the religion-nation bond, the levels of religiosity, religious affiliation, religious practice, the presence of religious education classes in public schools and in the inter-generational transmission of religious tradition, and the scope and intensity of religion in the party politics. The third section argues that maintenance and preservation of the hegemonic religious nationalism able to block the legal recognition of the family life of same-sex couples in the Baltic States depends on the input of both religious and secular actors. The fourth part argues that the right of homosexuals to religious practice and to religiously sanctioned forms of family is dependent mostly on the religious elites of the three dominant religious traditions of Baltic societies—Catholicism, Lutheranism and Orthodoxy. Finally, the last section concludes with a discussion of the two "condition variables"—the policy legacy of the Communist period and the level of attained socioeconomic development—that explain the persisting conservative value orientations of those segments of the population which, particularly in Estonia, have retained neither a formal nor an active relationship with Christian churches.

### Phases and Dimensions of the Recognition of Same-Sex Family Life

In the Baltic States, the recognition of same-sex family life is unrealized in three dimensions: legal, cultural, religious. Until October 2014, Latvia and Lithuania had not adopted a legislation recognizing the family life of same-sex couples in any form. On 9 October 2014, the Estonian Parliament ratified a gender-neutral Cohabitation Law, but its implementation provisions still require the support of an absolute majority of the MPs.

The cultural recognition of same-sex family life aims at a situation where the social value orientations are predominantly supportive of granting the partnership of homosexual couples a status equal to traditional marriage. The prevailing cultural value orientations in Baltic societies, however, are not supportive of the legal recognition of the family life of same-sex couples. While same-sex couples tend to be excluded from the category of "the family" in all Baltic societies, heterosexual un-married couples tend to be included in the category of "the family" in Estonia, but excluded from the notion of "the family" in Lithuania. To illustrate, in December 2013, the Lithuanian Parliament endorsed a constitutional amendment limiting the application of the constitutionally protected concept "the family" only to married heterosexual couples. This move indicated the widespread unwillingness of the Lithuanian MPs to recognize unmarried heterosexual partnerships as families. In Estonia, where the majority of children are born "outside of wedlock" (that is to say, to unmarried mothers), such a move would neither be endorsed nor understood by the Estonian population. In both Estonia and Lithuania, however, homosexual couples tend to be excluded from the category of "the family." Additionally, the social opposition to the legal recognition of same-sex unions has recently been rising.

Religious recognition refers to the situation *within* religious institutions where rituals such as marriage and other religious services are provided on an equal basis to hetero- and homosexual couples, and religious institutions do not discriminate among their members on the basis of sexual orientation.

The religious recognition of same-sex family life depends primarily on religious institutions, which have a degree of autonomous control over the access of homosexuals to religious services (including religious marriage). Even in cases when laws of the nation recognize the family life of same-sex couples and the social value orientations support homosexuality, religious institutions still retain an autonomous leverege over the extent to which homosexuals have an access to religious services. For instance, in Denmark and Sweden, Lutheran Churches introduced religious same-sex marriages shortly after their parliaments had permitted same-sex marriage. In contrast, the Church of Norway does not marry same-sex couples (although the church ordains LGB persons as ministers). As a result, the religious rights of homosexuals are slightly more limited in Norway than in Denmark not because of state laws or social attitudes, but because of the related "policy choices" of the church hierarchy. In the Baltic States, vocal and uniform disapproval of the legal recognition of same-sex unions by the religious elites may not be sufficient to prevent the legal change. Religious elites, however, are capable of limiting the access of same-sex couples to religious services and hindering the effective practice of the right of homosexuals to free exercise of religion.

In Western history, the recognition of the family life of same-sex couples has occurred simultaneously in three of these dimensions. In principle, national parliaments may recognize the family life of same-sex couples *without* significant changes in social value orientations, *without* the support of religious institutions and *without* a decline in the levels of church-related religiosity. For example, in April 2014, the parliament in Malta legalized same-sex unions and gay adoptions despite the vocal and active opposition of the Catholic Church and the low level of social support for such a move. Likewise, post-communist Hungary and Slovenia have legally recognized same-sex unions despite the relatively low level of social acceptance of homosexuality (Uitz 2012: 252). Countries that pass such laws without significant social support and without a "demand from below" are mostly present members of the European Union. Outside of the European Union, relatively high levels of social approval toward homosexuality are regularly present already at the moment of adoption of laws recognizing same-sex unions. For example, the first countries in South America to legalize same-sex civil unions (Uruguay in 2007) and same-sex marriage (Argentina in 2010) were the only "high tolerance" countries in the region (Encarnación 2011: 104–115). Additionally, the Western countries (both in Europe and in North America), that have legally recognized same-sex unions and marriages, have typically also enjoyed a degree of support from religious institutions, which have been split over the issue either internally or among themselves.

Though the recognition of the family life of same-sex couples has tended to proceed in three dimensions simultaneously, the extension of *religious* rights of the same-sex couples has primarily been dependent on the religious elites and the extension of *legal* rights of the same-sex couples has ultimately been dependent on the willingness of the political elites (Rom 2007: 3). The progress leading to the legal acceptance of same-sex marriage takes place incrementally (Aloni 2010: 114). In a typical case, the legalization of sexuality rights starts from the decriminalization of homosexuality and ends with the inclusion of homosexuals "as full and equal citizens," whose intimate relationships and parenting relationships are protected on equal grounds with heterosexuals (Roseneil *et. al.* 2013). The full recognition of the family life of same-sex couples presupposes a broader understanding of sexualities, where the earlier distinctions between hetero- and same-sex orientations are depoliticized (Kuwali 2014), and homosexual identity is transformed from deviant other into "mirror images of the ideal heterosexual" (Mepschen and Duyvendak 2012: 72–73).

Consequently, the legal recognition of the family life of same-sex couples is expected to take place by small changes where, for example, the debates over the right of association and "free speech" are expected to be preceded by full decriminalization of homosexuality. Similarly, the public debate over the legalization of same-sex marriage is hardly realistic while the majority of the population is still considering teaching about homosexuality in public schools a harmful propaganda of a deviant life-style and does not consider discrimination on the basis of sexual orientation at the work-place as a violation of human rights.

On this "incremental" continuum of the legal recognition of same-sex couples, same-sex marriage is currently not an object of public debate in the Baltic States: the progressive activists do not demand legal recognition of same-sex marriage and national parliaments have strengthened the legal status of heterosexual marriage. Shortly after accession to the EU, Latvia introduced a constitutional bar to same-sex marriage in 2005 (entered into force in 2006). The bar to same-sex marriage also exists in the Lithuanian constitution. Additionally, in 2008 the Lithuanian Parliament adopted the State Family Policy Concept, which defined "family" exclusively as a legal relationship between a married heterosexual couple and their children. Similarly, the Family Law Act of Estonia (entered into force in 2010) defines marriage as a contract between a man and a woman (§1.1), and considers marriage void when formed by persons of the same sex (§10.1). In Estonia, the public debates have arrived at a more advanced stage of legal recognition of gender-neutral cohabitations, while the public debates in Latvia and Lithuania still primarily focus on the dangers originating from "the propaganda of homosexuality," on the application of the rights of assembly and free speech by homosexuals.

## The Religious Assets of Religious Nationalism

As religious nationalism refers "to a community of religious people or the political movement of a group of people heavily influenced by religious beliefs" (Rieffer 2003: 225), religious nationalism is expected to be more vibrant in a society and politics where religion is more present. Three confessions—Catholicism, Orthodoxy and Lutheranism—dominate the religious sphere in Baltic societies. Lithuanian Catholicism is the only confession in its society that owns the allegiance of an absolute majority of the population. Only the Lithuanian population has retained a high level of religious affiliation, and most of the beliefs and practices of the traditional institutional religion (see Table 1). By contrast, among ethnic Estonians, the level of church-related religiosity is linearly declining. According to the Housing and Population Census, the percentage of ethnic Estonians admitting religious affiliation declined from 24% in 2000 to 19% in 2011. The percentage of self-identified Lutherans (overwhelmingly ethnic Estonians) declined from 14% to 10%, while the proportion of the Orthodox (mostly Russian-speaking minorities) respondents rose from 13% to 16.0% (Känd 2002: 292). In the Eurobarometer survey in 2006, Estonia scored lowest among the 25 member states of the European Union in weekly attendance of religious services (2.5%), daily prayer (12.4%) and self-identified religious persons (28.3%) (Smith 2009: 61–63). By contrast, the level of religious affiliation in Lithuania is either persisting or possibly rising. According to the Lithuanian census of 2011, only 6.1% of the population did not affiliate themselves with any religious community (down from 9.5% in the 2001 census; Ambrozaitienė 2013).

TABLE 1      *Religious affiliation and attendance (World Values Surveys, 1999)*

|                                              | Lithuania | Latvia | Estonia |
| -------------------------------------------- | --------- | ------ | ------- |
| Do you belong to a religious denomination? Which one? | 81.3      | 59.3   | 24.9    |
|    Catholic                   | 92.5      | 33.2   | 1.6     |
|    Protestant                 | 2.9       | 36.2   | 53.8    |
|    Orthodox                   | 3.5       | 28.3   | 41.0    |
| Attend religious services once a month       | 31.5      | 15.1   | 11.1    |
| Never attend religious services              | 16.0      | 34.6   | 37.8    |

Source: Halman 2001: 74–75, 78. Percentage of respondents who answered affirmatively to the listed questions.

TABLE 2     *Religious beliefs (World Values Survey, 1999)*

| Belief in ... | Lithuania | Latvia | Estonia |
|---|---|---|---|
| God | 86.5 | 79.5 | 51.4 |
| Life after death | 79.0 | 45.3 | 36.2 |
| Hell | 68.1 | 28.4 | 16.3 |
| Heaven | 70.6 | 33.3 | 19.1 |
| Sin | 90.5 | 73.6 | 52.4 |
| Reincarnation | 44.0 | 33.4 | 37.0 |
| Telepathy | 79.4 | 52.3 | 54.9 |

Source: Halman 2001: 86–92. Percentage of positive answers to questions: "Do you believe in ...". The question of belief in reincarnation was stated as follows: "Do you believe in re-incarnation, that is, that we are born into this world again?"

When respondents were asked about their religious beliefs one by one in the World Values Survey of 1999 (Table 2), the levels of belief were highest among Lithuanian respondents in all categories. The most telling indicator of the persisting religious authority is the belief in hell, which was not widespread among Estonian (16%) and Latvian (28%) respondents, but was affirmed by two thirds of Lithuanian respondents (68%).

The inter-generational variations in religious belonging, belief and practice are the largest in Estonia, where the 2011 Census demonstrated that more than 50,000 out of 108,513 residents who identified themselves as Lutherans were aged 65 and older. Among ethnic Estonians aged 15 to 29, only 4.9% identified themselves as Lutherans. Likewise, the data from the World Values Survey (1999) identified a strong inter-generational difference in religious affiliation, belief and practice among Estonians, almost non-existent inter-generational difference among Lithuanians, and a significant inter-generational gap in Latvia, with the qualification that the overall levels of religious belonging, belief and practice were slightly higher in all age clusters in Latvia than they were in Estonia (Smith 2009: 101–127).

The status of the religious education classes in the Baltic countries corresponds to this pattern. In Lithuania, nearly 98% of the pupils of primary schools attend classes on religion (Ralys 2010: 127), which according to the Article 17 of the Lithuanian Law of Education are provided exclusively by the religious communities or churches of traditional religions for the children whose parents or guardians have chosen these classes for their children. In contrast, the religious education classes in Latvia and Estonia are non-confessional or ecumenical in content, dependent on the choice of the parents of primary school pupils, and on the choice of pupils in secondary schools. In practice, classes of religious education exist in about one out of ten Estonian schools and only one percent of the pupils take these classes.

Religion (Catholicism) has been consistently more connected to politics and nationalism in Lithuania than (Lutheranism) in Latvia or Estonia (Johnston 1994: 27). Estonian and Latvian (Lutheran) Churches are weakly related to national identity and been largely absent from nationalist struggles (Bruce 2000: 41–43). In the 19th century, the Catholic clergy in Lithuania and Latvia were predominantly of native origin and supportive of the national awakening (Hoppenbrouwers 1999: 162–163), while the Lutheran clergy in Estonia and Latvia were mostly of German origin and not supportive of the national awakening movements. Later, the anti-communist dissident or semi-dissident movements in Estonia and Latvia were mostly defending the language, cultural heritage and civil rights rather than religion (Martin 2014: 7), while religious symbolism and church resources were highly important within the Lithuanian nationalist mobilization during the Soviet period (Johnston, 1992: 74–75).

The lower level of political secularization in Lithuania is also manifested in the success of parties that have appealed to the religious/secular divide among the electorate or have stood for the interests and values of traditional churches. In the 1990s, the Lithuanian Christian Democratic Party stood for religious values and for the Catholic Church (Krupavicius 1998: 490), and was the second largest party in terms of membership and the third most important party in the party system. It has also performed well since 2008, when a faction of the party merged with the large conservative party Homeland Union. Thereafter, the Homeland Union-Lithuanian Christian Democrats won the parliamentary (2008) and the European elections (2009). It has established itself as a party that emphasizes Christian family values, nationalism, a religious and culturally conservative social agenda, and favors the inclusion of the elites of the Lithuanian Catholic Church in the processes of political decision-making (Duvold and Jurkynas 2013: 132, 146).

In Latvia, Christian parties have remained mostly small and electorally unsuccessful. Nevertheless, from 2002 until 2011, Latvia's First Party occupied from 8 to 10 seats (out of 100) in the Latvian Parliament, had a significant representation of religious ministers among the founders and high-ranking leaders of the party, enjoyed a broad support of traditional (Lutheran, Catholic, Orthodox and Baptist) and new Charismatic churches, and was committed to combat the "atheization of society" and to protect Christian values (Teraud-kalns 2011: 13, Freston 2004: 44). Finally, in 2011, the party lost parliamentary representation. In 2006, however, Latvia's First Party initiated a bill in the Latvian parliament aiming at banning any mention of homosexuality in the mass media (Smith-Sivertsen 2010: 459). The Latvian parliament did not approve the bill.

Religious cleavage has manifested itself the least in Estonian party politics, where the national parliament has not included a party standing distinctively for the interests of the Church or primarily for religious values. In the Estonian party system, the only party perceived to speak for Christian values, has been the Estonian Christian People's Party (which changed its name to Estonian Christian Democrats in 2005). However, since its foundation in 1998 until 2012, when it ran into bankruptcy and was dissolved, it never succeeded to pass the 5% electoral threshold. Despite electoral failures, the electoral lists of this party included proportionally the highest percentage of clergy (primarily from Baptist, Methodist, Pentecostal and Free Churches, but also some high-ranking ministers from the Estonian Evangelical Lutheran Church) running for parliament. Its program was explicit in its commitment to interpret social and political processes according to the Bible and in its aim "to create a better society based on Christian values and to apply these values at all levels of society" (Kilp 2009: 73).

Despite the significant differences in social and political secularization as well as social value orientations, the elites of the dominant religious traditions—Catholicism, Orthodoxy and Lutheranism—tend to disapprove of homosexuality in all of the Baltic States. The levels of cultural traditionalism (e.g. social value orientations primarily supportive of traditionalist values) are relatively high in all of the Baltic States, even though slightly lower and decreasing more in Estonia than in Latvia or Lithuania. According to the World Values Survey (1999), 78% of Lithuanian, 77% of Latvian and 57% of Estonian respondents considered homosexuality "never justified." In 2006, when the Eurobarometer monitored the extent to which societies in the European Union support the introduction of homosexual marriages throughout Europe, this option was supported by 12% of respondents in Latvia (which was the lowest level among the member states of the EU), by 17% in Lithuania and 21% in Estonia (European Commission 2006).

The relatively widespread "unconcern" for legal and religious recognition of the family life of same-sex couples does not automatically mean that people in Baltic societies are strongly attached to traditional family in other dimensions of sexuality and morality. The percentages of live births outside of wedlock, for example, are linearly rising in all of the Baltic States (Table 3). The trend is the

TABLE 3    *Percentage of live births outside of*
           *marriage (Eurostat, 2010)*

|        | Lithuania | Latvia | Estonia |
|--------|-----------|--------|---------|
| 1990   | 7.0       | 16.9   | 27.2    |
| 1998   | 18.0      | 37.1   | 52.5    |
| 2008   | 28.5      | 43.1   | 59.0    |

Source: Eurostat (2010).

most advanced in Estonia, where children born outside of wedlock constitute an absolute majority.

Additionally, in Lithuania, unmarried heterosexual partnerships are perceived not to fall into the category of "the family" (Duvold and Aalia 2012: 414). By contrast, the Estonian population does not exclude from the category of "the family" the one third of heterosexual couples living together in *de facto* unions without being married (Olm 2013: 104). In Latvian and Lithuanian societies, the level of anti-gay prejudice is high (Mole 2011, O'Dwyer and Schwartz 2010, Duvold and Aalia 2012: 44, Tereškinas 2007). The Resolution of the European Parliament (24 May 2012) "on the fight against homophobia in Europe" did mention instances of violation of the freedom of expression and freedom of assembly of homosexuals in both Latvia and Lithuania. In 2009, when Lithuania adopted a "Law on the Protection on Minors," which sought to protect children from negative influences by limiting various types of information that might otherwise be available to them, including information that "promotes homosexual, bisexual and polygamous relations" (Duvold and Aalia 2012: 42), this move was condemned by the European Parliament which responded with a resolution "on the Lithuanian Law on the Protection of Minors against the Detrimental Effects of Public Information." Similarly, in 2006, a couple of weeks after Latvia had constitutionally limited marriage to heterosexual couples, the European Parliament called for "tough action" against Latvia on the grounds of Article 13 of the EU Treaty, which had given the EU an authority to combat homophobia (Belien 2007).

A recent EU-wide survey of the LGBT people's experiences of discrimination organized by the EU Agency for Fundamental Rights identified the highest proportion of respondents who felt discriminated or harassed because of their sexual orientation in Lithuania (61%), while the related percentage of respondents in Estonia (44%) was below the EU average (47%) (ILGA-Europe 2014: 65). In Estonian society, the perceptions of discrimination on the basis of sexual orientation and the negative attitudes towards homosexuality have slightly declined over past two decades. In 1990, more than three quarters (76%) of the respondents to the World Values Survey thought that homosexuality is never justified. In 2010 the corresponding indicator was 48% (Realo 2013: 55).

Opposition to legal recognition of same-sex families, however, has been increasing in both Estonia and Lithuania over the last years. In Estonia, the public opinion polls conducted in August 2014 demonstrated that electorates of all parliamentary parties were inclined not to support the introduction of the Cohabitation Bill—the rate of disapproval was highest (72%) among the electorate of centre-left Centre Party and lowest (51%) among the electorate of the liberal-right Reform Party. In general, the legal initiative was supported by 34% (down from 40% in 2012) and opposed by 58% of the respondents. A similar trend also exists in Lithuania, where according to a survey conducted by the Public Opinion and Market Research Centre VILMORUS, the opposition to legal recognition of registered same-sex partnerships rose from 74% in 2012 to 79% in 2013 and its support declined from 10% to 7%.

### The Interplay of the Religious and the Secular in the Maintenance of Hegemonic Religious Nationalism

In Lithuania, political initiatives to introduce bills recognizing the family life of same-sex unions have been unable to counteract effectively the anti-gay rhetoric and moral agenda of the Catholic Church and its political ally, the Homeland Union/Lithuanian Christian Democrats (Duvold and Jurkynas 2013: 146), which after forming a governmental coalition in 2008 made homophobic discourse hegemonic in the Lithuanian Parliament (Duvold and Aalia 2012: 40, 43). The majority of MPs in the Lithuanian Parliament have been condemning homosexuality (Stan and Turcescu 2011: 113). The most radical MPs have recently even compared homosexuality to necrophilia and pedophilia (ILGA-Europe 2013: 140–141). Importantly, the widespread homophobic attitude was not confronted by the later centre-left governmental coalition (the Labor Party and the Order and Justice Party), which also expressed commitment to Christian values and willingness to protect people from legislation initiatives originating from Europe (including the ones related to sexual minorities) that contradict the Lithuanian character. The only party in the Lithuanian Parliament which has expressed public support for legal recognition of same-sex partnership is the relatively small Liberal Movement of the Lithuanian Republic. The Lithuanian political class tends to support the position of the Roman Catholic

Church against homosexual behavior (Stan and Turcescu 2011: 112), and there exists "no domestic, political or social forces willing or able to counteract the efforts to establish homophobic notions in Lithuanian legislation and society" (Duvold and Aalia 2012: 43).

Latvia introduced a constitutional bar to same-sex marriage in 2005 pre-empting the pressure coming from European institutions, which expect member states to recognize same-sex couples in some form or another. The first Riga Gay Pride Parade in July 2005 led to a multi-confessional protest (Hoppenbrouwers 2006: 90), where leaders of Latvia's Evangelical Lutheran Church, Roman Catholic Church, Orthodox Church, and Baptist Congregation warned about the potential for the moral degradation of Latvia if gay parades were to take place (Riga 2005). Similar to Lithuania, the Latvian anti-gay rights coalition has included religious elites, parties relying on religious appeal (e.g. Latvia's First Party), and secular social actors and political forces anxious about the preservation of national traditions and demographic community (O'Dwyer and Schwartz 2010: 239). Similar to Lithuania, the Latvian Parliament also lacks any significant party advancing gay rights (Mole 2011: 554), and besides gay activists, "there has been little desire to reconsider existing sexual norms or to emulate Western Europe's" (O'Dwyer and Schwartz 2010: 236). At present, governments and legislatures in Latvia and Lithuania face neither a clear-cut social demand nor a political incentive to grant legal recognition to same-sex unions. In contrast, if the dominant parties do not preserve the status quo in this policy area, they risk losing the support of their constituencies.

The Estonian political elite, however, began to fracture over the prospects of the legal recognition of same-sex unions in 2009, when the Ministry of Justice started to prepare the draft of the Cohabitation Act granting same- and opposite-sex couples a right to conclude a cohabitation contract covering issues related to property, inheritance and care obligations toward each other (Olm 2013: 109). Until Spring 2014 the draft of the Cohabitation Act did not find sufficient support from parties of the right-wing governmental coalition, but stirred up a vocal social reaction from churches and from a group consisting mostly of lay Catholics who formed the Foundation for the Protection of Family and Traditional Values committed to fight homosexual relations as immoral acts in conflict with "the law of nature." By May 2013, the Foundation had collected 38,000 signatures to the public call for protection of traditional family values and handed it over to the Parliament.

Finally, in Spring 2014, after the right wing coalition government was replaced by the coalition of the Social Democrats and the Reform Party, April 17, 2014, 40 members of the Estonian Parliament submitted a Cohabitation bill regulating financial, inheritance, care and visitation rights for cohabiting couples regardless of their sex. Thus, in contrast to the Lithuanian political class, which consults in the policy area of gender and sexuality preferably with pro-family and pro-Church associations instead of gender-oriented NGOs (Duvold and Aalia 2012: 44), the Estonian political class started to confront and test the social authority of the religious elite in this area of public policy.

The Churches in Estonia have been as vocal and active in rejecting proposals seeking the legalization of same-sex unions as they are in Lithuania or Latvia. From April until October 2014, the Cohabitation Act was repeatedly denounced by the Council of Estonian Churches, which represents not only the numerically largest and historic Christian denominations of Estonia, but also Christian denominations of more recent origin—the Estonian Evangelical Lutheran Church, the Union of Evangelical Christian and Baptist Churches of Estonia, the Estonian Methodist Church, the Roman Catholic Church, the Estonian Christian Pentecostal Church, the Estonian Conferences of Seventh-Day Adventists Church, the Estonian Congregation St. Gregory of the Armenian Apostolic Church, the Estonian Apostolic Orthodox Church, the Estonian Orthodox Church of Moscow Patriarchy, and the Charismatic Episcopal Church of Estonia. In addition to joint statements by the Council of Estonian Churches, the Cohabitation Act was also denounced by individual addresses by the Metropolitan Stephanus (of the Estonian Apostolic Orthodox Church), the Estonian Orthodox Church of the Moscow Patriarchate, the United Methodist Church in Estonia, the Union of Evangelical Christian and Baptist Churches of Estonia, the Estonian Christian Pentecostal Church, who sent their own public letters to the Estonian parliament. In their addresses the churches considered the toleration of homosexual relationships as not biblical. Homosexuality was labeled as a sin and vice, which should not be socially recognized, justified or legalized; the adoption of the gender-neutral Cohabitation Act as an attempt to redefine the meaning of family, to depart from traditional European values and to undermine the social order.

In Latvia and Lithuania, traditional churches are the strongest, most outspoken and often perceived to be the most powerful social forces opposing changes in the "sex/gender" order (Waitt 2005: 167, 170; Mole 2011: 543; Stan and Turcescu 2011: 98). Particularly in Lithuania, the negative attitude of the Lithuanian Catholic Church toward homosexuality and same-sex marriage has found increasing support from the Lithuanian political class (Stan and Turcescu 2011: 112). Estonian churches are also strongly opposed to homosexuality and the legal recognition of same-sex couples, but they have largely lost the support of the Estonian political class.

### Religious Elites Blocking the Right to the Religious Family of Homosexuals

All three dominant religious traditions in the Baltic States—Catholicism, Lutheranism and Orthodoxy—are strongly disapproving of the extension of the legal protection of same-sex couples so that their intimate relationships will be valued on equal grounds with heterosexual couples.

The negative attitude of the Orthodox toward homosexuality is least controversial and the negative attitudes of Baltic Lutheran Churches requiring most explanation, because traditionally Orthodox societies are regularly the least approving of homosexuality, while predominantly Protestant societies tend to be most approving. A study by Aleksander Štulhofer and Ivan Rimac demonstrated that four of the five least homo-negative countries were predominantly Protestant, while four of the five least accepting countries (Lithuania, Romania, Ukraine, Russia, and Belarus) were Eastern Orthodox (Štulhofer and Rimac 2009: 27). At present, no culturally Orthodox country in Europe has legally recognized same-sex union. Additionally, traditionally Orthodox Romania was the last of the current EU member states to decriminalize homosexual conduct fully in 2001 (private homosexuality was decriminalized in 1996) (Kochenov 2007: 483).

Despite the principled homophobic positions proclaimed by universal Catholicism, traditionally Catholic societies of Europe are *split within* the postcommunist region. Hungary and Slovenia have legally recognized same-sex unions, while Poland and Lithuania have not. With the exception of Italy, however, all traditionally Catholic countries in Western Europe offer legal protection of same-sex unions or marriages.

The most puzzling are the traditionally Lutheran societies, which are *split between* the European West and the European East in terms of both social values and the value orientations of the national Lutheran churches. The 1999/2000 round of the World Values Surveys demonstrated a vast rift in the social values of traditionally Lutheran Latvia, Estonia and the Scandinavian societies. When only 9 % of Swedish respondents considered homosexuality to be "never justifiable," the Swedes were close to respondents from other Scandinavian societies (12 % in Iceland, 13 % in Finland and 21 % in Denmark). In this respect, however, every Scandinavian country stood in stark contrast to the patterns of opinion expressed by the Estonian (57 %) and Latvian (77 %) respondents (Kilp 2009: 68). In contrast to Lutheran Churches in Denmark and Sweden, which have not only adjusted to changes in social value orientations, but have also introduced religious ceremonies for same-sex couples in their churches, the Lutheran Churches of Estonia, Latvia and Lithuania are clearly opposed to any expansion of religious or legal rights of same-sex couples. In a joint statement in November 2009, they denounced those member churches of the Lutheran World Federation, which "approve of religious matrimony for couples of the same gender" and "ordain non-celibate homosexual persons for pastoral or episcopal office" (Message 2010). Earlier, in March 2007, in reaction to the decision of the Swedish (Lutheran) Church to bless same-sex partnerships in church services, the Archbishop of Estonian Evangelical Lutheran Church, Andres Põder, confirmed that "homosexual behavior is a sin" and blessing of the partnership of the same-sex couples is inconceivable in the Estonian Lutheran Church (Ammas 2007).

### Conclusions

In all of the Baltic States, the process of recognition of the family life of same-sex couples is incomplete in the three main dimensions: the legal recognition of the family life of same-sex couples is missing; prevailing cultural perceptions exclude same-sex couples from the category of "the family"; the religious rights of homosexuals are limited not primarily because of state laws, but because of internal regulations of the religious institutions and policy choices of the religious elites.

At present, the prospects for legal recognition of same-sex unions are highest in Estonia, where the "blocking coalition" has lost most of its allies in the Estonian Parliament, despite the still hegemonic social and religious anti-gay activism. Attempts to introduce legal recognition of the family life of same-sex couples have been difficult to effect in the Baltic States as a result of both the policy legacy of the Communist period and the relatively low level of economic affluence.

The European empirical pattern of the legal recognition of same-sex unions and same-sex marriage has proceeded in accordance with the small changes theory (incrementalism). The time span since the decriminalization of homosexuality in post-Soviet Baltic States (1992 in Latvia and Estonia, 1993 in Lithuania) is significantly shorter than it was between the decriminalization of homosexual conduct in Hungary (in 1960s) and Slovenia (in 1976) and the legal recognition of registered partnerships (2006 in Slovenia and 2009 in Hungary). Additionally, the situation of homosexuals in the Soviet Union was far more repressive than it was in communist Czechoslovakia, Hungary or Yugoslavia.

The prospects for the enactment of legislation recognizing the family life of same-sex unions is also conditioned by the level of socioeconomic development. Several studies confirm the existence of a correlation between economic modernization and cultural value shifts from materialist, traditional, authoritarian and survival value orientations to post-materialist self-expression and tolerance values, where the former limit sexual relationships to the nuclear family and heterosexual marriage, and the latter tend to reshape both religious orientations, gender roles, sexual norms and patterns of cohabitation (Inglehart *et. al.* 2004: 9–10). At higher levels of economic security, more permissive and tolerant attitudes towards sex, abortion and homosexuality replace traditional norms that formerly regulated the institutions of marriage, the relations of gender and the norms of sexuality (Štulhofer and Rimac 2009). According to this explanation, the likelihood of the legal recognition of family life of homosexuals depends primarily on the dynamics of the economic development and on the resulting sense of material security. If this is true, then the prospects for legal recognition of same-sex couples remain low until the end of the economic crises that began in 2008.

How important then are the economic factors and "the policy legacy of the Communist period" in hindering the legal recognition of the family life of same-sex couples? Particularly for Estonia, the persistence of traditional conservative attitudes regarding homosexuality cannot be explained solely by the presence of church religion, when only one quarter of the population is religiously affiliated. Economic factors and "the policy legacy of the Communist period" explain the persisting conservative value orientations of those segments of the population that have retained neither formal nor active relationship with Christian churches.

All in all, it is reasonable to expect that the prevailing pattern of the legal recognition of same-sex unions and marriages in traditionally Catholic and Lutheran societies of Europe will also be followed in the Baltic countries. The public discussions over rights of association of homosexuals and free expression of homosexuality seem to be a past stage in Estonia, which is closer to legal recognition of family life of same-sex couples than in Latvia and Lithuania, where homophobic sentiments are more spread among religious, social and political elites, and legislative debates focus more on homosexuality in public education and on the rights of association of homosexuals.

### References

Aloni, Erez. 2010. "Incrementalism, Civil Unions, and the Possibility of Predicting Legal Recognition of Same-Sex Marriage." *Duke Journal of Gender, Law and Policy* 18: 105–161.

Ambrozaitienė, Dalia. 2013. "Lithuania is inhabited by people of 154 ethnicities." Press release of *Statistics Lithuania*, March 15, 2013. Retrieved April 18, 2014. http://www .baltic-course.com/eng/analytics/?doc-71945.

Ammas, Anneli. 2007. "Eesti luteri kirik Rootsi eeskujul homoabielusid sõlmima ei hakka." *Eesti Päevaleht* (March 27).

Belien, Paul. 2007. "Europe's Culture War; Secularism on the March." (May 23). Retrieved April 28, 2014. http://www.brusselsjournal.com/node/2144.

Brubaker, Rogers. 2012. "Religion and Nationalism: Four Approaches." *Nations and Nationalism* 18: 2–20.

Bruce, Steve. 2000. "The Supply-Side Model of Religion: The Nordic and Baltic States." *Journal for the Scientific Study of Religion* 39: 32–46.

Duvold, Kjetil, and Inga Aalia. 2012. "Fear and Loathing in Lithuania." *Baltic Worlds* 4: 40–47.

Duvold, Kjetil and Mindaugas Jurkynas. 2013. "Lithuania." Pp. 125–166 in S. Berglund, J. Ekman, K. Deegan-Krause, and T. Knutsen (eds.), *The Handbook of Political Change in Eastern Europe*. Cheltenham: Edward Elgar.

Eastwood, Jonathan, and Nikolas Prevalakis. 2010. "Nationalism, Religion, and Secularization: An Opportune Moment for Research." *Review of Religious Research* 52: 90–111.

Encarnación, Omar G. 2011. "Latin America's Gay Rights Revolution." *Journal of Democracy* 22: 104–118.

European Commission. 2006. "Eurobarometer 66: Public opinion in the European Union—first results." Retrieved October 10, 2013. http://ec.europa.eu/public_ opinion/archives/eb/eb66/eb66_highlights_en.pdf.

European Parliament. 2012. "European Parliament resolution of 24 May 2012 on the fight against homophobia in Europe." Retrieved October 10, 2013. http://www.europarl .europa.eu/sides/getDoc.do?type=TA&language=EN&reference=P7-TA-2012-222.

Eurostat. 2010. "Europe in figures—Eurostat yearbook 2010." September 9, 2010. Retrieved October 10, 2013. http://www.nbbmuseum.be/doc/seminar2010/nl/ bibliografie/inleiding/eurostatyearbook2010.pdf.

Freston, Paul. 2004. *Protestant Political Parties: A Global Survey*. Burlington: Ashgate.

Friedland, Roger. 1999. "When God Walks in History: The Institutional Politics of Religious Nationalism." *International Sociology* 14: 301–319.

———. 2011. "The Institutional Logic of Religious Nationalism: Sex, Violence and the Ends of History." *Politics, Religion and Ideology* 12: 65–88.

Halman, Loek. 2001. *The European Values Study: A Third Wave. Source book of the 1999/ 2000 European Values Study Surveys*. Tilburg: EVS/WORC, Tilburg University.

Hoppenbrouwers, Frans. 1999. "Romancing Freedom: Church and Society in the Baltic States since the End of Communism." *Religion, State and Society* 27: 161–173.

———. 2006. "Current Developments: The Baltic Area." *Journal of Eastern Christian Studies* 58: 85–104.

ILGA-Europe. 2013. *Annual Review of the Human Rights Situation of Lesbian, Gay, Bisexual, Trans and Intersex People in Europe.* Retrieved April 18, 2014. https://dl .dropboxusercontent.com/u/15245131/2013.pdf.

———. 2014. *Annual Review of the Human Rights Situation of Lesbian, Gay, Bisexual, Trans and Intersex People in Europe.* Retrieved September 20, 2014. http://www.ilga -europe.org/home/news/for_media/media_releases/rainbow_europe_2014.

Inglehart, Ronald, Miguel Basáñez, Jaime Diez-Medrano, Loek Halman, and Ruud Luijkx. 2004. *Human Beliefs and Values: a Cross-Cultural Sourcebook Based on the 1999–2002 Values Surveys.* México: Siglo XXI Editores.

Johnston, Hank. 1992. "Religious Nationalism: Six Propositions from Eastern Europe and the Former Soviet Union." Pp. 67–79 in M. Misztal and A. Shupe (eds.), *Religion and Politics in Comparative Perspective: Revival of Religious Fundamentalism in East and West.* Westport: Praeger.

———. 1994. "Religio-Nationalist Subcultures under the Communists: Comparisons from the Baltics, Transcaucasia, and Ukraine." Pp. 17–32 in W.H. Jr. Swatos (ed.), *Politics and Religion in Central and Eastern Europe: Traditions and Transitions.* Westport: Praeger.

Juergensmeyer, Mark. 1996. "The Worldwide Rise of Religious Nationalism." *Journal of International Affairs* 50: 1–20.

———. 2008. *Global Rebellion: Religious Challenges to the Secular State, from Christian Militias to al Qaeda.* Berkeley: University of California Press.

Känd, Kristina. 2002. *2000 Population and Housing Census IV: Education. Religion.* Tallinn: Statistical Office of Estonia.

Kilp, Alar. 2009. "Secularization of Society after Communism: Ten Catholic-Protestant Societies." *ENDC Proceedings* 12: 194–231. Retrieved April 18, 2014. www.ksk.edu.ee/ toimetised/kvuoa-toimetised-nr-12/.

Kochenov, Dimitry. 2007. "Democracy and Human Rights Not for Gay People?: EU Eastern Enlargement and Its Impact on the Protection of the Rights of Sexual Minorities." *Texas Wesleyan Law Review* 13: 459–495.

Krupavicius, Algis. 1998. "The Post-communist Transition and Institutionalization of Lithuania's Parties." *Political Studies* 46: 465–491.

Kuwali, Dan. 2014. "Battle for Sex? Protecting Sexual(ity) Rights in Africa." *Human Rights Quarterly* 36: 22–60.

Martin, David. 2014. "Nationalism and Religion—Collective Identity and Choice: The 1989 Revolutions, Evangelical Revolution in the Global South, Revolution in the Arab World." *Nations and Nationalism* 20: 1–17.

Mepschen, Paul, and Jan Willem Duyvendak. 2012. "European Sexual Nationalisms: The Culturalization of Citizenship and the Sexual Politics of Belonging and Exclusion." *Perspectives on Europe* 41: 70–76.

Merdjanova, Ina. 2000. "In Search of Identity: Nationalism and Religion in Eastern Europe." *Religion, State and Society* 28: 233–262.

"Message from the Meeting of the Baltic Lutheran Bishops." 2010. *Concordia Theological Quarterly* 74: 151–152.

Mole, Richard. 2011. "Nationality and Sexuality: Homophobic Discourse and the 'National Threat' in Contemporary Latvia." *Nations and Nationalism* 17: 540–560.

O'Dwyer, Conor, Katrina Z.S. Schwartz. 2010. "Minority Rights after EU Enlargement: A Comparison of Antigay Politics in Poland and Latvia." *Comparative European Politics* 8: 220–243.

Olm, Andra. 2013. "Non-married Cohabiting Couples and Their Constitutional Right to Family Life." *Juridica International* 20: 104–111.

Ralys, Kestutis. 2010. "Social Activity of the Roman Catholic Church in Lithuania." *Socialinis Ugdymas* 12: 120–129.

Realo, Anu. 2013. "Values." Pp. 48–58 in M. Heidmets (ed.), *Estonian Human Development Report 2012/2013: Estonia in the World*. Tallinn: Eesti Koostöökogu.

Rieffer, Barbara-Ann J. 2003. "Religion and Nationalism: Understanding the Consequences of a Complex Relationship." *Ethnicities* 3: 215–242.

"Riga cancels 'pride' parade, but debate continues." *Latvians Online*, July 20, 2005. Retrieved April 18, 2014. http://latviansonline.com/riga-cancels-pride-parade-but -debate-continues/.

Rom, Mark Carl. 2007. "Introduction: The Politics of Same-Sex Marriage." Pp. 1–38 in C.A. Rimmerman, and C. Wilcox (eds.), *The Politics of Same-Sex Marriage*. Chicago: University of Chicago Press.

Roseneil, Sasha Isabel Crowhurst, Tone Hellesund, Ana Cristina Santos, and Mariya Stoilova. 2013. "Changing Landscapes of Heteronormativity: The Regulation and Normalization of Same-Sex Sexualities in Europe." *Social Politics* 20: 165–199.

Smith-Sivertsen, Hermann. 2010. "Baltic states." Pp. 447–472 in S.P. Ramet (ed.), *Central and Southeast European Politics since 1989*. Cambridge: Cambridge University Press.

Spohn, Wilfried. 2003. "Multiple Modernity, Nationalism and Religion: A Global Perspective." *Current Sociology* 51: 265–286.

Stan, Lavinia and Lucian Turcescu. 2011. *Church, State, and Democracy in Expanding Europe*. New York: Oxford University Press.

Storm, Ingrid. 2011. "Ethnic Nominalism and Civic Religiosity: Christianity and National Identity." *Sociological Review* 59: 827–846.

Štulhofer, Aleksander and Ivan Rimac. 2009. "Determinants of Homonegativity in Europe." *Journal of Sex Research* 46: 24–32.

Teraudkalns, Valdis. 2011. "Religion and Politics in Latvia at the Beginning of the 21st Century." *Religion in Eastern Europe* 31: 10–18.

Tereškinas, Artûras. 2007. "Lithuanian Gays and Lesbians' Coming Out in the Public/Private Divide: Sexual Citizenship, Secrecy and Heteronormative Public." *Sociologija. Mintis ir veiksmas* 19: 74–87.

Uitz, Renáta. 2012. "Lessons from Sexual Orientation Discrimination in Central Europe." *The American Journal of Comparative Law* 60: 235–264.

Waitt, Gordon. 2005. "Sexual Citizenship in Latvia: Geographies of the Latvian Closet." *Social and Cultural Geography* 6: 161–181.

Wood, James. E. Jr. 1968. "The Problem of Nationalism in Church-State Relationships." *Journal of Church and State* 10: 249–264.

CHAPTER 7

# "Gays as a Weapon of the Antichrist": Religious Nationalism, Homosexuality and the Antichrist on the Russian Internet

*Magda Dolinska Rydzek and Mariecke van den Berg*

"Gays as a weapon of the Antichrist": these words, here in translation, are from Maxim Schevchenko (2013), one of the most prominent Russian journalists and an expert in ethno-cultural and religious policies. These words are just one of many examples of how sexual minorities in Russia are being associated with the notion of the "Antichrist" on RuNet—the term by which in this chapter we refer to the Russian segment of the Internet.

The Antichrist did not (as some apocryphal writings suggest) come falling out of the blue. Rather, this apocalyptic figure invokes a long tradition of Russian cultural imagery, where over the centuries he has undergone numerous historical and semantic transformations (Ewertowski 2010). He was understood as God's enemy, the false Messiah, the usurper of the tsar's power (*lzhe-tzar*), the embodiment of evil forces, and an individual who falsely interprets Christian values.

In particular the 17th century and the *Raskol*[1] contributed to the vivid presence of the concept of the Antichrist in Russian cultural cognition. In this period those who came to be known as "Old Believers" interpreted the reformist Patriarch Nikon's actions, which were supported by tsarist authorities, as the beginning of the Antichrist's rule (Crummey 1970). Moreover, the Antichrist and his presence in the world were an important subject of Russian philosophy of the late 19th century, which was then under the strong influence of Nietzsche's critique of Christianity. In their numerous works, authors and philosophers such as Dostoyevsky, Berdyaev, Solovyov, Rozanov, Merezhkovsky, and Leontiev appealed to the concept of the Antichrist as an allegory of immanent evil, present both in the human and the surrounding world (Korolev 2004, Ewertowski 2010). Since the introduction of Christianity in Russia, the concept of the Antichrist has been used to designate "the other" in many differ-

---

1  The split in Orthodox Church, triggered in 1653 by the reforms of Patriarch Nikon, who tried to establish uniformity between Greek and Russian practice.

ent contexts—e.g. theological, philosophical, literary, and historical. Russian historiosophy has seen the Antichrist in individual figures such as Napoleon, Rasputin and Peter the Great, in political and social systems such as Russian autocracy (*samoderzhavie*), socialism, communism or liberal democracy, and in social groups such as Roman Catholics, Jews, Muslims and (other) immigrants. Each epoch of Russian history created its own vision of Antichrist, visions which often have little in common with the Beast from the book of Revelation (Korolev 2004). Now, finally, the Antichrist is gay.

The different interpretations of the figure of the Antichrist in Russian history suggest that the social meaning of this rhetorical figure, as well as the normative and emotional responses he is supposed to evoke, are subject to change. While presented as quite a massive theological and social concept, the historical fluidity gives reason to suspect that in present-day discourses the rhetorical effects of the Antichrist may not be quite as unequivocal as intended. Indeed, his rhetorical function might at times even fail, opening up the heteronormative discourse he is supposed to support to "cracks" where, according to Michel Foucault (1998), the possibility for resistance resides. In this chapter we will therefore scrutinize present-day discursive formations of the Antichrist in Russia, not only focusing on how the notion of the Antichrist is employed by Russian religious nationalists, but also assessing its religious provenance in a secular context. We will first explain our use of the method of Critical Discourse Analysis. We will proceed by discussing the specificity of the space of Russian Internet, followed by a discussion of religious nationalism in general, and Orthodox nationalist approaches to homosexuality in particular. We will then present our materials, in which homosexuality is equated with the Antichrist in RuNet, and our analysis of how these equations may be understood. In the final paragraph we offer some concluding suggestions on how Antichrist-based heteronormative discourse may be understood and valued.

### Critical Discourse Analysis as a Set of "Conceptual Tools"

The theoretical approach in this chapter, Critical Discourse Analysis (CDA), forms a suitable point of departure for our research intentions, but is hard to pin down in a simple definition. According to Gilbert Weiss and Ruth Wodak (2003: 6), "there is no such thing as a uniform, common theory formation determining CDA." Other scholars dealing with CDA have similarly argued that this framework should be approached as a set of "conceptual tools" rather than a consistent theory (Van Dijk 1985, Mottier 2002). The main aim of these tools is to de-mystify ideologies implicitly embedded in a discourse, constructed in a certain socio-political context (Hajer 2006b, Van Dijk 2003, Fowler 2003). Therefore, above all, CDA should try to integrate sociological and linguistic positions, mediate between texts and institutions, as well as analyze communication and its structure (Weiss and Wodak 2003). Maarten Hajer (2006a) argues that discourse should be understood within CDA in a way proposed by Michel Foucault—as "patterns in social life." He defines discourse as an ensemble of ideas, concepts and categories, through which the meaning of phenomena is produced and reproduced (Hajer 2002). In this context, language is viewed as an important means of social power, which not only contains hidden patterns of discrimination and inequalities, but also mediates social values (Caldas-Coulthard 2003, Van Dijk 2003). Moreover, discourse reflects reality and simultaneously shapes it by creating meaning out of signs and symbols (Hajer 2006b). Therefore, signs and representations should never be approached as neutral or innocent (Caldas-Coulthard 2003, Weiss and Wodak 2003, Rochefort and Donnelly 2013).

Crucial to the study of the workings of language in CDA is attention to the power which is exercised through dominant discourses over what is rejected. Often such exclusions happen by ways of creating oppositions that give benefits to some groups in society at the expense of others. Jacob Torfing (2002: 9), for instance, argues that discourse "is a result of *hegemonic articulations* that aim to establish a political as well as moral-intellectual leadership in society." In his understanding, *hegemonic articulation* is mainly based on a construction of social antagonism that creates a threatening exterior in order to unify and stabilize internal discourse. Therefore, certain discursive strategies of altering "the other" often refer to "common evils" and are supposed to set clear boundaries between "us" and "them" to construct a national or a political identity (Torfing 2002; Mottier 2002).

Critical Discourse Analysis, while initially applied to the study of traditional discourses, can also be applied to media discourses. These, according to Carmen Rosa Caldas-Coulthard (2003: 274), are "culturally dependent and reflect what 'goes on' in society in many aspects." It means that media discourse is not only constructed by, but in turn also influences, social reality. Due to the asymmetrical relation between producers and recipients of media discourse, the controlling group may strongly influence the knowledge, attitudes and ideologies of the rest of society (Caldas-Coulthard 2003, Van Dijk 2003). The example of such a situation may be the development of policies on sexuality in the Russian Federation. Here, since the passing of the "anti gay-propaganda law,"[2]

---

2   A Federal Law signed by Vladimir Putin on July 30, 2013 in order to protect children from

sexual minorities are excluded from official discourse while their capability to participate in creating it was strictly limited. In this chapter, we intend to investigate how the rhetorical use of the figure of the Antichrist in religious nationalist discourses promotes certain social values rather than others, and how this creates a social reality in which different groups in society (notably religious nationalists and sexual minorities) are placed in opposition to one another.

### Uniqueness of RuNet

It is a truism to claim that in recent years the Internet has become a relevant medium of communication. "Web 2.0" has evolved from a static information platform to the site where information and opinions are mutually shared, and where to an increasing extent people's social lives take place. In this regard RuNet is no exception: it is one of the most important and developed parts of the global Web. In 2013 Russian exceeded German as the second most frequently used language on the Internet, following English (Gelbman 2013). One year later, in 2014, the portal The Runet estimated the audience of Russian Internet to stand at about 69 million users (The Runet 2014). Moreover, according to the project Runward:Track that analyzes platforms, instruments and technologies of the Russian Internet, in November 2014 there were almost 5 million pages with a .ru domain (Runward:Track 2014). The vivid evolution of the Russian Internet and the fact that the name of RuNet entered not only colloquial speech, but also academic discourse, shows the significant impact it has on different layers of Russian society.

The status of RuNet as an "object of research" is, however, complicated (Etling et al. 2010). First, it has to do with the many aspects present within the Internet as such and, second, with the unique character and relative isolation of the Russian segment of the Internet. Many scholars have pointed at its specific socio-cultural context (Alexanyan 2009, Etling et al. 2010, Nocetti 2011). RuNet can be seen as a social phenomenon defined by aspects as diverse as geography (Russian Federation), language (web-pages in Russian), or culture and tradition (Konradova and Schmidt 2014). And whereas some see RuNet predominantly

---

information popularizing the rejection of "traditional family values." Similar laws were passed before in some regions of the Russian Federation, among others St. Petersburg; in some regions this law was passed together with the laws against the "propaganda of pedophilia" (Federal'nyy zakon No. 135-FZ, 2013).

as a "social space," emphasizing its function as a platform for social exchange (Bowles 2006), others such as Zizi Papacharissi (2002) emphasize the collective function, considering RuNet to be a kind of "public sphere" and a "virtual mirror" reflecting social relations. By contrast, Floriana Fossato (2008) claims that the internet in Russia should be approached as an "adaptation tool" to a political reality which users otherwise consider inaccessible. Since the majority of Russian citizens perceive their influence on the political and economic situation to be marginal, RuNet may be the only platform that enables them to articulate explicit beliefs and ideas freely and influence reality in some way (Fossato 2008). Whichever approach is applied, it must be realized that in recent years RuNet has developed "from a free space of creative articulation, into a fully-fledged mass medium of a national significance" (Konradova and Schmidt 2014: 36).

Over the past years, however, Russian authorities have gradually attempted to reestablish a hierarchical structure through the Russian Internet, which considerably limits freedom of expression (Konradova Schmidt 2014). "Nationalization" as well as attempts to establish firmer and more sophisticated control over RuNet, in many respects aim at "recreating the state online" (Nocetti 2011). In this way, RuNet has become the subject of constant scrutiny from the Kremlin. Russian authorities perceive the Internet as a link between the public and the state. By investing in digital structures they not only intend to connect a maximum number of Russian citizens, but also to construct a "Russian identity formula" online. Nocetti (2011) argues that such endeavors construct an "imagined community" (Anderson 2006) which exceeds the Russian border and includes the Russian-speaking diaspora all over the world. In this line of argument, Dirk Uffelman (2014) approaches RuNet as a tool of "a Russian post-imperial thalassocracy" and a medium for colonization and imperialism. He claims that it not only has an ideological influence on Russian-speaking users of the Internet all over the globe, but may also be used as an instrument of extending "Russkiy mir"[3] and "Orthodox civilization."[4] At any rate, since the internet is significantly changing the dynamics of political communication in Russia (Etling et al. 2010), apart from quantitatively investigating its impact, RuNet

---

3   Russkiy mir: "Russian World"—the conception of the transnational community conjoining all Russian-speaking people who identify themselves with Russian culture. In this conception the Russian language is understood as the language of the "historical brotherhood of nations" that "preserves numerous world-wide achievements" (Tishkov 2007).

4   All transcriptions in the article are done according to the BGN/PCGN System (U.S. Board on Geographic Names and Foreign Names Committee Staff 1994: 93–94).

should be also analyzed as a kind of a "battlefield" of many various ideologies and discourses, where liberal and conservative, dominant and oppositional, religious and secular discourses clash (Kondratova Schmidt 2014).

### The Phenomenon of Religious Nationalism

Secularization theses have claimed that religion and religiosity were to disappear from the public space as a consequence of modernization. However, religious factors remain an important part of modern nation-building processes. Due to the great capability of religion as a constitutive element of nationalism as well as an effective mobilizing force, it still plays a significant role in contemporary states, especially in Central and Eastern Europe (Barker 2009). Since we suspect that both religious and nationalist motives underlie discourses of the Antichrist, it will be good to clarify how in this chapter we conceive of religious nationalism.

Nationalism, often called "secular religion," is a phenomenon that emerged in 19th century as a result of industrialization, modernization and the philosophy of romanticism that served as a reservoir of national myths (Gellner 1997). It was mainly based on the concept of "nationhood"—an "imagined" as well as an "invented" community (cf. Anderson 2006, Gellner 1997). Despite its secular character, as Anderson argued, nationalism understood as an ideology belongs to "kinship" and "religion" rather than to "liberalism" or "fascism." Both religion and nationalism provide society with its prophets, myths, rites, sacred spaces, social organization, and moral sanctions—as well as symbolic and real violence (Juergensmeyer 1994). Being both "ideologies of order," they may be perceived as potential rivals. However, since religion as well as nationalism respond to the same social need of belonging to a collective that enforces moral authority and ultimate loyalty, some scholars argue that they rather complement each other (Brubaker 2011, Friedland 2011).

Rogers Brubaker (2011) proposed four approaches to the interrelation between religion and nationalism: explaining nationalism through religious notions, tracing how religious traditions have shaped nationalism; considering religion to be a part of nationalism, and a specific combination of those two phenomena that resulted in the emergence of a "distinctive kind of nationalism"—religious nationalism. According to Brubaker, nationalism that derives Its values from religion proposes a certain program for ordering and regulating social, public and private life. Focusing on the questions of family, gender and sexuality in particular, it not only promotes restrictive regulations of sexuality, but also generates strict moral rules concerning social reproduction and socialization. In case of Russia, Juergensmeyer links the emergence of religiosity as well as religious nationalism to the collapse of the Soviet Union:

> It is no mystery why religious nationalism has become so popular at this moment in history. In times of social turbulence and political confusion, which the collapse of the Soviet Union and the decline of American economic power and cultural influence have created around the world new panaceas abound. It was inevitable that many of these would involve religion, sometimes perceived as the only stable point in a swirl of economic and political indirection.
>
> 1994: 194

Sudden political and social transformations, Juergensmeyer argues, led to the resurgence of identities based on religion and ethnicity. Therefore, the appearance of religious nationalism was a response to the failure of secular nationalism that turned out to be an insufficient mobilizing force in times of crises. In a similar vein, Barker (2009) and Kinnvall (2004) argue that "religious revival" as well as "the outburst of religious nationalism" may be understood as a social reaction to the sense of insecurity generated by industrialization, as well as the protest against globalization and unification. Individuals that feel insecure tend to search for self-affirmation within collectives. Hence, the strength of nationalism and religion lies not only in the fact that they are strong individual identity markers, but also "in their ability to convey unity, security and inclusiveness in times of crisis" (Kinnvall 2004: 762).

The search for unity, however, comes at a cost. Roger Friedland argues that religious nationalism has a tendency toward bodily violence and a regulation of sexuality which derives from the institutional logic of religion. As a collective religious subject the nation-state seeks to "subordinate sexuality to divine law" (2011: 13). Moreover, by adopting religious language and modes of communication, it provides societies with well-established ideologies as well as discursive practices that promote group homogeneity, moral purity and clear-cut separation from racial or sexual "others." Hereby, acceptance or refusal of homosexuality becomes a kind of "identity marker." As a result, sexuality is constructed through a normative framework used to establish a clear division between "us" and "the others" (Vikkurnen 2010, Van den Berg et al. 2014). When one particular nation or sexuality is favored by the state institutions, the other is automatically ostracized. In other words, if national identity is constructed as a "hetero-male project," homosexuals and women automatically become "others," excluded from the "brotherhood" (Mayer 2000).

## Orthodox Fundamentalism and Homosexuality

As mentioned above, the "return" of religion in the public sphere is noticeable in particular in Central and Eastern Europe (Barker 2009, Tomka 2006). Though this process followed different trajectories in different states, a common feature is that it was a social reaction to the uncertainty caused by a sudden transformation of the political and economic order, such as the fall of the USSR and ongoing processes of globalization (Tsereteli 2010), inciting an anti-Western attitude (Juergensmeyer 1994: 1). In order to understand religious nationalist discourses on sexuality and their relation to anti-Western discourse, the role of the Russian Orthodox Church (ROC) needs further discussion.

According to ROC authorities, with Patriarch Kiryll in the lead, only religion has the power to form the essential mindset, which helps to stand against Western trends, lifestyle models and behavior patterns inseminating Russian society through media.

The ROC, then, is perceived as a "reservoir of the true Russian values and national soul," and has become one of the crucial public institutions, not only playing an important role in establishing attitudes toward minorities and opponents, but also influencing many spheres of Russian public life. The ROC and its followers regularly stood against gay parades in Moscow, contributed to the cancellation of the art exhibition "Ostrozhno, religiya!"[5] in 2003 and protested against "immoral" TV programs (Zhukova 2010, Van der Veer 1994, Ryklin 2006, Tsereteli 2010). According to Verkohvsky (2002, 2014) these are examples of how the ROC in many regards contributed to the dispersion of "aggressive nationalism" in contemporary Russia.

The rhetoric of the most radical and extreme wing within the ROC, "Orthodox fundamentalism," is strongly intertwined with national-patriotic movements and shares their attitudes toward democracy, liberalism and sexual morality (Kostyuk 2000, Verkhovsky 2002). It is one of the most influential variants of religious nationalism in Russia (de Lazari 1995). The ideology of Russian Orthodox fundamentalism is mainly based on mythologized notions and con-

---

5   The exhibition "Beware, Religion!," organized in 2004 in the Sakharov Centre for Human Rights, criticized "the mass perception of religious doctrines and iconography in contemporary Russia, where the Russian Orthodox Church has gradually replaced the old Communist party" (Zinik 2004). Shortly after its opening, the exhibition was vandalized by a group of religious nationalists supported by the Russian Orthodox Church's hierarchy. However, vandals were not the ones to be punished—soon after the happenings, the organizers of the exhibition together with the director of the Sakharov Centre were sued for "inciting of religious and racial hatred" (Zinik 2004, Ryklin 2006).

cepts derived from religious discourse. It is characterized by a negative attitude toward plurality, the West and Judaism. It concentrates instead on the eschatological role of "Holy Russia," and perceives the non-Orthodox world as ruled by the Antichrist (Verkhovsky 2003, Steeves 1994).

One of the most important identity markers of Russian religious nationalism, both in its moderate and its radical form, is its attitude toward (homo)sexuality. Appealing to nationalistic and xenophobic sentiments, the Kremlin and the ROC managed to mobilize Russian society successfully against "the nation's other"—in this case homosexual minorities (Greene and Robertson, 2004). In the context of the fight over "national purity" and "traditional Russian values" based on Orthodoxy, nationalists and religious activists portray themselves as the only force able to save the Russian Federation from the "global gay"—which in the majority of their discursive strategies is used to personify "Western cultural imperialism" (Virkkunen 2010). It seems, however, that more than "just" the rights of sexual minorities or the defense of the traditional family is at stake. Joni Virkkunen (2010) argues that the clashes between LGBT movements and religious nationalists in the Russian Federation could be interpreted as an illustration of ideological disputes within the entire Russian society. Numerous protests against "homosexual propaganda" are not only the result of "overall" homophobia of society, in which the "heteronormative character of the contemporary Russian state" is propagated, but also serve as instruments of national and territorial bordering. In this context the discussion on (homo)sexuality may be considered to be an excuse to control or influence "wider matters of social change and national identity" (Virkkunen 2010: 3).

### Is the Antichrist Gay?

Despite the fact that nationalists and religious activists in Russia promote an archaic and traditional outlook, the main channel through which their ideology reaches recipients is modern. Online, the border between the religious community and beyond is often crossed. Numerous interviews, analyses, scientific and quasi-scientific articles dealing with the problem of (homo)sexuality and religious nationalism in Russia may be found not only on Orthodox web-pages and blogs,[6] but also on official news portals.[7] This vast number of websites admin-

---

6   For example: http://www.pravmir.ru/, http://www.etika-prav.ru/, http://www.mgarsky
    -monastery.org/, http://www.zaweru.ru/, http://www.logoslovo.ru, and many others.

7   In this article content published on Vzglady http://www.vz.ru; Russia.net http://www.russia
    .net; and Russkie Novosti http://ru-news.ru/ were analyzed.

istered by Orthodox fundamentalists as well as other web-pages promoting analogous content in RuNet, may be the indicator of its ideological success in contemporary Russian society (Kostyuk 2000). Orthodox fundamentalist discourse predominately labels homosexuality as an abomination (Valeckiy 2011), a parasitic minority (Via-Midgrad 2012), a serious psychological illness (Zametalov 2010) or a plague (Newsland 2010). Perhaps the strongest term used to condemn homosexuality, however, has been referring to gays, lesbians and their supporters as the Antichrist. This labelling, and its symbolic and social implications, will be discussed in detail below.

One of the examples in which homosexuality is associated with the Antichrist and anti-Christian values, is a video circulating online, in which a prominent Russian journalist, Maksim Schevchenko, sharply criticizes French authorities for passing the law that legalizes same-sex marriages and enables same-sex couples to adopt children. Schevchenko argues that the law was passed against the will of the majority of French citizens, and jeopardizes the condition that "a human and the human law remain human." Moreover, he labels people supporting same-sex marriages as "servants of the Antichrist":

> I believe that this is a step toward the creation of a man of the Antichrist's era, the servant of the Antichrist, a man who is a held hostage by his own desires, wishes of which hostage he is, and which will determine the political formats of life.
>
> SCHEVCHENKO 2013

According to Schevchenko, passing the same-sex marriage law is evidence that the prophecy from the Book of Revelation finally finds its fulfillment— whereas religious people in secular Western Europe are prohibited to exhibit their faith, "homosexuals—harlots and sodomites" can openly display their "proclivities." Therefore, contemporary Europe is for Schevchenko the "anti-Christian space," the Kingdom of Sin, against which Russia has to defend itself. In this context, the French law sets the clear border between the Russian Federation and the world, which "pulverizes humanity in a human" and "makes contemporary human-alike beings hostages of their own passions." In his speech, Schevchenko not only strictly separates Russia and Western Europe, but also dehumanizes the homosexual minority.

> The response of the Russian Orthodox Church to the decision of the Evangelical Lutheran Church in Sweden to bless the single-sex unions in 2005, too, expressed a negative attitude toward homosexuality. The Holy Synod of the Russian Orthodox Church with "great disappointment" decided to

suspend relations with the Lutheran Church in Sweden. The resolution was justified with reference to the Base of the Social Concept of the Russian Orthodox Church from 2000, according to which any expression of homosexual propaganda should be condemned.

Pravoslaviye i mir 2009

In the public statement, the Smolensk and Kaliningrad Metropolitan of that time, Kiryll, who in 2009 become the Patriarch of the Russian Orthodox Church, claimed that after accepting homosexual marriages, the next step of Western societies will be "a discussion suggesting that pedophilia should be recognized as a norm." He described the acceptance of homosexuality as a result of the Antichrist's influence:

> The Antichrist will teach evil, teach that killing and violence are good. One would think: who would accept such a leader? However, today, it is being implemented in our consciousness that there is no objective difference between sin and virtue as in many countries same-sex marriages and normal marriages are legally placed on the same level.

Pravoslaviye i mir 2009

Following that line of argumentation, Olga Nikolaevna Chetverikova (2013), professor of Moscow State Institute of International Relations,[8] claims that the Antichrist will attain his power through the relativization and softening of true Christian values. In an interview with the portal Vzglady, she stated that such a process may already be observed in the Roman Catholic Church where, according to her, the Second Vatican Council had initiated a serious crisis of the Christian world-view. The election of Jorge Mario Bergoglio as the Pope was, according to Chetverikova, the consequence of this preceeding demoralization, intensified by the process of globalization and the dissemination of liberal values. As she argues, by accepting divorces, abortion, contraception and homosexual marriages, Pope Francis not only attempts to destroy the Catholic Church, but also to marginalize the influences of Christianity in Western Europe. Not only reforms undertaken by the Pope are perceived by Chetverikova as a potential threat to "true Christianity." She also argues that the global system of values, based on the principles of humanism, as established and maintained by such institutions as the Council of Europe or UNESCO, have resulted in considering tolerance to be a "new religious dogma." Broadening the outreach of this "new

---

8  One of the most prestigious institutions of higher education in Russia. http://www.mgimo.ru/.

religion" by means of globalization practices of Western elites, referred to by Chetverikova as "the Anglo-Saxons," tries to establish a new world order.

According to her, the ultimate consequence of this process will be the coming of the Antichrist:

> The Anglo-Saxons are now playing the role of globalists-destroyers, because the task of the organizers of the new order is now to maximize a disassembly. Then the Anglo-Saxons will finish and a figure, who will unite and reconcile, will come. After all, the antichrist will be a reconciler (from the fallen church, according to our tradition). This is why now there is a need to create an image of the Roman Pope as a reconciler in all this chaos, a sacred figure, embodying the image of a religious leader of all mankind. The Pope is for everyone—poor and rich, Christians and Muslims, believers and sinners.

Although Chetverikova does not explicitly label Pope Francis as the Antichrist, in the narration presented in the interview on the portal Vzglady, such a connection is easily recognized. Hence, Chetverikova not only clearly distinguishes "contaminated" Western Christianity and "pure Orthodox faith," but she also refers to the antagonism between two Christian churches that derives from the "Great Schism" in eleventh century. Like Maksim Schevchenko and Patriarch Kiryll, Olga Chetverikova considers "homosexual propaganda" to be a threat to the Russian Federation. Moreover, she argues that the prohibition of "gay propaganda among children" and resistance against "the dictatorship of tolerance" may be insufficient measures to restrain "the attack" of "anti-Christian" powers. According to her, the only effective "weapon" against dissolving true Christian values is to "call things by their names" and resist both external and internal hostile forces.

Other authors also point out the fact that acceptance of same-sex marriages foreshadows the Antichrist's coming. One of them is Oleg Valeckiy, who argues that sexual perversions are the instrument of political impact. In his text, published on the portal Russkiye Novosti, Valeckiy claims that LGBT movements have always been interrelated with anti-Christianity and heresy. Therefore homosexuality, and other sexual deviations, should be considered to be an element of a greater strategy that mainly aims at destroying Christian morals in Russian society. In this regard, the acceptance of same-sex marriages is the symptom of "Western societies' decay" as well as an omen of the Antichrist:

> According to the Christian logic, God allows such "revelries" as a punishment for man's sins, namely for what a man himself has come to. In

the past Romanian (Byzantine) Empire as well as in Ancient Rus' that adopted Orthodoxy, sexual perversions, of course known then as well, if they were generally accepted in the society, they were considered to be the last step to the rules of the Antichrist. Popular at this time, the "Revelation of Mefodiy Patarskiy" also describes the arrival of Antichrist, the important sign of which will be incest, representing for the author of "Revelation" an absolute evil ...

VALECKIY 2011

The Old Testament is another source where one can find anticipations of the arrival of the Antichrist. Leonid Kanochkin refers to the book of Daniel, the prophet in exile who in the eleventh chapter of his biblical book foresees a period of conflict and the rule of the "oppressor" (verse 20) who will do as he pleases. In verse 37 of that chapter, which Kanochkin literally quotes, it is stated that this oppressor "[...] will show no regard for the gods of his fathers *or for the desire of women*, nor will he show regard for any other god, for he will magnify himself above all."[9] From this verse, Kanochkin concludes that a political leadership can be imagined (and feared) in which non-traditional sexualities will be accepted. Such leadership, to Kanochkin, would require a degenerate society that accepts a deviant sexual moralality:

But since the time of Sodom and Gomorrah, homosexuals have never had the authority in society and it has never been possible that an open homosexual would be the leader, who would attract people. However, we know that the antichrist will be a leader attracting a huge mass of people. To make this possible, there has to take place a revolution in the consciousness of people. They should change their negative attitude towards homosexuality into a positive one. This is exactly what is happening now.

KANOCHKIN 2008

Another prophecy, this time by Nil Afonskiy Mirotochivyy, is evoked in an article published on the portal Zaveru. The prophesies of this 17th century saint have been extensively quoted and re-published by Orthodox fundamentalist

---

9   Taken from the New American Standard Bible, italics by the authors. Other translations have a different interpretation of the phrase "desire of women." The Contemporary English Version for instance speaks of "the god preferred by women," while the Good News Translation speaks of "the god that women love."

movements after the collapse of the Soviet Union. In this case his prophetic words are cited in an article that portrays homosexuality as illness and elaborates on the methods of treating it:

> By the middle of the 20th century, the people of that time will start to become unrecognizable. When the time of the Antichrist's arrival approaches, the people's minds will be darkened from the passions of the flesh and the lust and lawlessness will increase. The world will become unrecognizable, and it will be impossible to distinguish clearly man from woman, because of the shamelessness in clothes and haircut. These people will be wild and violent, like animals, because of the temptation of the Antichrist. There will be no respect for parents and elders, love will disappear. Christian pastors, bishops and priests will become vainglorious people, who cannot distinguish right from left. Then the customs and traditions of Christians and the Church will change. Modesty and chastity will disappear among people, and adultery and promiscuity will rule. Lies and avarice will reach an upper level, and woe unto them who amass treasures. Fornication, adultery, sodomy, secret affairs, theft and murder will rule in society.

Overall, homosexuality is associated not only with the Antichrist as an individual, but also with all the forces that are adverse to Orthodox Christianity.

Nevertheless, equating same-sex love with Antichrist is not the sole discursive strategy used by nationalist and religious movements—in RuNet one can find articles, in which homosexuals are portrayed as the servants of the dark forces. One of the examples is the article of Sergey Novokhatatskiy (2009):

> Although homosexuals externally resemble normal people, we are essentially dealing with a non-human, with the seed of antichrist. These are a special kind of intelligent animals, who are very similar to humans, but will never become one.

Novokhatatskiy not only labels sexual minorities as "seed of Antichrist," but also dehumanizes them. In that sense his is the firmest statement that we encountered: sexual minorities are not equated with Western values, the non-Russian or the non-Orthodox, but the non-human, and in this sense placed outside humankind.

## Conclusion

Is the Antichrist gay? On many occasions contemporary religious nationalism in Russia equates the (coming of) the Antichrist with sexual minorities
or the acceptance of non-hetero relationships. But the figure of the Antichrist
is believed to denote more, and the figurative speech is stretched to the whole
of society. Not just gays and lesbians, but also those who support them and
their legal rights, may count on the accusation of introducing the apocalypse
in Russia. Religious nationalist discourse seems to rely heavily on a number of
oppositions: gay/straight, Western/Eastern, non-Orthodox/Orthodox and, ultimately, non-human/human. As a result, issues like sexual orientation, national
identity and church denomination become intertwined. Homosexuality, western values and all non-Orthodox Christian traditions have become a package
deal. Moreover, as these oppositions become more and more entangled, they
come to strengthen each other. The Antichrist functions as an "all-purpose
word" that brings these different elements together and provides their mingling
with an internal logic and the emotional charge of ultimate evil. To resist such
a strong heteronormative discourse becomes a complicated task. The issue of
LGBT rights cannot be addressed in itself. Any lobbying for the right of sexual
minorities will necessarily also have to deal with nationalism and Orthodoxy.

The rhetorical strength of the figure of the Antichrist lies therein, first,
that he is not a stranger to Russian ears. In the introduction we have already
discussed the many shapes the Antichrist has taken in Russian history, and
though the often-foretold apocalypse is still awaited, this does not keep new
generations of Russian church leaders away from finding new incarnations of
the Antichrist in society. As diverse as interpretations of the Antichrist have
been, a common denominator is this: the Antichrist is "that which we do not
want to be." The Antichrist has thus become a religious concept that has many
secular connotations, a concept that can connect the religious and the secular.
In fact, it is a religious concept that has a long tradition of being used in defining
that which is secular, that which is outside of the borders of the (true) church
and thereby outside of the definition of what is truly Russian. As such, it is
incredibly useful in connecting nationalism and religion.

In addition, the Antichrist is a concept which does not require much Biblical
or traditional knowledge among the readership. In its combining of a massive
moral charge (describing ultimate evil) with secular implications (denoting the
non-Russian), it can function without being embedded in a well-thought-out
theological system, or foreknowledge of such a system. Sources such as the
Bible and religious authorities from the Russian Orthodox tradition are called
on, but these references are often wrenched from their contexts. Kanochkin's

use of the book of Daniel for instance, discussed earlier, is based on theology that has no regard for the historical or cultural context in which the text was written.

We would, however, like also to argue that the Antichrist does not always fulfill his rhetorical duties in religious nationalist discourse. On the Russian Internet, we get acquainted with a different face of the Antichrist which is not easily limited to "pure evil." The Antichrist we encounter is also an individual who will connect people, attract people. His words will sound right and reasonable. The Antichrist symbolizes not so much obvious evil, but evil that presents itself as good. This implies that the authors presume that their readership do not necessarily agree that the persons or social changes described in terms of the Antichrist (LGBT rights, Western values, non-Orthodox Christian faith) are wrong. The sexual morality through which the Russian national identity is negotiated is not automatically shared by the Russian users of the Internet. The authors, in turn, may be presumed at least to some extent to be able to understand why their readers would feel attracted to different values of sexuality, religion and national identity. Should there be any Foucauldian cracks in religious nationalist discourse of the Antichrist, it could be localized here: that the good through which the Antichrist presents himself is at least recognized and perhaps partly shared by those who invoke him to warn against his hidden evil agenda.

Finally: religious nationalists, by altering "the other" as the Antichrist, attempt to mobilize society against a common enemy—the homosexual minority. The underlying motives, however, might be more complex than "mere" homophobia. According to Mariya Akhmetova (2010), appealing to the Apocalypse or eschatological visions is a symptom of crisis. Evoking archetypes such as Antichrist of the Apocalypse aims at explaining complex problems in an easy way. In this context, homophobia may be a factor consoling a society traumatized not only by the collapse of the Soviet Union, but also by the ideological and economic crisis of the 1990s. It is much easier to explain failures by means of "homosexual plots" than to introduce reforms. The strategy for resistance may also be found in developing ways of confirming Russian identity, while addressing such national traumas without falling back on oppositional pairings and othering practices.

### References

Akhmetova, Mariya. 2010. *Konec sveta v odnoy otdelno vzyatoy strane*. Moskva: Obedinennoe Gumanitarnoe Izdatelstvo.

Akopov, Petr, and Chetverikova, Ol'ga Nikolayevna. 2013. "Vatikan razmyvayet khristian-skiye tsennosti." *Vzglyady.ru*. November, 7. Retrieved September 18, 2014. http://www .vz.ru/world/2013/11/7/658459.html.

Alexanyan Karina. 2009. "The RuNet—Lost In Translation." *Russian Analytical Digest*, No. 69, 2–4. Retrieved September 17, 2014. http://www.css.ethz.ch/publications/ pdfs/RAD-69.pdf.

Anderson, Benedict. 2006. *Imagined Communities*. London: Verso.

Barker, Philip W. 2009. *Religious Nationalism in Modern Europe: If God Be With Us*. New York: Routledge.

Bowles, Anna. 2006. *The Changing Face of the Runet*. Retrieved September 18, 2014. http://tepaardnaarsintpetersburg.nl/wordpress/wp-content/uploads/2012/10/runet -today-an-abstract-by-Bowles.pdf.

Brubaker, Rogers. 2011. "Religion and Nationalism: Four Approaches." *Nations and Nationalism*. Retrieved 16 September, 2014. http://www.sscnet.ucla.edu/soc/faculty/ brubaker/Publications/religion_and_nationalism_forthcoming.pdf.

Caldas-Coulthard, Carmen Rosa. 2003. "Cross-Cultural Representation of 'Otherness' in Media Discourse". Pp. 272–296 in G. Weiss and R. Wodak (eds.), *Critical Discourse Analysis: Theory and Interdisciplinarity*. Hampshire: Palgrave Macmillian.

Crummey, Robert. 1970. *Old Believers and the World of Antichist*. Madison: University of Wisconsin Press.

De Lazari, Andrzej. 1995. *Czy Moskwa będzie Trzecim Rzymem?* Katowice: Śląsk

Etling, Bruce, Karina Alexanyan, John Kelly, Robert Faris, John Palfrey and Urs Gasser. 2010. "Public Discourse in the Russian Blogosphere: Mapping RuNet Politics and Mobilization." *Berkman Center Research Publication*, No. 2010–2011. Retrieved 18 September, 2014. http://cyber.law.harvard.edu/teaching/ilaw/2011/sites/teaching/ images/Public_Discourse_in_the_Russian_Blogosphere_2010.pdf.

Ewartowski, Stefan. 2010. *Idea Antychrysta w kulturze współczesnej*. Olsztyn: Studio Poligrafii Komputerowej "SQL".

*Federal'nyy zakon № 135-FZ*. 2013. Retrieved 18 September, 2014. http://mhg-monitoring .org/sites/default/files/files/fz_no135_ot_30.06.2013_zashchita_detey_ot_informacii .pdf.

Fossato, Floriana. 2009. "Discussion: Is Runet the Last Adaptation Tool?" *Russian Cyberspace* 1(1). Retrieved September 14, 2014. http://www.digitalicons.org/issue01/pdf/ issue1/Web-as-an-Adaptation-Tool_N-Fossato.pdf.

Foucault, Michel. 1998. *The Will to Knowledge: The History of Sexuality*, vol. I. London: Penguin Books.

Fowler, Roger. 2003. "On Critical Linguistic." Pp. 3–14 in C.R. Caldas-Coulthard and M. Coulthard (eds). *Text and Practices: Readings in Critical Discourse Analysis*. London: Routledge.

Friedland, Roger. 2011. "The Institutional Logic of Religious Nationalism: Sex, Violence and the Ends of History." *Politics, Religion Ideology*, 12(1). Retrieved 10 September, 2014. http://www.religion.ucsb.edu/Faculty/Ends2011.pdf.

Gelbmann, Matthias. 2013. "Russian is now the second most used language on the web." Retrieved September 18, 2014. http://w3techs.com/blog/entry/russian_is_now _the_second_most_used_language_on_the_web.

Gellner, Ernest. 1997. *Nationalism*. New York: New York University Press.

Greene, Samuel A., and Graeme B. Robertson. 2014. "Identity, Nationalism, and the Limits of Liberalism in Russian Popular Politics." *PONARS Eurasia Policy Memo* No. 323 Retrieved September 14, 2014. http://www.ponarseurasia.org/sites/default/files/ policy-memos-pdf/Pepm323_GreeneRobertson_June2014.pdf.

Hajer, Maarten A. 2002. "Discourse Analysis and the Study of Policy Making." Pp. 61–65 in J. Newell and M. Rhodes (eds.) *Discourse Analysis and Political Science* Florence: European Consortium for Political Research.

———. 2006a. "Doing Discourse Analysis: Coalitions, Practices, Meaning". Pp. 65–74 in M. van den Brink and T. Metze (eds.) *Words Matter in Policy and Planning: Discourse Theory and Method in Social Sciences*. Utrecht: Netherlands Graduate School of Urban and Regional Research.

———. 2006b. "Ordering Through Discourse." Pp. 251–268 in M. Moran, M. Rein, and R. Goodlin (eds.) *The Oxford Handbook of Public Policy*. New York: Oxford University Press.

Juergensmeyer, Mark. 1994. *The New Cold War?: Religious Nationalism Confronts the Secular State. Comparative Studies in Religion and Society*. Berkeley: University of California Press.

Kanochkin, Leonid. 2008. "Gomoseksualizm v sovremennom mire." Retrieved September 18, 2014. http://www.foru.ru/slovo.18165.1.html.

Kinnvall, Catarina. 2004. "Globalization and Religious Nationalism: Self, Identity, and Search for Ontological Security." *Political Psychology* 25(5). Retrieved August 31, 2014. http://identities.org.ru/readings/Religion_globalsiation_and.pdf.

Konradova, Natalija, and Henrike Schmidt. 2014. "From the Utopia of Authonomy to a Political Battelfield of the 'Russian Internet'." Pp. 34–54 in M.S. Gorham, I. Lunde, and P. Pulsen (eds) *Digital Russia: The Language, Culture and Politics of New Media Communication*. New York: Routledge Chapman Hall.

Korolev, Vardan B. 2004. "Obraz antikhrista v russkoy istoriosofskoy mysli." Retrieved September 18, 2014. http://www.pravaya.ru/faith/11/74.

Kostyuk, Konstantin. 2000. "Pravoslavnyy fundamentalizm: sotsial'nyy portret i istoki." *Polis No. 5*. Retrieved September 10, 2014. http://krotov.info/libr_min/11_k/os/tyuk .htm.

Mayer, Tamar. 2000. "Gender Ironies of Nationalism: Setting the Stage." Pp. 1–33 in T. Mayer (ed.) *Gender Ironies of Nationalism: Sexing the Nation*. London: Routledge.

Mottier, Véronique. 2002. "Discourse Analysis and the Politics of Identity/Difference."

Pp. 57–60 in J. Newell and M. Rhodes (eds.) *Discourse Analysis and Political Science*, Florence: European Consortium for Political Research.

Newsland. 2010. "Yevrope khochet·sya podelit'sya s det'mi prelestyami gomoseksualizma." Retrieved November 2, 2014. http://newsland.com/news/detail/id/566014/.

Nocetti, Julien. 2011. "Digital Kremlin: Power and the Internet in Russia." *Russia/NIS Center*. Retrieved September 10, 2014. http://www.ifri.org/downloads/ ifrinocettirussianwebengmars2011.pdf.

Novokhtatskiy, Sergey. 2009. "Golubyye rastiteli- v liberal'nom zakone." Retrieved September 18, 2014. http://pomnimvse.com/296pb.html.

Papacharissi, Zizi. 2002. "The Virtual Sphere: The Internet as a Public Sphere." *New Media Society*, 4 (9): 9–27.

Rochefort, David A. and Kevin P. Donnelly. 2013. "Agenda-Setting and Political Discourse: Major Analytical Frameworks and Their Application." Pp. 189–203 in E. Ararar et al. (eds.) *Routledge Handbook of Public Policy*. London: Routledge.

The Runet. 2014. "Pul's Runeta." Retrieved November 25, 2014. http://therunet.com/ pulse.

Ryklin, Mikhail. 2006. *Svastika, krest, zvezda. Proizvedeniye iskusstva v epokhu upravlya-yemoy demokrati*. Moscow: Logos.

Pravoslaviye i mir. 2009. "Ne-Zakonnoye venchaniye." Retrieved September 18, 2004 http://www.pravmir.ru/katolicheskie-i-pravoslavnye-cerkvi-shvecii-osudili -reshenie-lyuteranskoj-cerkvi-strany-o-venchanii-odnopolyx-par/.

Shevchenko, Maksim. 2013. "Gei kak oruzhiye antikhrista" [Video file]. Retrieved September 1, 2014. http://www.russia.ru/hero/shevchenko/.

Steeves, Paul D. 1994. "Russian Orthodox Facism after Glasnost." Presented at the Conference on Faith and History. Harrisburg, Pennsylvania, 8 October 1994. Retrieved 25 November, 2014. http://www2.stetson.edu/~psteeves/rusorthfascism.html.

Tishkov, Valeriy. 2007. "Russkiy mir: smysl i strategii." *Strategiya Rossii*. Retreived September 2, 2014. http://sr.fondedin.ru/new/fullnews_arch_to.php?subaction= showfullid=1185274651archive=1185275035start_from=ucat=14.

Torfing, Jacob. 2002. "Discourse Analysis and Post-structuralism of Laclau and Mouffle." Pp. 54–56 in J. Newell and M. Rhodes (eds.) *Discourse Analysis and Political Science*. Florence: European Consortium for Political Research.

Track.Ruward. 2014. "Sistemy veb-analitiki." Retrieved November 25, 2014. http://track .ruward.ru/analytics.

Tsereteli, Tamar. 2010. *Nationalism and Representations of Gays and Lesbians in Post-Soviet Georgia*. Master's Thesis, Department of Gender Studies, Central European University. Retrieved August 21, 2014. http://minority.ge/wp-content/uploads/2010/ 12/Tsereteli-Tamar-nationalism-and-the-representation-of-gl-in-georgia.pdf.

Uffelman, Dirk. 2014. "Is There a Russian Cyber Empire?" Pp. 266–284 in M.S. Gorham, I. Lunde, and P. Pulsen (eds.) *Digital Russia. The Language, Culture and Politics of New Media Communication*. New York: Routledge Chapman Hall.

U.S. Board on Geographic Names Foreign Names Committee Staff. 1994. *Romanization systems and Roman-Script Spelling Conventions*. Retrieved September 11, 2014. http://libraries.ucsd.edu/bib/fed/USBGN_romanization.pdf.

Valeckiy, Oleg. 2011. "Seksual'nyye izvrashcheniya kak instrument politicheskogo vliyaniya." *Russkiye Novosti*. Retrieved September 18, 2014. http://ru-news.ru/seksualnye-izvrashheniya-kak-instrument-politicheskogo-vliyaniya/.

Van Dijk, Teun. 1985. "Critical Discourse Analysis." Pp. 352–371 in D. Tannen, D. Shiffrin, and H. Hamilton (eds) *Handbook of Discourse Analysis*. Oxford: Blackwell.

———. 2003. "Discourse, Power and Access." Pp. 84–104 in C.R. Caldas-Coulthard and M. Coulthard (eds.) *Text and Practices: Readings in Critical Discourse Analysis*. London: Routledge.

Van den Berg, Mariecke, David J. Bos, Marco Derks, Ruard R. Ganzevoort, Milos Jovanovic, Anne-Marie Korte, and Srdjan Sremac. 2014. "Religion, Homosexuality, and Contested Social Orders in the Netherlands, the Western Balkans, and Sweden." Pp. 116–134 in *Religion in Times of Crisis*, edited by G. Ganiel, H. Winkel, C. Monnot. Leiden: Brill.

Van der Veer, Peter. 1994. *Religious Nationalism*. Berkeley: University of California Press.

Verkhovsky, Aleksandr. 2002. "The Role of the Russian Orthodox Church in Nationalists, Xenophobic and Antiwestern Tendencies in Russia Today: Not Nationalism but Fundamentalism." *Religion, State and Society* 30(4). Retrieved September 17, 2014. http://biblicalstudies.org.uk/pdf/rss/30-4_333.pdf.

———. 2003. "The Orthodox in the Russian Radical Nationalist Movements." SOVA *Center*. Retrieved November 25, 2014. http://www.sova-center.ru/en/religion/publications/2003/04/d354/.

Via-Midgrad. 2012. "Ot gomoseksualizma do pedofilii." Retrieved September 18, 2014. http://via-midgard.info/blogs/18398-ot-gomoseksualizma-do-pedofilii.html.

Virkkunen, Joni. 2010. "Politics of Pride: Ethnosexual Conflict of Nationalisms in post-Soviet Russia." Retrieved November 23, 2014. http://www.eastbordnet.org/working_papers/open/documents/Virkkunen_Politics_of_Pride_101105.pdf.

Weiss, Gilbert, and Ruth Wodak. 2003. "Introduction: Theory, Interdisciplinarity and Critical Discourse Analysis." Pp. 1–32 in *Critical Discourse Analysis: Theory and Interdisciplinarity*. Hampshire: Palgrave Macmillian.

Zametalov, Artem. 2010. "Vsya pravda o gomoseksualizme." Retrieved September 18, 2014. http://www.existense.ru/vsya-pravda-o-gomoseksualizme.html.

Zaveru. "Lecheniye khomoseksualizma." Retrieved November 25, 2014. http://www.zaweru.ru/news/1459-.html.

Zhukova, Ludmila. 2010. "Religion and Ideology in Modern Russia." Retrieved September 1, 2014. https://src-h.slav.hokudai.ac.jp/rp/publications/no13/13_5-1_Zhukova.pdf.

Zinik, Zinovy. 2004. "The Neighbors Hence." Retrieved January 15, 2015. http://old.sakharov-center.ru/museum/exhibitionhall/religion_notabene/zzinik2004.htm.

# CHAPTER 8

# Religion, Homosexuality and Nationalism in the Western Balkans: The Role of Religious Institutions in Defining the Nation

*Tamara Pavasović Trošt and Koen Slootmaeckers*

While the relative closed-mindedness of South East European societies towards LGBT issues (Takacs and Szalma 2011, Uitz 2012) has been a topic of much interest among researchers, the question of the interaction between national and ethnic identities on the one hand, and homosexuality on the other, has received less attention. Yet, it is precisely during highly public debates on LGBT rights where the most vocal opponents of LGBT rights receive a platform to voice their opposition. The discourse used in justifying anti-LGBT attitudes is frequently *explicitly national or ethnic in character*: Homosexuality is, in this discourse, directly tied to what it means to be a "true" member of a nation, or of espousing values compatible with the nation's ethnic and cultural identity. Arguments against LGBT rights—most heavily employed in recent discourse regarding the Pride parades in Serbia and Montenegro and the referendum on marriage in Croatia—frequently utilize nationalist rhetoric and call for preserving the "true" Serbian/Croatian nation against Western "ailments" such as homosexuality. When this kind of nationalist rhetoric is embraced by religious institutions as "defenders" (or representatives) of the nation, this interplay becomes even more relevant. Thus, in addition to the anti-gay arguments found in such debates in other geographical contexts, in the Balkans the national and ethnic dimension becomes particularly salient. As such, examining the relationship between religious institutions and homosexuality, in particular in their reliance on nationalism and ethnic identity arguments, is of high relevance.

In this chapter, we survey the relationship between religious institutions, nationalism and homosexuality, by examining how the major religious institutions in Bosnia and Herzegovina, Croatia, Montenegro and Serbia are playing a role in defining the nation through their statements about homosexuality. Considering the increasing prominence of religious institutions in everyday life in post-Yugoslav countries and the rising rates of religiosity in general, the examination of how these prominent institutions play a role in defining discourse about the nation (and accordingly, who does and does not belong in this idea of the nation) is of central relevance to nationalism research.

The importance of the connection between sexuality and nationalism is by now well-established by researchers: "sex and nation combine to produce notions, both real and imagined, of other nationalities' sexual character and threat, and ideals of virility, fecundity and respectability" (Pryke 1998: 529).[1] The interconnections between sexuality and nationalism include national sexual stereotypes, the issue of sexuality in times of conflict and sex during nation building. These in turn raise other intricate questions, such as the definition of nations through gendered sexuality(Pryke 1998: 531, see also Žarkov 1995). They also include discussions of who belongs to the nation and who does not, and particularly whether the advancement of LGBT rights is compatible with this imagined nation (Van den Berg et al. 2014). Nationalist rhetoric frequently draws upon notions of sexuality in identity-making ways: "nationalist rhetoric centered around homosexuality promises to deliver to the nation what is most elusive: identity" (Dudink 2011: 263). This is particularly stark in the Balkans, where discourse about the LGBT community is directly connected with core national questions: patriotism and religion, economic problems, poverty, the Kosovo crisis, and EU integration (Van den Berg et al. 2014).

Indeed, public claims about national and sexual identities can influence the degree to which those identities are compatible or not. Sexual diversity can be presented as a complement to national identity, if the national identity is centered upon virtues of tolerance or diversity (such as in the case of Sweden or the Netherlands; see Puar's [2007] work on *homonationalism*). It can also be seen as incompatible with a particular national identity, when identity claims are based on masculinity and purity as in the Balkans (Van den Berg et al. 2014). In either case, "debates about religion and homosexuality serve to define the nation's cultural identity, including some groups and excluding others," where religious groups make the struggle over homosexuality issues a salient identity marker (Van den Berg et al. 2014: 116; see also Bates 2004, Cobb 2006). As such, the discourse utilized by religious officials becomes particularly important. This chapter examines religious institutions in the Balkans (specifically the Catholic Church in Croatia, the Serbian Orthodox Church in Serbia and Montenegro, and the Islamic Community in Bosnia) and how they are playing a role in *defining the nation* through their statements about homosexuality. The contribution of this chapter is that, unlike previous studies examining the relationship between sexual and religious identities via implicit "othering," we

---

1   For a discussion of the challenges of studying nationalism and sexuality, as well as a review of previous works on this topic, see Pryke (1998).

focus on instances where who "belongs" to the nation—and what belonging to the nation means—is explicitly discussed, and whether and how these discursive strategies vary across the region.

In the following sections, we first provide a theoretical overview of the literature on nationalism and sexuality, focusing on their interplay with religion in the Western Balkans context, followed by a brief discussion on the current state of religion and religiosity in the region. We then turn to the four countries— Bosnia and Herzegovina, Croatia, Montenegro and Serbia—focusing on the most prominent recent events in which religious institutions played an important role in shaping public discourse on LGBT issues: debates over marriage and family laws in Croatia, pride parades in Serbia and Montenegro, and the queer film festival in Bosnia.

### Theoretical Background

In his seminal work, *Imagined Communities: Reflections on the Origin and Spread of Nationalism*, Benedict Anderson (1983: 7) defines the nation as imagined as a community, "always conceived as a deep, horizontal comradeship. Ultimately it is this *fraternity* that makes it possible [...] for so many millions of people, not so much to kill, as willingly to die for such limited imaginings" (italic added). Although Anderson's reference to *fraternity* alludes to the gendered structure of nationalism,[2] it is with the feminist critique on this literature that the gender dimension of nationalism moves to the center of the debates. The feminist critique seeks to unravel the consequences of nationalism for women, highlighting, for example, the specific roles of women within the nationalist project. Nyra Yuval-Davis, for example, argues that women are not only the biological reproducers of the nation, but are also in charge of cultural reproduction. Moreover, women often perform the role of the "symbolic bearers of the collectivity's identity and honour, both personally and collectively" (Yuval-Davis 1997: 45). The "burden of representation" that rests on the women of the nation makes it the interest of the national project to control not only

---

2  The reference to the gendered aspects of nationalism can be found in other seminal works on nationalism. For example, in his work *Ethnic Groups in Conflict*, Donald L. Horowitz (1985) asks why groups move from the family to ethnicity as their basis for group loyalty. He argues that ethnic ties, as kinship ties, are an extension of family ties. Nationalism, according to Horowitz, is the process by which kin loyalty is extended to the ethnicity and the nation, i.e., the nation is seen as an extension of the family.

women's behavior, but also their body and sexuality—a role ascribed to the male bodies of the nation. Within the patriarchal family, the gendered division of labor follows a pattern in which women are perceived as the passive bearers of the family/national honor, and men are the active defenders of their women's and nation's honor (Nagel 1998). Within this feminist literature, although not ignored, the role of men, and the impact of nationalism on men and masculinity, has been explored to a much lesser extent. As Wendy Bracewell (2000: 566) argues, "[a]ttempts to theorise nations and nationalism from a gendered perspective [...] have to often treated men and masculinity as stable, undifferentiated categories, and have posited a straightforward equation between male interests, masculinity and nationalism." However, as (hegemonic) masculinity is idealized as the foundation of the nation and society (Mosse 1985), this power struggle between masculinities becomes imperative to the study of nationalism.

Masculinity, as a configuration of practice, is a relational concept. As R.W. Connell argues, it has become common to recognize multiple forms of masculinity, which all relate to each other in a specific way. One relationship of particular relevance is that of hegemonic and subordinate masculinities. Hegemonic masculinity is the "masculinity that occupies the hegemonic position in a given pattern of gender relations," and is defined as "the configuration of gender practice which embodies the currently accepted answer to the problem of the legitimacy of patriarchy" (Connell 2005: 76–77).[3] While hegemonic masculinity is at the top of the masculine gender hierarchy, the subordinate masculinities are at the bottom. The dominance of the former is gained by the marginalization of the latter. Something that becomes very clear in the semiotic approaches of defining masculinity (see Connell 2005: 70) is defining masculinity in negative terms, by defining what men are not. Masculinity, then, is defined as not-feminine, and is sharply contrasted by masculine countertypes, whether they are *racial or sexual* (Nagel 1998, our emphasis). This process of subordinating racial and sexual masculine countertypes also characterizes nationalism in the Western Balkans.

As mentioned previously, the interplay between nationalism, masculinity and sexual identities is particularly stark in this region. Analyzing the break-up of Yugoslavia, Dubravka Žarkov argues that ethnicity in the Western Balkans has been created via male and female bodies. She shows that "without notions of masculinity and femininity, and norms of (hetero)sexuality, ethnicity could

---

3  See Connell and Messerschmidt (2005) for a critical reformulation of the concept of hegemonic masculinity.

have never been produced" (2007: 8). Within the wars of the disintegration of Yugoslavia, the different nations used (heterosexual) (hyper)masculine norms to illustrate national superiority and pride, while simultaneously ascribing characteristics of the subordinate (homosexual) masculinities to the other nations. In her analysis of media representations in the Croatian and Serbian press of sexual violence against men, Žarkov (2001, 2007) argues that the different representation of the male body in stories about sexual violence against men contributed to the construction of the ethnic *self* and the ethnic *other*. Although stories about male victims of sexual violence were rare, she argues that the selected presence of some male bodies is significant.

She finds, for example, that within the Croatian press, male victims were (made) invisible. This invisibility, Žarkov (2001: 80) argues, "points to the significance of positioning a heterosexual power at the core of the definition of the ethnic Self in the Croatian media. The raped or the castrated Croat man [...] would undermine the construction of the Croat nation as virile and powerful." Bosnian Muslims (Bosniaks), on the other hand, were always depicted as the victims, and both their masculinity and heterosexuality were systematically questioned (for a detailed analysis see Žarkov 2001: 77–79). Serbs, in the Croatian reports on sexual violence against men, were always depicted as the perpetrators. Although their masculinity was not brought into question (as perpetrators, their acts are interpreted in terms of power), it was defined as significantly different from Croat masculinity. Serbs were depicted as perverts and primitives. Images of masculinity were thus used to signify the boundaries between the different nations. The de-masculinization and homosexualization of Bosniaks in the media representation excludes them from the Croatian nation, whilst Serbs were excluded because their masculinity was perverted and primitive, and thus lesser than the powerful, heterosexual masculinity of the Croat men/nation.

Another poignant example of the strong link between nationalism and sexuality can be found in the internal "othering" following the rise of (hyper)masculine nationalism in Serbia. The first signs of ethnicization and masculinization in Serbia are found in the rise of nationalist rhetoric concerning Kosovo in the late 1980s. Wendy Bracewell (2000), highlights the sexualization of the "Kosovo problem"—including debates on sexual violence in Kosovo as national rape— as a catalyst for political mobilization based on nationalism that draws from, and reinforces, traditional gender role patterns, which were inspired by the traditional and hetero-normative, patriarchal pre-socialist past. Using Bracewell's (2000: 584) words, it linked the "ideology of the nation to ideas of motherhood and female submissiveness, of male dominance and power, and of uncompromising heterosexuality, [and by doing so] reversed the official socialist ideology of gender equality, reinforcing male privilege, [...] and marginalising men and women who did not conform to the imperatives of nation and gender." When the wars broke out, this nationalist rhetoric not only mobilized male Serbs to volunteer to fight (see Milićević 2006), it also labeled the (male) opponents of the war as "traitors of their nation [and] traitors to their gender: cowardly, weak, effeminate and *probably homosexual*" (Bracewell 2000: 580, our emphasis). The (hyper)masculine traits of Serbian nationalism appealed to those experiencing a crisis of masculinity (caused by, for example, the growing insecurity of employment) and provided the grounds to re-assert their alignment with the hegemonic masculinity via "othering" based on, among others, homophobia (Bracewell 2000; see also Greenberg 2006).

Even after the fall of Milošević, Serbian nationalism remains masculinized and related to homophobia. Jessica Greenberg (2006: 321–322), for example, argues that masculine nationalism has been a "resource that the people in Serbia, and in other post-socialist context, have drawn on in times of social and political crisis." Analyzing the alignment of nationalism and homophobic violence during the 2001 Belgrade Pride, Greenberg (2006: 336) argues that the homophobic violence occurred at the "intersection of different modes of belonging, entitlement, action and politics." Marek Mikuš (2011) makes a similar observation for the 2010 Belgrade Pride. He asserts that the homophobic violence, and the riots following the Pride, occurred at the clash of "two Serbias"—where the "first Serbia" represents those adhering to the old system of belonging, based on conservative and nationalist views, and the "other Serbia" stands for a system of belonging based on liberal democracy, cosmopolitanism and anti-nationalism (see also Rossi 2009, Stakić 2011, Pavasović Trošt and Kovačević 2013). Homosexuality, thus, has become a symbol for the "other Serbia," which clashes with the system of belonging rooted in the nationalist legacies of 1990s.

### Religious Institutions and LGBT Issues in the Western Balkans

In the countries explored in this chapter, the official religious institutions are *de facto* unified in their opposition to LGBT rights; a situation most clear in the multiple joint statements by leaders of the otherwise opposing major religious communities (Catholic, Orthodox, and Muslim) about positions toward Pride parades and laws preserving the "sanctity" of marriage. In terms of the connection between religion and homosexuality, it has long been established, both within the Balkans and out, that religiosity is one of the stronger predictors of individual homophobia (Adamczyk and Pitt 2009, Marsh and Brown

2009, Slootmaeckers and Lievens 2014).[4] This does not apply to only the religious individual. A country's religious tradition also affects those who "share the same cultural space in which the religious traditions are embedded" (Kuhar 2013: 6). Štulhofer and Rimac (2009) found that religious tradition is one of the key determinants of countries' levels of homophobia, and further argued that Eastern Orthodox countries, such as Serbia, are among the most homophobic countries in Europe. Štulhofer and Rimac link this to the more troublesome, destructive political and socio-economic transitions of Eastern Orthodox countries, a context in which the Church became a "tool for re-building personal and collective identity in a rapidly changing social environment" (Štulhofer and Rimac 2009: 7). The process of re-traditionalization, which Kuhar (2013: 8) defines as "'coming home' to the true (patriarchal) values of the nation, previously erased by the communist regime," is not separate nor distinct from nationalism and religion. It intensified the role of both processes, thereby contributing to a (hyper)masculine and heteronormative culture, in which the homosexual body is seen as a national threat (Kuhar 2013; see also Van den Berg et al. 2014).[5]

The process of re-traditionalization, which came hand-in-hand with a revival in religiosity, has occurred both at the state level and in terms of actual on-the-ground religiosity (Perica 2002). During the wars of the 1990s and the nation-building that followed, religion became the new dominant ideology that filled the void left from Marxism to nationalism (Kleman 2001: 25), and religious communities became the stabilizing factor of the nation (Cvitković 2013: 19). In the post-Yugoslav states, the region has witnessed an increase in the intertwining of religious and official affairs, as evidenced by the introduction of religious education in schools, the heavy presence of religious leaders at state and official events and in political campaigns, and the introduction of new religious holidays into previously secular national calendars. This makes the utilized discursive strategies ever so important, as they are not occurring at the fringes of society, but in mainstream media and very much at the forefront of public attention. The involvement of religious figures in issues related to LGBT rights—namely referendums on marriage and the right to hold pride

---

4  It is not our intent to argue that homophobia is part of religion, as we follow Wilcox's argument that, given the historical evidence, it "has become more difficult [...] to claim that homophobia, biphobia, and transphobia are intrinsic and 'natural' to any given religious tradition" (2012: 81).

5  The idea that homosexuality is a threat to the nation has already been used by the Christian Right in the 1990s in the United States of America (see Herman 1997).

parades—is particularly visible, and is, thus, the main focus of the empirical work in this chapter.

Some important differences in the religious landscape across the Balkans exist, however, which are important prior to considering the case studies. First, the development of religious institutions during the Communist regime somewhat differs across the region. During this period, religious institutions, in all of the countries, took a backseat, and religiosity rates among the population fell continuously during from the 1950s through the 1970s. Very low rates of religiosity—measured as religious identification, participation in religious rites, and respect and perceived importance of the institution—persisted, particularly, in the Orthodox areas of Serbia and Montenegro (see Pantić 1993, Perica 2002, Đorđević 2007, Blagojević 2008).

In Croatia, the Catholic Church took over as the preserver of the Croat nation, following the mass Communist crackdown during the Croatian Spring (see Pavasović Trošt 2012), so the relationship between the Catholic Church and Croatian national identity already became particularly intimate in the 1980s. In Bosnia, by contrast, its multi-ethnic composition and continued insistence on shared brotherhood and unity narratives persisted through the breakup (Mihajlović Trbovc and Pavasović Trošt 2013). Second, the connection with the EU is also of high relevance, as Slovenia and Croatia are both EU member states. The remaining countries are on a slow, seemingly never-ending, journey to EU membership—a perception of ceaseless demands, of which human rights and the rights of sexual minorities are perceived by many average people as the most prominent (Pavasović Trošt and Kovačević 2012). The perception of the EU and the compatibility of national/ethnic identities with EU values differs across the region, and what are perceived as EU values (including rights of sexual minorities) are compatible with the Slovenian national identity and, to a larger extent than in other Balkan countries, with Croatian national identity (Subotić 2011). This in addition to the fact that events such as the NATO bombing of 1999 and the West's support of Kosovo's unilateral declaration of independence in 2008 cemented the perception of the West as Serbia's enemy, making it extremely easy—and in fact strategically useful—for the Church to get support for anti-LGBT issues.

Hence, the connections between national belonging and sexual diversity— as something the "malevolent EU" is trying to impose—are expected to be higher in countries farther from, and/or more opposed to, membership in the EU, and vary depending on the country's historical relationship with the West. Finally, the Eastern Orthodox Churches are national churches—that is, they are explicitly national/ethnic in character, as contrasted to the Catholic Church in Croatia, which falls under the jurisprudence of Rome. Finally, the legal framework of the states, which certainly affects the parameters within which the religious institutions operate, also differs across the countries—both in regards to when (if at all) homosexuality ceased to be listed as a mental disorder, or in the classification of homosexual relations as a criminal offense in the criminal code. For instance, the Croatian Medical Chamber took homosexuality off of its list of mental diseases as early as 1973, while Serbia's medical society did so only in 2008; such examples of disparate legal frameworks (particularly in terms of adoption of anti-discrimination laws) abound across the Balkans.

### Croatia

The biggest involvement of the Roman Catholic Church in Croatia with LGBT issues occurred during the Croatian constitution referendum in 2013; when, in reaction to the left-wing coalition government's attempt to legalize same-sex partnerships, an initiative named "In the Name of Family" was organized by the Catholic Church and several conservative groups. Other recent events in which the Catholic Church has been vocal include the yearly organization of Pride parades in Zagreb and Split, and the proposed new curriculum for health education, in 2014—whose fourth module included sexual education. The Church's public stances towards these issues are described below.

The "In the Name of Family" referendum was held in late 2013, upon gathering over 700,000 signatures in May 2013, with the aim of defining marriage exclusively as a union between a man and a woman. Thirty-eight percent of the population voted, of whom almost two-thirds voted yes. Leaders of virtually all of Croatia's religious groups joined the Catholic Church in a common statement of support for the referendum. It was signed by officials from the Serbian Orthodox Church, the Macedonian Orthodox Church, the Reformed Christian (Calvinist) Church, the Baptist Union of Croatia, the Evangelical Pentecostal Church, the Bet Israel Jewish Community, and the Mesihat of Croatia (see *Glas Koncila* 2013). The Evangelical Lutheran Church opposed the referendum, stating that real democracies do not exclude any minority, and that Christians in general and Lutherans, in particular, were also discriminated against and persecuted in the past; making Lutheran Protestants particularly sensitive toward questions of human rights, freedom and equality (*Tportal* 2013a). The joint statement and symposium "The Preventative and Curative Aspects of Preserving Marriage and Family in Croatia—Experiences of Religious Communities," appealed to "all believers: Catholics, Orthodox, Protestant, Jew, Muslim and others" to "ensure with their vote the constitutional protection of marriage, given that marriage as a relationship between a woman and a man is the best place for receiving and rearing children and maintaining the basis of the family, which is the fundamental unit of any society" (*HKV* 2013). While the Catholic Church was formally not an organizer of the referendum, the links between the church and the independent group "In the Name of the Family" was led by people connected to the Church or Church-related organizations.

What is immediately clear from this discourse, particularly in comparison to similar statements by religious officials in Serbia and Montenegro, is a higher reliance of themes portraying the LGBT community as a threat to *the family*—and less as a sickness, or a question of national purity, as similarly found by Sremac et al. (2014: 259). The main advocate for the Church's position toward the referendum, Zagreb Archbishop Cardinal Josip Bozanić—who was incidentally named "homophobe of the year" at the 2013 (12th) pride parade in Zagreb—has maintained a temperate and neutral discourse. His statements about the referendum, and LGBT issues in general, heavily relied on family-centered rhetoric, "marriage is the basis of the family, a cell of society," "we should not neglect the primary right of children, who are the only ones who should be privileged," and were accompanied without exception by explicit non-discrimination statements. For instance, upon insisting that marriage was exclusively a union between a man and a woman, different from a same-sex relationship, he adds, "but being different does not mean limiting anyone's rights, but respecting them" (Župa Soblinec 2014).

Nonetheless, even in the temperate statements by Cardinal Bozanić, several themes connecting the nation to LGBT issues are present. First, the question of same-sex marriage is not only a religious, but a *civilizational question*—"We will invite our parishioners to get involved in this democratic and far-reaching civilizational undertaking" ... "This is a first-class civilizational question." and so on. (*KHV* 2013). Relatedly, *the future of the Croatian nation* is frequently alluded to. For example, Cardinal Bozanić underscored the Church's wish to defend the institution of marriage and the family socially for "the future of the Croatian nation and its good people" (*Index* 2013), and called believers "not to deny the truth and the future of Croatian generations to come" (*Večernji* list 2013).

Third, the omnipresent Homeland (*Domovina*) and *responsibility to the Homeland* even appears in the most non-national of speeches. Cardinal Bozanić, for instance, while speaking in Vukovar about the importance of voting for the referendum, said, "I feel a responsibility to say this here in Vukovar, because from this place it is easier to hear and feel the responsibility to the Homeland" (*HKV* 2013), and frequently mentioned that the referendum was a "serious question for our Homeland" (*Večernji list* 2013). Naturally, where the Homeland is discussed, the allusion to *Croatia's thousand-year statehood* was also mentioned. The Catholic Bishops Conference stated, "the bishops maintain that the [signing of the referendum] is in accordance with the general human and gospel values and with the thousand-year tradition and culture of the Croatian people" (*Jutarnji* 2013a).

Finally, while certainly far from mainstream, several Catholic officials, mostly from smaller parishes, came out with far-reaching statements on the Croatian nation and LGBT issues. These include the priest Andro Ursić, Dr. Adalbert Rebić, Bishop Valentin Pozaić, and Franjo Jurčević, who was convicted for spreading hate speech after explicitly condoning the violence following the Belgrade pride parade (see *Tportal* 2011a). In the statements by these pastors, we can find language very similar to the far-right ones in Serbia and Montenegro. First, Don Ursić has propagated the idea that the EU is purposely "spreading in all directions a pandemic of homosexualism," and that Pride parades represent a "disoriented and lunatic Europe ... spreading a contemporary leprosy over the entire continent" (*Tportal* 2011b). Second, that LGBT issues will lead to the *destruction of the nation*: Dr. Adalbert Rebić, for instance, speaks about the "sexual anti-Croat conspiracy," stating that "with these moral politics, small nations are condemned to destruction. Destruction will come to all of us if we allow that this to happen to Croatia, though it seems to me that it will be difficult to resist this faggot 'conspiracy'" (*Jutarnji* 2013b).[6] A related theme appears, which is absent in the other countries analyzed, namely that of *a conspiracy of Communists* against the Roman Catholic Church and Croatia. This theme was arguably *more present* in some ultra-religious circles than the threat of the LGBT population. Valentin Pozaić, for instance, compared the left-leaning government with Communism, noting additionally that Nazism also came to power through democratic elections (*Jutarnji* 2013d). The theme of the threat of Communism is, nonetheless, not drastically different from statements of the editor of *Glas Koncila*, the Catholic weekly newspaper, who stated that all circles of Croatian society should recognize that, instead of removing obstacles to the development of the Croatian economy, energy was being spent on "turning back the wheel of time and reviving the continuity, political and ideological, of the 1980s" (Miklenić 2012).

### Serbia
In Serbia, the event of focus in our analysis is the organization of the Pride parade—most notably the notorious parade in Belgrade in 2010 secured by 5,000 police officers and followed by widespread looting and violence—and

---

6   Throughout the chapter, we use the word "gay" for the translation of "gej" and "faggot" for the translation of "peder."

also those organized (successfully or not) in subsequent years, toward which the Serbian Orthodox Church has always taken a particularly rigid stance. In 2010 particularly, Church representatives utilized extreme nationalist discourse and did little to distance themselves from the hooligan and ultra-right groups advocating for violence toward the Pride participants (see Nielsen 2013). Indeed, although the Serbian Orthodox Church officially condemned any violence toward parade participants, the rhetoric used by several bishops and priests was strikingly similar to the rhetoric of the ultra-right groups and hooligans. It has been argued that, by aligning itself with the attitudes of several ultra-right organizations, the Church provided legitimacy for extreme homophobia (Pavasović Trošt and Kovačević 2013). As in the other countries of the region, in Serbia all of the major religious communities came together in their position against the Pride parade. As recently as 2014, the Center of the Archdiocese Belgrade-Karlovac organized a public debate on the topic of "How to Speak about Homosexuality Today." The speakers included representatives of the Catholic, Jewish, and Muslim communities (Holy Assembly of Bishops 2014).

In an official statement by the Holy Synod, the Serbian Orthodox Church stated that it is against public displays of sexual orientation "especially if it insults the right of citizens to privacy and family life, their religious beliefs, and inviolability of human dignity." It added that violence is condemned, "even toward persons or groups which, by the teachings of the Church, sin against moral norms or threaten public morale" (Holy Assembly of Bishops 2010). Already in this official statement, the bases for the statements of other more extreme religious figures are present. Interestingly, among the religious officials most vocal in their condemnation of the parade, Montenegrin Bishop Amfilohije Radović especially stands out with his statements and de facto calls for violence. He frequently referred to the parade as the "parade of shame" or "parade of Sodom and Gomorrah," and said "the tree that doesn't bear fruit [reproduce] should be cut and thrown into the fire" (Bojić 2009), culminating in his statement after the parade: "Yesterday we watched the stench poisoning and polluting the capital of Serbia, scarier than uranium." Instead of condemning violence, he attributed the blame to the participants of the gay parade (B92 2010).

The statements of the Orthodox Church—both officially and coming from particularly opinionated priests—are worrisome given the authoritative position the Church plays in everyday life. The Serbian Orthodox Church has played a role in providing credibility to right-wing movements, including its reverence of Bishop Nikolaj Velimirović, an anti-Semite, xenophobe and zealous nationalist. "By assimilating their extremist political views within the ideology of an esteemed religious figure, organizations such as Obraz are able to present themselves as reasonable and respectable" (Byford 2002: 50). The media played a particularly troublesome role, publishing headlines such as "The Church is Only Defending Morality" (Kazimir 2009). The media's unquestioning representation of these positions is what makes this situation stand out in comparison to Croatia, where the media were much more critical of such extreme headlines.

When examining statements that explicitly link the Serbian nation and homosexuality, several themes appear. First, the Church makes the connection between *homosexuality as something European and Western*, thus inherently opposed to traditional Serbian values. The threat to traditional national values comes from the "decadent West" (Tucić 2011:45), and the move towards local LGBT rights is supported by the "international gay lobby," the U.S., and "deviant Europe where gay lobbies rule" (Pavasović Trošt and Kovačević 2013: 1066). The Holy Synod recently discussed the new "post-Christian" world order, where an increasing number of countries have taken benevolent positions toward "unusual" phenomena, such as homosexuality. These countries are led forward by "European and Euro-Atlantic countries" (and later "a part of the Protestant population, especially in European countries"), who allow same-sex marriages with the open threat and tension to spread (Holy Assembly of Bishops 2014). The Patriarch also pointed to the fact that paedophilia (which is unsurprisingly equated with homosexuality) was "massively spread in the Western world" (B92 2014).

Relatedly, the parade was *"imposed"*—sometimes explicitly, sometimes implicitly, by the West, the EU, the U.S., "international gay lobbies," or NGOs—a statement present even in official statements by the Holy Synod. The Synod, for instance, has ascribed the imposition as coming from "certain media and nongovernmental organizations" (Assembly of Bishops 2010). In a statement of the SOC, signed by Patriarch Irinej, the SOC maintains that the parade is "forcefully imposed" onto Belgrade and Serbia, and that the organizers of this parade and "their mentors from Europe" apparently do not wish to learn the lesson from previous parades (B92 2014). On a similar note, the Church has also advanced the popular notion that gays are "materially well-situated" and purposely trying to corrupt the "innocent, scared and weak persons ... especially uncorrupted children and inexperienced youth" (Holy Assembly of Bishops 2014).

Third, while the Catholic Church in Croatia also frequently refers to same-sex marriage or parades as threats to the "healthy" family, in Serbia it is emphasized that they *threaten the healthy, Serbian, traditional family*. The Holy Assembly of Bishops (2014) stressed, "in the healthy Serbian family traditional atmosphere, a relationship is deeply engrained toward everything that is verified, weighed and that lasts" ([*provereno, odmereno i što traje*]). Patriarch Irinej similarly pointed out that "a healthy family is the basis for a healthy society, healthy nation, healthy education, and healthy culture," and called for an increased presence of the Church in the "spiritual and moral renewal of the Serbian nation" (RTS 2013a). The notion that *Serbian traditional symbols do not belong to the LGBT population* was also evident in the outcry of the SOC against the organizers of Belgrade's Pride week for using the icon of the "White Angel," a fresco in the Serbian Monastery of Mileševa, appealing to the government of Serbia for protection of the church's holy objects. The SOC blamed the organizers for "spitting on Orthodoxy," which is the "source of the live water that made us literate, enlightened, and educated us, and took us into the cultural heritage of worldly nations" (*Alo* 2013a). Amfilohije Radović has also spoken about the "abuse" of Christian symbols ("such as the cross and others") in gay parades, which he sees as "permanent violence over the majority," and a "more or less hidden fight against Christianity and the Christian faith, and against all-religious values on which humanity has built its collective historical memory and existence through centuries" (*Pečat* 2010).

Finally, the *survival of the Serbian nation* is called into question. Patriarch Irinej stated that, in this day and age, nothing is more threatened than marriage and the family, which are being deliberately destroyed, "especially by the gay parade," and this scourge [*pošast*] is the only remaining thing the Serbian nation needs to disappear from the face of the earth (RTS 2013a). Similarly, discussions about the Church's role in promoting natality, spirituality and the moral renewal of the Serbian nation are frequently mentioned side-by-side with discussions on LGBT issues (*Novi Magazin* 2013). The SOC's statement captures the idea that the Serbian nation is on the edge of survival, only to be pushed over by gays: "You have a right to parade, but only at your own cost and the cost of your customers [*nalogodavaca*], whatever they may be called, for the parade, as well as for the security, but not at the cost of Serbia—bombed, ravaged, morally and economically crippled, impoverished, flooded, nailed to the pillar of shame" (B92 2014). Apart from pointing to gays as the potential downfall of the Serbian nation, this statement also underscores an appeal to patriotism, and the implicit statement that, if anyone truly cared about Serbia, she or he would not parade. The parade, itself, is thus inherently unpatriotic and nationally treacherous. The connection between the parade and the destruction of Serbia reached an almost humorous dimension in May 2014, following the floods that devastated the entire region. They were interpreted, by Patriarch Irinej, as God's warning to "stay away from the path of vice, wickedness, and lawlessness," specifying that he is referring to the parade being organized in Belgrade, which represents "great lawlessness and an abominable vice" (Mihajlović 2014).

### Bosnia

In Bosnia and Herzegovina, the situation regarding LGBT rights is even starker. The notion of holding any semblance of a Pride parade is all but non-existent (Banović and Vasić 2012). Thus, we analyze here the incident related to the first Sarajevo Queer Festival in 2008, since it represents one of the few organized LGBT events in Bosnia. The Sarajevo Queer Festival in 2008 was organized by the Q organization, and was supposed to be a cultural five-day event including broadcasting of several LGBT-issue films. Protesters, purported to be mainly from the extremist Wahhabist movement, were later joined by football hooligans, and attacked journalists and participants at the event. The event was then closed after the opening night, with eight people injured. In addition to the Queer Festival, we also examine media statements of the Islamic Community regarding LGBT rights, whether connected to a particular event or not.

As in Serbia, but to an even greater extent, the media in Bosnia and Herzegovina has amplified the situation and given extremist statements visibility.[7] The titles of the articles themselves are already indicative of the unmistakable position. In 2008, *Dnevni Avaz*, a daily non-religious newspaper, published two articles with particularly problematic titles: "Who is imposing the gay gathering upon Bosniacs during Ramadan?" (*Dnevni Avaz* 2008a) and "Mufti Smajkić: Freedom should not be used as promotion of that garbage from the West" (*Dnevni Avaz* 2008b). The Islamic periodical *Saff*, which describes itself as the "Islamic Youth Review," published articles with titles such as "Masters of Faggotism Promoted in Sarajevo: 44 Experts for Debauchery" (*Saff* 2011), and other *Saff* articles, before and after the event, included similarly colorful discourse. While these articles do not represent official statements of the Islamic Community, their inclusion in *Saff* implies their condoning of the viewpoints presented. Maša Durkalić, an analyst of Bosnian media, concludes: "The ideological messages sent through these publications is a terrifying point of how it is possible to change any idea which does not in accord with the prevalent opinions rooted in tradition and patriarchate (which are still represented as the greatest moral values), by using careful editor manipulation into open hatred" (2012: 160).

As can be seen from the article titles, several of the themes are similar to the ones discussed in the cases above. The first is the idea that *homosexuality comes from the deviant West*. One of the *Dnevni Avaz* articles cited Mufti Smajkić saying, "I think that freedom and democracy should not be used to promote grotesque ideas and that garbage which is imported from the West" (*Avaz*

---

7   For a review of the media situation in regard to LGBT issues in Bosnia, see Huremović (2012), and Zurovac (2012).

2008b). This mirrors the language used by protesters at the Queer Festival, "May dear Allah let you live to see your children taken by two faggots from the Netherlands and make porn movies with your children" (Huseinović 2008). Mufti Smajkić frequently referred to the "spirit of Bosnia" and the "vision of Bosnia" in which these kinds of Western-imported ideas do not belong (*Dnevni Avaz* 2008b). The Islamic daily, *Saff*, unsurprisingly takes these statements quite a few steps further, blaming the European Union for the "gay evil" threatening Bosnia, and projecting a future Bosnia within the EU—where the "European Muslim" will need to, "apart from consuming pork, also support faggots, if he wants to achieve anything in the Christian hierarchy" (*Saff* 2008a). Other *Saff* articles have similarly called out the countries believed to have supported the festival: the Netherlands, Switzerland, the U.S., as well as certain local media (*Saff* 2008b). The sentiment that the event was forcefully imposed onto Bosniacs, and is a "provocation" (*Dnevni Avaz* 2008c), is a recurrent theme in both *Dnevni Avaz* and *Saff* articles.

While the *Saff* article mentioned above does not explicitly combine national identity themes, professor of Islamic theology Abdusamed Nasuf Bušatlić, nonetheless appeals to Bosniac patriotism by *clear demarcation between Bosniacs and ethnic "others."* He quotes the statement of the president of the Radical Party in Republika Srpska, who claimed that Sarajevo was indeed the proper site for such a festival, because Republika Srpska would "never allow debauchery and perversion on its streets, nor does it support unnatural affinities" (*Saff* 2008d). In this way, Bušatlić appeals implicitly, but unambiguously, to ethnic sentiments (Durkalić 2012: 171). After the parade, he made an explicit differentiation between "citizens of Sarajevo, and especially Muslims during the mubarak month of Ramadan," on the one hand, and the festival organizers and participants, on the other. The included group is, thus, comprised of "all those who believe in ... Allah ... and follow the path of Islam which is sheer purity, goodness and virtue," while the excluded group not only includes members of the LGBT community, but also atheists, communists and secularists in general (*Saff* 2008e). He proceeds to draw a binary between those who supported the festival—or simply condemned the violence—as "seething Islamophobes with insatiable hatred and antipathy towards Islam and Muslims," comparing them to the "black hand of Communism and aggressive atheism" (*Saff* 2008e). By stressing that secularism has reached "the status of a religion whose perverted principles have become holy and untouchable," including an insistence on understanding and tolerance "toward the worst forms of twistedness and deviation" (*Saff* 2008e), he draws a clear binary between those who practice Islam on the one hand, and members of the LGBT community, their supporters and atheists on the other (see also Durkalić 2012).

Other *Saff* articles make similar comparisons: a letter to the editor refers to the journalists at the event as "demuslimized journalists" and the event itself as "organized anti-Muslim action" (*Saff* 2008f). In the *Saff* articles, Bušatlić further *appeals to fears of internal division of Bosniacs* by pointing to the fragmentation of the daily newspaper *Avaz* (in reference to an internal disagreement of *Avaz* journalists on journalistic standards in relation to the festival reporting), concluding that they are "each on their own" and divided (*Saff* 2008c). With this, *Saff* "actually attempted to point to the disunity in the bastion of the defense of Bosniacness itself—the *Dnevni Avaz*" (Durkalić 2012:175). This is connected to the idea that Bosnia is *at risk of losing its tradition or assimilation*: a published letter to the editor states that Muslim blood is being shed "in barrels" all over the world, while Bosnia "worries about a few broken noses" (of the journalists at the Queer Festival [*Saff* 2008f]). On a similar note, radical Islamist Fatmir Alispahić contends that, in addition to homosexuality being purposely driven to Bosnia by the destructive West, this is being aided by "Serbian and Croatian intelligence services, as well as the international factor," who are together driving Bosniacs to accept homosexuality instead of "their own tradition" (*Saff* 2008a). The elements of a conspiracy theory are clearly present, even more so when the author blames these forces for their "fascist plan to blame the most tolerant and open society in the Balkans for closed mindedness, terrorism, Wahhabism, and much else" (*Saff* 2008a). As Durkalić points out, this argument contains the idea that Western forces, along with the penultimate enemies Croats and Serbs, are trying to infiltrate the traditional bastion of Bosniac society through the Queer Festival (2012: 177). Sremac et al. (2014: 257) and Vlaisavljević (2009: 78) similarly point to the constant reproduction of the fear of assimilation or extermination by repeated ethnic narratives with the same internal logic.

### Montenegro
In Montenegro, the bulk of the public performance of religious officials in regard to LGBT rights occurred in response to the Pride parades. While the 2014 parade in Podgorica occurred more or less peacefully, the first two parades, held in Podgorica and Budva in 2013, were marred by violence. Bishop Amfilohije Radović has been the most outspoken in regards to LGBT issues, although his statements only represent variations to the themes of the official positions of the Serbian Orthodox Church,[8] as discussed in previous sections.

---

8  The Montenegrin Orthodox Church is a fairly small, newly established and controversial church, which has not been recognized by other Orthodox churches. It is typically attributed

The first theme that appears in statements regarding the Pride parade is that allowing homosexuality indicates a *loss of national honor*. During the mass Bishop Radović held in Podgorica to "cleanse the streets" following their "defilment" by the Pride parade, Bishop Radović proclaimed that the parade "dishonored" Montenegro, and that Podgorica needed its honor restored (*24sata* 2013a). The Mass itself was presented as a Mass for "Montenegrin honor [referred to by two words: *čast* and *obraz*], the sanctity of marriage and of bearing children" (*RTS* 2013b). Indeed, "dishonored" and "dishonorable" were a common theme in regard to many different concepts by Bishop Radović. The parade dishonored the mustache of Montenegrins, which represented "the symbol of the centuries-long humanity and morality of Montenegro." (Pride organizers used mustaches as a symbol of the parade. *Novosti* 2013). The police found itself in a "dishonored" position because it had to protect Pride participants (*Alo* 2013d). A related theme is that the parade represents an *attack on Montenegrin identity and dignity*. Bishop Radović sated that the organizers of the parade had to be aware that their way of life and behavior "threaten the identity and dignity" and the "ethical, moral and spirtual being" of the large majority of the Montenegrin people (*Blic* 2013). Appeals to identity also included drawing a contrast between the "ecological state" of Montenegro, which was now in danger of becoming a "sodom" state (*Alo* 2014).

The *biological survival of the nation* is similarly called into question. The discursive strategies used to promote this concept are numerous. They include discussing abortion simultaneously with LGBT rights, and warning about the dangers of homosexuality and abortion side-by-side, in the same discussion. In the same sermon about the Pride parade, Radovic warned mothers against abortion (which he refers to as "infanticide" [*čedomorstvo*]): "Without children, dead is the temple, dead is the land, dead is the nation" (*24sata* 2013a). Frequent reference to the impossibility of biological reproduction of gays, a theme that was already heavily present in Radović's comments about the Belgrade 2010 Pride parade, in which he stated that everything that exists, exists to bear fruit, and that "the tree that doesn't bear fruit [reproduce] should be cut and thrown into the fire" (Bojić 2009; *24sata* 2013b). As such, pride parades are described as "parades of death," behind which "suicidal tendencies" are hidden. Another way

---

to the political nationalist project in Montenegro. The majority of Orthodox Montenegrins declare themselves as Serbian Orthodox, while those declaring a Montenegrin national identity tend to lean toward the Montenegrin Orthodox Church. In this chapter we refer to statements of the Serbian Orthodox Church as official positions of the Church, since it is still officially has jurisprudence over Orthodox believers in Montenegro. Bishop Amfilohije Radović is the current bishop of Montenegro and the Littoral.

of emphasizing the connection between the biological survival of the nation and the parade is by repeated reference to the parade as "violence" over the nation. By holding the parade, "we all lost and are left defeated in front of the spiritual-moral and physical violence that befell the capital city of Montenegro" (*Novosti 2013*).

Finally, the aforementioned theme of *gay lobbies and the deviant EU*, which stand in opposition to the purity of the Montengrin nation, is heavily present here as well. According to Radović, gay parades in the region are a result of propaganda imposed by the West, including the EU (*Alo* 2013c), and the Montenegrin government was forced to hold the parade under pressure from the "European faggot lobbies" (*24sata* 2013b). He pointed to the fact that there were "LGBT members" in the top leadership of the EU, but that nobody, not even officials of the EU, "under influence of gay lobbies," has the right to impose their will about something that is unhealthy and morally unpermissible, to "threaten the ethical being of entire nations" (*Blic* 2013). That accepting the EU's demands to hold Pride parades was a form of *national subjugation* was also mentioned. Europe's will "finally to put Montenegro under itself, as a sign of her full fulfilment of integration conditions" (*Alo* 2014).

## Conclusion

In this chapter we have analysed how religious institutions and actors in the Western Balkans have taken up the role of the "defender" of the nation, by looking at their discourse on homosexuality. With the disintegration of Yugoslavia, nationalism (and ethnic identities) became very linked to the question of masculinity, which was often defined against subordinate homosexual masculinities. Within this context of new nation-building, religious institutions became more prominent, becoming the new dominant ideology that filled the void left by the demise of socialism, increasingly intertwined with the politics of the new nations. In our analysis, we explored how the religious institutions, in contemporary events, continuously take on the role of upholding the dominant ideology not only to defend the nation, but also define the nation through their statements on homosexuality.

Several themes can be found in the religious discourse on homosexuality. First, homosexuality (and the LGBT related events we analyzed) is depicted as a *threat to the nation*. While this debate in Croatia is centered around the question of the survival of the family (i.e., the central unit of the nation), which needs to be protected from the vices of the LGBT community, the discourse in the other countries is about the threat to the morality of the nation, as well as its health and honor. In Serbia, Montenegro and Bosnia, the stress is also on the *biological survival of the nation*, citing the impotency of homosexual relationships and linking LGBT issues to the declining birth rates.

Another theme we distinguished is the *linkage of homosexuality to the "deviant" West/EU* and the general idea that the parades are methodically imposed by the West. Pride parades (in Serbia and Montenegro) and the Queer festival (in Bosnia) are presented by the religious institutions as a vice forced upon the countries by the EU, opposing the values of their respective countries. This discourse is absent in Croatia, however, which is expected, given Croatia's closer relationship to the EU and the perceived compatibility between Croatian and European identities. Finally, religious leaders use homosexuality to *define ethnic boundaries*. In Serbia, for example, the Church denies the LGBT population the use of traditional Serbian symbols and claims that homosexuals are not truly Serbian, hence the parade is presented as unpatriotic and nationally treacherous. In Bosnia the issue of homosexuality is used to mark the distinction between Bosniacs and ethnic others, inherently linking homosexuality with Islamophobia, secularism, Communism and atheism. This theme is likely the most troublesome finding of our chapter, as it suggests that LGBT rights have slim prospects of advancing, as long as they are perceived as a Western-imposed ailment (or without a meaningful change in the public's perception of the West). It further underscores the ease with which religious institutions can manipulate feelings about LGBT rights when they are bundled up in anti-EU discourse, given the general public's feelings of dissatisfaction with the current political and economic situation and impatience with the EU's never-ending demands upon them for achieving membership.

Finally, some important distinctions surfaced. While nationalist rhetoric and intolerant attitudes can also be found in statements of Catholic officials, in Croatia these are limited to the margins of society—in smaller parishes, on blogs of lesser-known priests, and without support from higher levels of the Church leadership, whose statements are unmistakably temperate. In Serbia and Montenegro, by contrast, startlingly extremist (and frequently unconstitutional) discourse can be found in statements of the very highest level of the Serbian Orthodox Church leadership. In these two countries, and in Bosnia, the situation is compounded by the unprofessional conduct of the media, who report on these statements unquestionably, practically condoning them, hence only further inflaming public discourse. Ultimately, while our findings do not allow for an examination of the *effects* of religious institutions on public discourse, and certainly not their effect on the actions of everyday people, we can observe clear patterns between the statements of religious leaders on the one hand, and populist sentiments of everyday people, hooligans and ultra-right groups on the other—groups to which the religious leaders advertently or inadvertently provide legitimacy.

## References

Adamczyk, Amy and Cassady Pitt. 2009. "Shaping Attitudes About Homosexuality: the Role of Religion and Cultural Context." *Social Science Research* 38: 338–351.

*Alo.* 2013a. "Crkveni sud manastira Mileševa: Gejevi su pljunuli na Belog Anđela!" *Alo.rs* 24 September. Accessed at http://www.alo.rs/vesti/aktuelno/crkveni-sud-manastira -mileseva-gejevi-su-pljunuli-na-belog-andela/31856, 7 November 2014.

———. 2013b. "Nadam se da je kraj sa gej paradama!" *Alo.rs* 1 August. Accessed at http:// www.alo.rs/vesti/aktuelno/nadam-se-da-je-kraj-sa-gej-paradama/26439, 7 November 2014.

———. 2013c. "Amfilohije: Crna Gora da se ugleda na Srbiju i zabrani Prajd!" *Alo.rs* 29 September. Accessed at http://www.alo.rs/vesti/aktuelno/amfilohije-crna-gora -da-se-ugleda-na-srbiju-i-zabrani-prajd/32337, 7 November 2014.

———. 2013d. "Gej paraderi obeščastili crnogorski brk!" *Alo.rs* 21 October. Accessed at http://www.alo.rs/vesti/aktuelno/amfilohije-gej-paraderi-obescastili-crnogorski -brk/34563, 7 November 2014.

———. 2014. "U Podgorici danas Parada ponosa." *Alo.rs* 2 November. Accessed at http://www.alo.rs/vesti/svet/u-podgorici-danas-parada-ponosa/72983, 7 November 2014.

Anderson, Benedict. 1983. *Imagined Communities: Reflections on the Origin and Spread of Nationalism.* London: Verso.

Banović, Damir and Vladana Vasić. 2012. "Seksualna orijentacija i rodni identitet u kontekstu ljudskih prava u BiH." Pp. 57–68 in *Izvan Četiri Zida Priručnik za novinarke i novinare: o profesionalnom i etičkom izvještavanju o* LGBT *temama,* edited by Lejla Huremovic. Sarajevo: Sarajevski otvoreni centar.

Bates, Stephen. 2004. *A Church at War: Anglicans and Homosexuality.* London: Tauris.

Blagojević, Mirko. 2008. "Desecularization of contemporary Serbian society." *Religion in Eastern Europe* 28: 37–50.

*Blic.* 2010. "Crkva dala vetar u leđa protivnicima gej parade." *Blic.rs* 9 October. Accessed at http://www.blic.rs/Vesti/Tema-Dana/211033/Crkva-dala-vetar-u-ledja -protivnicima-gej-parade, 7 November 2014.

———. 2013. "Amfilohije: Gejevi iz vrha EU sole pamet i ugrožavaju etičko biće čitavih naroda." *Blic.rs* 1 August. Accessed at http://www.blic.rs/Vesti/Drustvo/396712/ Amfilohije-Gejevi-iz-vrha-EU-sole-pamet-i-ugrozavaju-eticko-bice-citavih-naroda, 7 November 2014.

———. 2014. "Gej parade su parade smrti i nose nasilje u sebi." *Blic.rs* 9 October.

Accessed at http://www.blic.rs/Vesti/Drustvo/501219/Amfilohije-Gej-parade-su
-parade-smrti-i-nose-nasilje-u-sebi, 7 November 2014.

Bojić, B. 2009. "Skandalozno: Amfilohiju sude zbog gej parade?!" *Press Online* 24 September. Accessed at http://www.pressonline.rs/info/politika/80702/skandalozno
-amfilohiju-sude-zbog-gej-parade.html, 7 November 2014.

Bracewell, Wendy. 2000. "Rape in Kosovo: Masculinity and Serbian Nationalism." *Nations and Nationalism* 6: 563–590.

Byford, Jovan. 2002. "Christian Right-Wing Organisations and the Spreading of Anti-
Semitic Prejudice in Post-Milosevic Serbia: The Case of the Dignity Patriotic Movement." *East European Jewish Affairs* 32: 43–60.

B92. 2010. "Govor mrznje: Parada kao uranijum." *B92Online* 14 October 14. Accessed at
http://www.b92.net/info/vesti/index.php?yyyy=2010&mm=10&dd=14&nav_id=
465324, 7 November 2014.

———. 2014. "SPC: Paradirajte, ali od svog novca." *B92Online* 23 September. Accessed
at http://www.b92.net/info/vesti/index.php?yyyy=2014&mm=09&dd=23&nav_id=
902904, 7 November 2014.

Cobb, Michael. 2006. *God Hates Fags: The Rhetorics of Religious Violence*. New York: New
York University Press.

Connell, R.W. 2005. *Masculinities* (2nd ed.). Cambridge: Polity Press.

——— and James. W. Messerschmidt. 2005. "Hegemonic Masculinity—Rethinking
the Concept." *Gender & Society* 19: 829–859.

Cvitković, Ivan. 2013. *Encountering Others: Religious and Confessional Identities in Bosnia and Herzegovina*. Niš: Yugoslav Society for the Scientific Study of Religion.

*Dnevni Avaz*. 2008a. "Ko Bošnjacima podvaljuje gej okupljanje u ramazanu?" *Dnevni
Avaz* 28 August.

———. 2008b. "Ef. Smajkić: Slobodu ne treba koristiti za promociju tog smeća sa
Zapada." *Dnevni Avaz* 2 September.

———. 2008c. "NAJAVE Uprkos protivljenju javnosti Queer Festivalu: Gejevi u Sarajevu
i u noći Lejletu-l-kadr!" *Dnevni Avaz* 23 September.

Dudink, Stefan. 2011. "Homosexuality, Race, and the Rhetoric of Nationalism." *History of
the Present* 1: 259–264.

Durkalić, Masha. 2012. "Bosanskohercegovački mediji i Queer Sarajevo Festival." Pp.
167–187 in A. Spahić and S. Gavrić (eds.) *ČITANKA lezbejskih, gej, biseksualnih i
transrodnih ljudskih prava*, 2nd edition. Sarajevo: Heinrich Böll Foundation.

Đorđević, Dragoljub B. 2007. "Religious-Ethnic Panorama of the Balkans." Pp. 79–93 in
N.S. Arachchige Don and L. Mitrović (eds.) *The Balkans in Transition*. San Francisco:
International Research Foundation for Development.

*Glas Koncila*. 2013. "Izađimo na referendum i osigurajmo ustavnu zaštitu braka." *Glas
Koncila* 24 November. Accessed at http://www.glas-koncila.hr/index.php?option=
com_php&Itemid=41&news_ID=23573, 7 November 2014.

Greenberg, Jessica. 2006. "Nationalism, Masculinity and Multicultural Citizenship in Serbia." *Nationalities Papers* 34: 321–341.

*HKV.* 2013. "Kardinal Bozanić: Crkva podupire inicijativu "U ime obitelji"." *HKV* 29 April. Accessed at http://www.hkv.hr/vijesti/hrvatska/15003-kardinal-bozanic-crkva -podupire-inicijativu-u-ime-obitelji.html, 7 November 2014.

Holy Assembly of Bishops. 2010. "Saopstenje Svetog Arhijerejskog Sinoda povodom najava gej parade u Beogradu." Statement of the Holy Synod of Bishops on the occasion of the announcement of the Gay Parade in Belgrade, at the Serbian Orthodox Church in Belgrade, 8 October 2010. Accessed at http://www.spc.rs/sr/saopstenje _svetog_arhijerejskog_sinoda_povodom_najava_gejparade_u_beogradu, 7 November 2014.

———. 2014. "Трибина на Коларчевом универзитету." 25 February. Accessed at http://www.spc.rs/sr/tribina_na_kolarchevom_univerzitetu, 7 November 2014.

Horowitz, Donald L. 1985. *Ethnic Groups in Conflict*. Berkeley: University of California Press.

Huremović, Lejla. 2012. "LGBT teme u bosanskohercegovačkim štampanim medijima u 2011. Godini." Pp. 91–96 in L. Huremovic (ed.) *Izvan Četiri Zida Priručnik za novinarke i novinare: o profesionalnom i etičkom izvještavanju o LGBT temama*. Sarajevo: Sarajevski otvoreni centar.

Huseinović, Samir. 2008. "Homoseksualci napadnuti "u Alahovo ime"." *Deutsche Welle* 25 September. Accessed at http://www.dw.de/homoseksualci-napadnuti-u-alahovo -ime/a-3669493, 7 November 2014.

*Index.* 2013. "Bozanić: Brak je u opasnosti da bude diskriminiran." *Index* 21 November. Accessed at http://www.index.hr/mobile/clanak.aspx?category=&id=712608, 7 November 2014.

*Jutarnji.* 2013a. "BISKUPI 'Izađite na referendum i glasajte ZA—time ne ugrožavate nikoga'." *Jutarnji* 19 November. Accessed at http://www.jutarnji.hr/hrvatska -biskupska-konferencija-izadite-na-referendum-i-glasajte-za-time-ne-ugrozavate -nikoga-/1140710/, 7 November 2014.

———. 2013b. "Teolog Adalbert Rebić: 'Urota pedera, komunista i lezbi uništit će Hrvatsku!'" *Jutarnji* 9 January. Accessed at http://www.jutarnji.hr/adalbert-rebic -razni-stulhoferi-pederi-i-lezbe-zele-nam-nametnuti-svoj-manjinski-moral-koji-ce -upropastiti-drustvo-/1077363/, 7 November 2014.

———. 2013c. "Biskup pozvao na oružano rušenje vlasti. Vlada: Iz Crkve dolazi govor mržnje! KAPTOL: Nitko nas neće zaustaviti u pobuni protiv vlasti!" *Jutarnji* 10 January. Accessed at http://www.jutarnji.hr/vlada-iz-crkve-dolazi-govor-mrznje-kaptol -nitko-nas-nece-zaustaviti-u-pobuni-protiv-sdp-ove-vlasti-/1077724/, 7 November 2014.

———. 2013d. "VIDEO, SKANDALOZAN ISTUP! BISKUP USPOREDIO VLADU S NA-CISTIMA: 'Treba nam nova Oluja za svrgavanje vlasti!'" *Jutarnji* 9 January. Accessed at http://www.jutarnji.hr/biskup-usporedio-vladu-s-nacistima/1077502/, 7 November 2014.

Kazimir, Velimir. 2009. *Nasilje u sportu i mediji*. Ebart Media Documentation Research Paper prepared for the Serbian Center for Free Elections and Democracy (CeSID) and the Serbian Ministry of Youth and Sport.

Kleman, Olivije. 2001. *Pravoslavna crkva*. Beograd: Plato.

Kuhar, Roman. 2013. "In the Name of Hate: Homophobia as a Value." *Southeastern Europe* 37: 1–16.

Marsh, Timothy and Jac Brown. 2009. "Homonegativity and Its Relationship to Religiosity, Nationalism and Attachment Style." *Journal of Religion and Health* 50: 575–591.

Mihajlović, Branka. 2014. "Patrijarhova nečuvena zloupotreba katastrofalne nesreće." *Radio Slobodna Evropa* 22 January. Accessed at http://www.slobodnaevropa.org/content/patrijarhova-nečuvena-zloupotreba-katastrofalne-nesreće/25387368.html, 7 November 2014.

Mihajlović Trbovc, Jovana and Tamara Pavasović Trošt. 2013. "Who Were the Anti-Fascists? Multiple Interpretations of WWII in Post-Yugoslav Textbooks." Pp. 173–192 in C. Karner and B. Mertens (eds.), *Use and Abuse of Memory: Interpreting World War Two in Contemporary European Politics*. New Brunswick, NJ: Transaction Publishers.

Miklenić. Ivan. 2012. "Kakva će biti prekretnica?" *Glas Koncila* 13 January. Accessed at http://www.glas-koncila.hr/index.php?option=com_php&Itemid=41&news_ID=21775, 7 November 2014.

Mikuš, Marek. 2011. "'State Pride': Politics of LGBT Rights and Democratisation in 'European Serbia'." *East European Politics & Societies* 25: 834–851.

Milićević, A. Sasha. 2006. "Joining the War: Masculinity, Nationalism and War Participation in the Balkans War of Secession, 1991–1995." *Nationalities Papers* 34: 265–287.

Mosse, George L. 1985. *Nationalism and Sexuality: Middle-Class Morality and Sexual Norms in Modern Europe*. Madison: University of Wisconsin Press.

Nagel, Joane. 1998. "Masculinity and Nationalism: Gender and Sexuality in the Making of Nations." *Ethnic and Racial Studies* 21: 242–269.

Nielsen, Christian. 2013. "Stronger than the State? Football Hooliganism, Political Extremism and the Gay Pride Parades in Serbia" *Sport in Society* 16: 1038–1053.

*Novi Magazin*. 2013. "Crna Gora: Najavljeni protesti protiv Parade, organizatori se ne boje nereda." *Novi Magazin* 18 October. Accessed at http://www.novimagazin.rs/svet/crna-gora-najavljeni-protesti-protiv-parade-kacin-amfilohijev-govor-mrznje, 7 November 2014.

*Novosti*. 2013. "Crkva u CG: Nismo odgovorni za nasilje na Prajdu." *Novosti* 21 October. Accessed at http://www.novosti.rs/vesti/planeta.300.html:459960-Crkva-u-CG-Nismo-odgovorni-za-nasilje-na-Prajdu, 7 November 2014.

Pantić, Dragomir. 1993. "Promene religioznosti građana Srbije." *Sociološki pregled* 27(1–4): 177–204.

Pavasović Trošt, Tamara. 2012. "Construction and Contestation of Ethnic Identity: Identity Discourse among Serbian and Croatian Youth." Ph.D. dissertation, Harvard University.

——— and Nikola Kovačević. "Football, Hooliganism and Nationalism: The Reaction to Serbia's Gay Parade in Reader Commentary Online." *Sport in Society* 16: 1054–1076.

*Pečat.* 2010. "Kolo smrti na ulicama Beograda." *Pečat* 7 October Accessed at http://www.pecat.co.rs/2010/10/mitropolit-amfilohije-kolo-smrti-na-ulicama-beograda/, 7 November 2014.

Perica, Vjekoslav. 2002. *Balkan Idols: Religion and Nationalism in Yugoslav States*. New York: Oxford University Press.

Pryke, Sam. 1998. "Nationalism and Sexuality, What are the Issues?" *Nations and Nationalism* 4: 529–546.

Puar, Jasbir K. 2007. *Terrorist Assemblages: Homonationalism in Queer Times*. London: Duke University Press.

Rossi, Michael. 2009. "Resurrecting the Past: Democracy, National Identity, and Historical Memory in Modern Serbia." Ph.D. dissertation, State University of New York.

*RTS.* 2013a. "Patrijarh Irinej protiv Parade ponosa." *RTS* 24 September. Accessed at http://www.rts.rs/page/stories/sr/story/125/Društvo/1402510/Patrijarh+Irinej+protiv+Parade+ponosa.html, 7 November 2014.

———. 2013b. "Amfilohije: Gej parada zagadila Podgoricu." *RTS* 26 October. Accessed at http://www.rts.rs/page/stories/sr/story/11/Region/1428935/Amfilohije%3A+Gej+parada+zagadila+Podgoricu.html?email=yes, 7 November 2014.

*Saff.* 2008b. "Skandalozno: U zadnjoj trećini ramazana u Sarajevu će se održati veliki skup homoseksualaca." *Saff* 22 August.

———. 2008d. "Ramazan je mjesec pokajanja, ne orgijanja." *Saff* 5 September.

———. 2008c. "Kako administrator web foruma *Dnevnog avaza* piše protiv svojih novina." *Saff* 10 October.

———. 2008f. "Napredak unazad ili degeneracija čovječanstva." *Saff* 10 October.

———. 2008a. "Pederland." 10 October.

———. 2008e. "'Crna ruka' ateizma iznad Sarajeva." *Saff* 20 October.

———. 2011. "U Sarajevu promovirani magistri pederizma: 44 eksperta za razvrat." *Saff* 28 October.

Slootmaeckers, K., and J. Lievens. 2014. "Cultural Capital and Attitudes Toward Homosexuals: Exploring the Relation Between Lifestyles and Homonegativity." *Journal of Homosexuality* 61: 962–979.

Sremac, Srđan, Zlatiborka Popov-Momčinović, Miloš Jovanović, and Martina Topić. 2014. "Eros, Agape i Ethnos: Predlog za kriticku analizu javnog diskursa o religiji, homoseksualnosti i nacionalizmu u kontekstu Zapadnog Balkana." Pp. 247–269 in D. Valić-Nedeljković, S. Sremac, N. Knežević and D. Gruhonjić (eds.) *The Role of*

*Media in Normalizing Relations in the Western Balkans*. Novi Sad: University of Novi Sad Press.

Stakić, Isidora. 2011. "Homophobia and Hate Speech in Serbian Public Discourse: How Nationalist Myths and Stereotypes Influence Prejudices Against the LGBT Minority." *The Equal Rights Review* 7: 44–65.

Subotić, Jelena. 2011. "Europe is a State of Mind: Identity and Europeanization in the Balkans." *International Studies Quarterly* 55: 309–330.

Štulhofer, Aleksandar, and Ivan Rimac. 2009. "Determinants of Homonegativity in Europe." *Journal of Sex Research* 46: 24–32.

Takács, Judit, and Ivett Szalma. 2011. "Homophobia and Same-Sex Partnerships Legalization in Europe." *Equality, Diversity and Inclusion: An International Journal* 30: 356–378.

*Tportal*. 2011a. "Kastavski župnik osuđen zbog poticanja na nasilje i mržnju." *Tportal.hr* 23 March. Accessed at http://www.tportal.hr/vijesti/hrvatska/118405/Kastavski-zupnik-osuden-zbog-poticanja-na-nasilje-i-mrznju.html, 7 November 2014.

———. 2011b. "Don Ursić proglasio gay osobe—gubavcima!" *Tportal.hr* 10 January. Accessed at http://www.tportal.hr/vijesti/hrvatska/105491/Don-Ursic-proglasio-gay-osobe-gubavcima.html, 7 November 2014.

———. 2013. "Luteranska crkva protiv referenduma o braku." *Tportal.hr* 17 November. Accessed at http://www.tportal.hr/vijesti/hrvatska/299194/Luteranska-crkva-protiv-referenduma-o-braku.html, 7 November 2014.

Tucić, Živica. 2011. "SPC u novom veku (3): Homoseksualnost i pedofilija—Greh pohote." NIN 3137: 42–45.

Uitz, Renata. 2012. "Lessons from Sexual Orientation Discrimination in Central Europe." *American Journal of Comparative Law* 60: 235–264.

Van den Berg, Mariecke, David J. Bos, Marco Derks, R. Ruard Ganzevoort, Miloš Jovanovič, Anne-Marie Korte and Srđan Sremac. 2014. "Religion, Homosexuality, and Contested Social Orders in the Netherlands, the Western Balkans, and Sweden." Pp. 116–134 in *Religion in Times of Crisis*, edited by G. Ganiel, H. Winkel, and C. Monnot. Leiden: Brill.

*Vecernji list*. 2013. "Bozanić: Referendumom se ne ide protiv nikoga." *Vecernji list* 24 November. Accessed at http://www.vecernji.hr/za-i-protiv/bozanic-referendumom-se-ne-ide-protiv-nikoga-904796, 7 November 2014.

Wilcox, M.M. 2012. "Outlaws or In-Laws?" *Journal of Homosexuality* 52: 73–100.

Yuval-Davis, Nira. 1997. *Gender & Nation*. London: Sage.

Žarkov, Dubravka. 1995. "Gender, Orientalism and the History of Ethnic Hatred in the Former Yugoslavia". Pp. 105–121 in P. Lutz and N. Yuval-Davis (eds.) *Crossfires, Nationalism and Gender in Europe*. London: Pluto Press.

———. 2001. "The Body of the Other Man: Sexual Violence and the Construction of Masculinity, Sexuality and Ethnicity in the Croatian Media." Pp. 69–82 in C.O.N. Moser and F.C. Clark (eds.) *Victims, Perpetrators or Actors?: Gender, Armed Conflict and Political Violence*. London: Zed Books.

————. 2007. *The Body of War: Media, Ethnicity, and Gender in the Break-Up of Yugoslavia*. Durham: Duke University Press.

Zurovac, Ljiljana. 2012. "Analiza primljenih žalbi Vijeću za štampu u BiH na pisanje printanih i online medija o LGBT temama." Pp. 111–122 in L. Huremovic (ed.) *Izvan Četiri Zida Priručnik za novinarke i novinare: o profesionalnom i etičkom izvještavanju o LGBT temama*, edited by Lejla Huremovic. Sarajevo: Sarajevski otvoreni centar.

Župa Soblinec. 2014. "Kardinal: Usprkos krizi, želja za obitelji je i dalje živa". 15 December 2014. Accessed at http://www.zupa-soblinec.com/novost/kardinal-bozanic -usprkos-krizi-zelja-za-obitelji-je-i-dalje-ziva/132, 10 January 2015.

*24sata*. 2013a. "Amfilohije: Gej parada zagadila Podgoricu." *24sata.rs* 26 October. Accessed at http://arhiva.24sata.rs/vesti/aktuelno/vest/amfilohije-gej-parada-zagadila -podgoricu/111270.phtml, 7 November 2014.

————. 2013b. "Drvo koje ne daje ploda ...: Amfilohije protiv podgoričkog Prajda." *24sata.rs* 17 October. Accessed at http://arhiva.24sata.rs/vesti/svet/vest/drvo-koje -ne-daje-ploda-amfilohije-protiv-podgorickog-prajda/110131.phtml, 7 November 2014.

# Contributors

*Mariecke van den Berg*
studied Theology and Gender Studies at Utrecht University and obtained a
Ph.D. in Public Administration at the University of Twente, Netherlands. She
currently works as a post-doctoral researcher at VU University Amsterdam.
Within the project *Contested Privates* she compares oppositional constructions
of homosexuality and religion in public discourse in Sweden, Spain and Serbia.

*Magda Dolinska Rydzek*
is a Ph.D. candidate at the Graduate Center for the Study of Culture (Justus-
Liebig University) in Giessen, where she works on the dissertation about the
idea of the Antichrist in post-Soviet Russia. Her research interest includes cultural history of Central and Eastern Europe, contemporary Russian culture as
well as state-church relations in the post-Soviet region. Her latest book (published in Polish) is *Rosjanie w Izraelu: Problem zaprogramowania kulturowego
repatriantów z ZSRR i Federacji Rosyjskiej* (2014).

*R. Ruard Ganzevoort*
is Professor of Practical Theology at VU University Amsterdam (NL) and politically active as member of the Senate of the Netherlands. He is president of the
*International Society for Empirical Research in Theology* and past president of
the *International Academy of Practical Theology*. An alumnus of Utrecht University (NL), Ruard had published extensively on topics like religion and trauma,
religion and sexuality, narrative approaches, psychology of religion, and popular culture. He is the director of the *Amsterdam Center for the Study of Lived
Religion* and of the research project *Contested Privates: The Oppositional Pairing
of Religion and Homosexuality in Public Discourse*, funded by the Netherlands
Organization for Scientific Research NWO.

*Dorota Hall*
is a cultural anthropologist and sociologist, an Assistant Professor at the Institute of Philosophy and Sociology, Polish Academy of Sciences, and the Vice-
President of the International Study of Religion in Eastern and Central Europe
Association (ISORECEA). She previously studied new spiritualties. Currently,
she is closing her ethnographic research project on LGBT Christians in Poland,
and she is preparing a book on the issue in Polish.

*Miloš Jovanović*
is a teaching assistant and a Ph.D. candidate at the Department of Sociology at the Faculty of Philosophy, University of Niš, with a thesis entitled *The Identity Problem of Religious LGBT Persons in Serbia*. He has also edited an issue of *Teme—Journal for Social Sciences* dedicated to Sociology of Queer Identity (2009), and a reader, co-edited with Dragoljub B. Đorđević, *The Possibilities and Limits of the Social Teaching of Orthodoxy and Orthodox Churches* in 2010.

*Alar Kilp*
is a lecturer in Comparative Politics at the University of Tartu, Estonia. His research specializes in religion and politics, and church-state relations in post-communist Europe. He obtained his Ph.D. in Political Science at Tartu in 2012 with a dissertation on *Church Authority in Society, Culture and Politics after Communism*.

*Marek Mikuš*
is a Research Fellow at the Institute of Social Anthropology of the Comenius University in Bratislava, Slovakia, and a member of the editorial board of *New Perspectives: Interdisciplinary Insight into Central & East European Affairs*. He completed his Ph.D. in anthropology at the London School of Economics in 1974 with a thesis that examines transformations of the government of society and individuals at the interface of the state and civil society in neoliberalizing and globalizing Serbia.

*Zlatiborka Popov-Momčinović*
studied sociology at the Faculty of Philosophy in Novi Sad, and defended her dissertention about the women's movement in post-Dayton Boznia and Herzegovina at the Faculty of Political Sciences in Belgrade in 2013. She is a docent at the Faculty of Philosophy University of East Sarajevo. Her main research focus is on gender and civil society as they overlap with religion and on role of religion in different processes of the de/re/construction of Boznia and Herzegovinian society, including reconciliation and politics of identity.

*Koen Slootmaeckers*
is a Ph.D. candidate at Queen Mary University of London and a research affiliate at Leuven International and European Studies (LINES) at KU Leuven, University of Leuven. He has published in, amongst others, *Journal of Homosexuality* and has a forthcoming volume coedited with Heleen Touquet and Peter Vermeersch entitled: *The EU Enlargement and Gay Politics: The Impact of Eastern Enlargement on Rights, Activism and Prejudice* due to be released in 2015.

### Srdjan Sremac

is a research fellow at the Department of Theology at VU University Amsterdam and a research member at the Amsterdam Center for the Study of Lived Religion at the same university. He is also the co-founder of the Centre for the Study of Religion, Politics and Society in Novi Sad, Serbia. Srdjan is the author of *Addiction and Spiritual Transformation* (2013), and co-editor of *Europe as a Multiple Modernity: Multiplicity of Religious Identities and Belonging* (2014), and *Lived Religion and the Politics of (In)Tolerance (forthcoming)*. His broad research interests include narrative psychology of religion, biographical-reconstructive research, religion and sexuality, war-related trauma, addiction and spirituality, lived religion of marginalized groups and post-conflict reconciliation studies. Within the project *Contested Privates* he focuses on religious and sexual nationalisms in the post-Yugoslav space. See www.srdjansremac.com.

### William H. Swatos, Jr.

serves as Executive Officer of the Religious Research Association and was also Executive Officer of the Association for the Sociology of Religion from 1996 to 2012, prior to which he served for six years as editor of *Sociology of Religion*, the ASR's official journal. He is a Senior Fellow of the Center for Religious Inquiry Across the Disciplines at Baylor University, serving as editor of the *Interdisciplinary Journal of Research on Religion*. A doctoral alumnus of the University of Kentucky, Bill is author, co-author, editor, or co-editor of over thirty books, including the *Encyclopedia of Religion and Society* (1998). With Kevin Christiano and Peter Kivisto, Bill has written the text *Sociology of Religion: Contemporary Developments*, now entering its third edition. He has served as editor of the Religion and the Social Order series since 2005. In 2010 he was named Canon Theologian of the Anglican Diocese of Quincy (Illinois), of which he is also senior priest by length of service.

### Mihai Tarța

is an independent scholar based in Warsaw, Poland. He received his doctorate in Religion, Politics and Society from Baylor University under the supervision of Daniel Payne. Since 2014 he is co-editor and author of blog "Mămăligă de Varșovia" covering social and cultural issues. His current research interests include political religion, civil religion, religious nationalism and religion and sexuality.

### Martina Topić

holds a PhD in Sociology. She has worked as a journalist for print media in Croatia, Slovenia and Italy, research fellow at the University of Zagreb, and as a researcher on two large international projects. In December 2013, she co-founded the Centre for Research in Social Sciences and Humanities, the *Journal of Culture and Religion* and a Working Paper Series in Religion and Culture. Since July 2014, she also works at the Leeds Beckett University.

*Tamara Pavasović Trošt*
is a Visiting Professor at the Centre for Southeast European Studies at the University of Graz and Teaching Assistant at the Faculty of Economics at the University of Ljubljana. She received her Ph.D. in Sociology from Harvard University, with a dissertation examining the interplay between history and ethnic identity among Croatian and Serbian youth. She has published about issues of everyday identity, populism, history education, collective memory, and sports and nationalism.

# Religion and the Social Order

Edited by *William H. Swatos, Jr.*
ISSN 1061-5210

The series *Religion and the Social Order* was initiated by the Association for the Sociology of Religion in 1991, under the General Editorship of David G. Bromley. In 2004 an agreement between Brill and the ASR renewed the series.

11.  *State, Market, and Religions in Chinese Societies*. 2005.
     Edited by Fenggang Yang and Joseph B. Tamney
     ISBN 978 90 04 14597 9
12.  *On the Road to Being There*: Studies in Pilgrimage and Tourism in Late Modernity. 2006.
     Edited by William H. Swatos, Jr.
     ISBN 978 90 04 15183 3
13.  *American Sociology of Religion*: Histories. 2007.
     Edited by Anthony J. Blasi
     ISBN 978 90 04 16115 3
14.  *Vocation and Social Context*. 2007.
     Edited by Giuseppe Giordan
     ISBN 978 90 04 16194 8
15.  *North American Buddhists in Social Context*. 2008.
     Edited by Paul David Numrich
     ISBN 978 90 04 16826 8
16.  *Religion and Diversity in Canada*. 2008.
     Edited by Lori G. Beaman and Peter Beyer
     ISBN 978 90 04 17015 5
17.  *Conversion in the Age of Pluralism*. 2009.
     Edited by Giuseppe Giordan
     ISBN 978 90 04 17803 8
18.  *Religion Crossing Boundaries*: Transnational Religious and Social Dynamics in Africa and the New African Diaspora. 2010.
     Edited by Afe Adogame and James V. Spickard
     ISBN 978 90 04 18730 6
19.  *Toward a Sociological Theory of Religion and Health*. 2011.
     Edited by Anthony J. Blasi
     ISBN 978 90 04 20597 0
20.  *History, Time, Meaning, and Memory*: Ideas for the Sociology of Religion. 2011.
     Edited by Barbara Jones Denison
     ISBN 978 90 04 21062 2

21. *How Prophecy Lives.* 2011.
    Edited by Diana G. Tumminia and William H. Swatos, Jr.
    ISBN 978 90 04 21560 3

22. *Mapping Religion and Spirituality in a Postsecular World.* 2012.
    Edited by Giuseppe Giordan and Enzo Pace
    ISBN 978 90 04 23022 4

23. *Testing Pluralism: Globalizing Belief, Localizing Gods.* 2013.
    Edited by Giuseppe Giordan and William H. Swatos, Jr.
    ISBN 978 90 04 25447 3

24. *Religion in Times of Crisis.* 2014.
    Edited by Gladys Ganiel, Heidemarie Winkel, and Christophe Monnot
    ISBN 978 90 04 27778 6

25. *Sociologies of Religion: National Traditions.* 2015.
    Edited by Anthony J. Blasi and Giuseppe Giordan
    ISBN 978 90 04 29729 6

26. *Religious and Sexual Nationalisms in Central and Eastern Europe: Gods, Gays and Governments.* 2015.
    Edited by Srdjan Sremac and R. Ruard Ganzevoort
    ISBN 978 90 04 29747 0